# SEX, LAWS,

## AND

# CYBERSPACE

FREEDOM AND CENSORSHIP ON THE

FRONTIERS OF THE ONLINE REVOLUTION

JONATHAN WALLACE & MARK MANGAN

*An Owl Book*
Henry Holt and Company
New York

**Henry Holt and Company, Inc.**
*Publishers since 1866*
115 West 18th Street
New York, New York 10011

Henry Holt® is a registered trademark
of Henry Holt and Company, Inc.

Published in Canada by Fitzhenry & Whiteside Ltd.,
    195 Allstate Parkway, Markham, Ontario L3R 4T8.

Library of Congress Cataloging-in-Publication Data
    Wallace, Jonathan D.
        Sex, laws, and cyberspace : freedom and regulation on the
    frontiers of the online revolution / by Jonathan Wallace and Mark
    Mangan. – 1st Owl Books edition
            p.    cm.
        ISBN 0-8050-5298-4
    "First published in hardcover in 1996 by Henry Holt and Company, Inc."
        1. Computer crimes– –United States.  2. Computer networks– –Law and
    legislation– –United States.  3. Internet (Computer network)
    4. Obscenity– –United States.  5. Freedom of speech– –United States.
    I. Mangan, Mark.  II. Title.
    KF390.5.C6W35   1996
    345.73'0268–dc20
    [347.305268]                                        96-2668
                                                          CIP

Henry Holt books are available for special promotions and premiums.
For details contact: Director, Special Markets.

First published in hardcover in 1996 by Henry Holt and Company, Inc.

First Owl Book Edition—1997

**Associate Publisher:** Paul Farrell    **Managing Editor:** Cary Sullivan
**Editor:** Andrew Neusner    **Technical Editor:** Lance Rose
**Copy Edit Manager:** Shari Chappell    **Copy Editor:** Michael Hughes
                    **Design & production:** Maya Riddick

Printed in the United States of America
All first editions are printed on acid-free paper. ∞

10 9 8 7 6 5 4 3 2 1
10 9 8 7 6 5 4 3 2 1 (pbk.)

# Dedication

*Jonathan Wallace:*

To Margaret King, Aaron Streiter, Beth Singer, Laimdota Mazzarins, Dean Alden Sayres, and the faculty and staff of a noble experiment, the Brooklyn College New School of Liberal Arts, circa 1972. You were the most encouraging people I ever met.

*Mark Mangan:*

To Michael J. Mangan and Jonathan Wallace, and *l'espace de raison* where conservatism and liberalism meet.

# ACKNOWLEDGMENTS

Our thanks to Wade Saadi, Ed Taylor, and Edgar Saadi—their indulgence made this possible.

We also wish to thank Paul Farrell and Andy Neusner of MIS:Press (Henry Holt), who gave us our opportunity (Andy also tenaciously kept us on schedule); online law expert Lance Rose, Esq., who commented on the manuscript; law student Mike Green, who spent many hours surfing Westlaw in search of precedents; Internet free speech heroes Mike Godwin and Brock Meeks, who took time out during an unusually eventful period to answer our questions on numerous matters; Jim Thomas of CuD, who filled in some details on the Marty Rimm story; Thomas Nolan, James Causey, Douglas Mulkoff, David Cahill, Kenneth Chadwell, Philip Dubois and other attorneys who first shared court files, then filled in gaps in the record; Meri Wallace, who responded to neglect by getting her own book contract; Joseph Wallace and Sharon AvRutick, who patiently advised us how to walk, talk, and think like authors; Michael P. Mangan, who played the devil's legal advocate; and William Keh, a benefactor and a good friend.

# CONTENTS

# INTRODUCTION

A postal inspector, a stockbroker, a United States senator, a fringe church, an FBI agent, a thirty-year-old college student...

These are the self-appointed censors of the Internet. Each of them has used the civil and criminal laws of the United States to try to silence speech—or has given others the ammunition to do it.

History is repeating itself. During the Civil War, a new technology, photography, led to the creation of nude photographs that were sent to soldiers at the front via the U.S. mails. The Postal Obscenity Law, which is currently being used to prosecute computer pornographers, was passed by Congress in 1873. Immediately following the law's enactment, volunteer censors such as Anthony Comstock enforced the laws by mercilessly hounding not only pornographers, but sex educators and novelists whose work they believed to be indecent.

Comstock was the founder of the New York Society for the Suppression of Vice. The U.S. Postal Service designated him as an unpaid special agent, giving him the right to go into any post office in the nation and open mail he believed to be obscene. Comstock lobbied Congress by entering its halls with a sack and dumping the contents on a table: obscene photographs, abortion aids, aphrodisiac powders—all of which had passed through the U.S. mails.

The modern-day Anthony Comstock is Senator James Exon. Instead of a sack, he prowls the halls of Congress with his Blue Book, a collection of obscene and indecent materials downloaded from the Internet. "Click, click, click," says Senator Exon. "Page after page...pornographers, predators, and pedophiles." He and others like him appear to think that the Internet is a million-armed hydra, reaching into every American household to corrupt the children.

There is obscenity on the Internet. There is also explicit but legal sexual material, which Senator Exon has outlawed with the vague provisions of his Communications Decency Act (CDA). There are bomb recipes, militia materials, hate speech of every stripe—mixed in small amounts with the political, legal, medical, technical, and sports-related resources, the rock music fan pages, the science fiction forums, the Fish Cam, and the Magic Eightball.

Free speech is sloppy. The reason the First Amendment protects almost all speech is that, with very limited exceptions, we have never succeeded in agreeing which speech is good and which is bad. Therefore, the First Amendment has been interpreted to say that we will not make content-based distinctions of speech; there should not be censorship; the cure for bad speech is to overwhelm it with good speech, but not to silence it.

For these reasons, hate speech is legal in the United States—the Nazis were permitted to march in Skokie, Illinois. Pornography that falls short of the legal definition of obscenity may be freely distributed. Many grotesque things—denials of the Holocaust, catalogs of S&M materials, a talk show host's advice on the best way to shoot federal agents—are all protected by the First Amendment. If these materials are legal off the Internet, what is the justification for treating them differently on the Internet?

Senator Exon argues that these grotesqueries are pervasive because they come into the house. Ten-year-old children who understand computers better than their parents can find them.

But we have previously crossed this bridge. In 1957, the Supreme Court held that the state of Michigan could not set the acceptable level of public discourse at what was fit for children. Opponents of the Communications Decency Act point out that parents cannot abdicate their responsibility to know and to regulate what their children are doing with the computer any more than they can ignore the movies their children are seeing. When parents cannot monitor their children's computer activities, new software is available to lock pornography and violence out of computers.

This book's first chapter tells the story of a pair of computer pornographers from Milpitas, California, who were indicted and convicted in Memphis, Tennessee. Robert and Carleen Thomas are married and have two sons. Together, they ran the Amateur Action Bulletin Board, from which they distributed GIF images that are explicit and, in some cases, repellent, violent, and grotesque.

Today, they are both in prison. When you have read their story, you may conclude that they deserve it—if you believe that obscenity laws should exist, you certainly will believe that some of the material they distributed (involving rape and torture) was obscene. So why should we care about them?

For two reasons. First, the obscenity laws mandate that local community standards—the standards of the community where the jurors reside—must be applied to the material in question. This rule, promulgated by the Supreme Court in 1973, made minimal sense then. Today, as you will see from the Thomas case, it permits Memphis, Tennessee, to establish itself as the arbiter of all cyberspace.

Secondly, there really is a slippery slope; it is not just a fantasy of the ACLU, the NRA, and other organizations that would have you believe that a little regulation (of speech, guns, or whatever) will lead to total prohibition. The proof is in the story of Anthony Comstock whose mission began with banning obscene photographs. In his forty-year career, however, he prevented the publication in this country of novels by Zola and Balzac, and he drove an early sex educator, Ida Craddock, to suicide.

Yes, you say, but those were the wild old days; we know better, and it can't happen now. Wrong: the modern-day Comstock and his colleagues will do everything the original Comstock did, if permitted. In the last few years, for example, the curator of an art museum was indicted for displaying the explicit works of a respected photographer and a rap group was prosecuted for its lyrics. Cyberspace presents a new playground, a new field of endeavor, for censorship as it does for speech. The new and extraordinarily vague rules of the CDA will allow prosecutors to go after anything "indecent." If you think Zola, Balzac, James Joyce, Henry Miller, and Lenny Bruce could never be prosecuted again, think twice. To paraphrase Pastor Niemoller: First they come for Robert and Carleen Thomas, then they come for you.

Why do the would-be censors find the Internet so frightening? Because it is a cheap, easily accessible means of communication that is almost free of social control.

If you have an idea—good, bad, indifferent—that you want to communicate to 250 million Americans, your choices are very limited. To get your idea into the *New York Times*, *Time*, *60 Minutes*, the *Rush Limbaugh Show*, a movie from Paramount, or a book from Henry Holt, you will have to convince someone—usually an older, white male in an office in Manhattan or Los Angeles—that your idea has merit. He will examine your idea from two perspectives: first, to see how it fits with his own preconceptions and prejudices; second, to determine if it has commercial appeal and is likely to attract an audience or sponsors and make money for his company. Government censors sift out the limited types of speech (obscenity, fighting words, threats) that are illegal under the First Amendment. But the vast, remaining mass of speech—ostensibly free and protected—is in reality controlled by the preconceptions and commercial judgments of the people who stand as gatekeepers to the means of communication.

The Internet is a forum without gatekeepers. Anyone with a computer and an Internet account can be a publisher. On the Net, you can reach tens of millions of potential readers at low cost and without having to persuade anyone—editor, publisher, reporter, producer—that your information deserves to see the light of day.

This panics the censors. Phrases like "sink of depravity" are being tossed around. If you can't institute your own social controls, we are told—if we can't make the Internet and all of cyberspace more sedate, more "decent," more like older, mainstream forms of publishing and communication—the government will step in and do it for us.

In this atmosphere, the would-be censors have an opening. They are lining up at the courthouse doors to try to chase from cyberspace the forms of speech that irritate them most. Everyone has a bogeyman who "doesn't deserve" First Amendment protection. For postal inspector David Dirmeyer, it was on-line pornographers. Stockbrokerage Stratton Oakmont was upset by postings about its public offerings on Prodigy. A grand jury is investigating a cryptographer for a real Catch-22—writing software that he should have foreseen someone else would upload to the Internet. The Church of Scientology is unhappy that some of its internal documents wound up in Usenet and on the World Wide Web. The FBI didn't think a college student should be posting violent fiction to the **alt.sex.stories** newsgroup. A college student saw an opportunity to profit from the hype and make himself famous with some "statistics" regarding on-line pornography.

That student, Marty Rimm, was a long-time member of the Thomases Amateur Action board. His "research" wound up in a cover story in *Time* that Senator Exon waved on the Senate floor. In the wide-ranging debate on Exon's act in the Senate, the Thomas and Prodigy cases came up repeatedly. Other legislation has been introduced dealing with cryptography and with bomb recipes. The varied strands are being woven together in Congress; the resulting tapestry will determine the future of the Net. Will it continue to be a wild frontier of ideas, some good, some grotesque, competing for attention? Or will it become an intellectual wasteland like broadcast television, subject to the regulations of the FCC?

In the following chapters, we will study several cases of unsuccessful and successful attempts at censorship, by government agents and self-appointed citizen censors alike. Along the way, we review the forms censorship takes in cyberspace—the seizure of computers, gag orders, damage awards, prison terms, and the "FUD" (fear, uncertainty, and doubt)—spread by all of the above. In the final section, we will make our own recommendations for sensible solutions that will allow society to exclude the truly illegal forms of speech on the Net, while allowing the Net to remain what it is and what makes it so valuable today: a wild medium in which everyone can be publisher, reader, and distributor of information without requiring the permission of anyone in authority.

# CHAPTER

# I

# MEMPHIS RULES

## ACT I—THE STING

Postal Inspector David Dirmeyer of Memphis, Tennessee, was trolling for pornographers. Dirmeyer was a lanky man with a Tennessee twang. He had 15 years of government service and a collection of genuine child pornography, seized by the Postal Service more than 10 years before. Dirmeyer had a tested routine. Using a pseudonym, he would contact pornographers, order material from them, and, via telephone conversations or the mail, attempt to interest them in some "action mags." If they expressed interest, he would mail them the magazines, and then perform what he called a "controlled delivery." Armed with a search warrant, Dirmeyer would show up at the suspect's house on the day the magazines were delivered, seize the contraband, and execute a search of the premises.

Dirmeyer had received special training in combatting child pornography and obscenity, and had participated in approximately one dozen investigations of pornographers, of which about half had involved controlled deliveries. In July of 1993, Dirmeyer reeled in Robert and Carleen Thomas of Milpitas, California—his first computer pornographers. Robert Thomas has been married to Carleen for 21 years, and together they have two teenage sons. In early July 1995, serving time in a federal prison in Tennessee, Robert wrote a poignant appeal on behalf of his wife, then awaiting sentencing:

"I'm requesting your assistance in helping my wife Carleen remain free on bond pending the outcome of the appeal process. ... My wife and I have up until now, successfully attempted to raise two sons with the best education, values and hopes that can be. ... Both boys have so far avoided every imaginable pitfall that faces growing up in this generation. ... My greatest hope is that at the least my wife be allowed to be there to help them get through the important changes in their lives."

Thomas concluded his letter, which was distributed in newsgroups on the Internet, with an appeal to readers to send letters in support of Carleen Thomas to her attorney, James Causey in Memphis. "No matter who you are or where you live on this earth, your thoughts are important and it can make things happen. Thank you all for listening." At the time of this emotional appeal, Thomas was serving three years in a Tennessee prison for serving up lewd graphic files on his California-based electronic bulletin board system ("BBS").

Dirmeyer first learned of the Thomases' Amateur Action bulletin board system ("AABBS") in late July 1993, when he was contacted by Earl Crawley of Gleason, Tennessee. Crawley was a hacker who had stumbled into the public section of the board. The Thomases had been running their electronic pornography store since 1991 and went to some trouble to run it carefully. It was a membership-only system; only one file, containing a text description of some 17,000 Graphic Interface Format ("GIF") files, was available to nonmembers. To join, a user printed a form from the BBS, filled it out and mailed it to the Thomases in Milpitas. The form included the user's address and telephone information. One of the Thomases, usually Robert, would then call and speak to the applicant before signing him up as a member. Generally, from the handwriting on the form and the applicant's voice on the telephone, Robert would be able to make a careful judgment of whether the applicant was over eighteen. He testified at trial that he frequently had refused membership on this basis.

On AABBS's main menu, an option entitled "Legal Issues" pointed to a file directed at law enforcement officers who might be investigating the board. The file stated that the operation was legal, having been investigated and cleared by the San Jose police department in 1992. This file had been prepared by J. Keith Henson, a software developer and Internet activist who became involved with the Thomases after their high-tech operation's first confrontation with the law. Another legally prudent feature of AABBS was that no uploads were accepted. Robert Thomas was afraid that someone would upload something illegal, such as child pornography, on his system.

The material he made available was carefully screened. Though many of the GIFs he captioned as involving pre-teens, Robert Thomas went to lengths to be sure that the women in the pictures were all 18 or older. He distributed a certain amount of "naturist" material—nudist camp footage of children in nonsexual situations—which at trial was acknowledged to be legal in all 50 states. But he was careful to stay away from any images of children in sexual situations. On the other hand, he knew what his customers wanted and would suggestively hint at underage sex and incest. At the same time, he openly solicited requests from his members, and made efforts to fulfill their graphics and video desires.

Robert Thomas had found a pretty good formula for marketing explicit sexual materials on-line. Several membership plans were available, allowing users to spend a certain amount of time on the BBS, or download a certain number of files. The text was a tease for the GIFs, and the GIFs were primarily a come-on for the videos from which they were taken. In the first nine months of 1993, almost $240,000 had passed through one of the Thomases' bank accounts, and there may have been other accounts. The business was run from three locations: the house, where the computers, printers, and 32 modems were kept; a warehouse, where the videotapes, the duplication bank of 32 VCRs, the car and the boat were located; and a Mailboxes Etc. store that received their business mail.

The Thomases had collected the full gamut of sexual images including bestiality, rape, torture, and incest. Many of the GIFs on AABBS were taken from publicly available videotapes. For the corresponding text descriptions, Robert Thomas often copied words from the box; other times he would set his imagination free. A video of an older man and woman having sex with people half their age, for example, became "She Sucks Her Son's Cock. Father is Fucking His Daughter." Images of very young-looking women would invariably be tagged with lewd, pedophilic descriptions. Robert Thomas was shrewd and thought he knew where the legal line was. Ironically, it was this kind of false advertising that attracted Dirmeyer's attention. Dirmeyer was specifically looking for child pornography—his favorite prosecutorial challenge. Though he was never able to uncover any on AABBS, he easily found enough vulgar material to shock the Tennessee court.

Dirmeyer, who had not previously had much contact with computers, dialed into AABBS for the first time on a borrowed machine in his office in Memphis. At first look, he must have seen enough to rush the blood of even the most jaded porno-seeking postal inspector. The public files seemed to point to a slew of pictures of little girls and boys engaged in all kinds of illegal sex acts. Dirmeyer took no action for a couple of weeks, but on August 20 he called AABBS again, armed with a false name and a firm plan to go undercover.

In his communications with the Thomases, Dirmeyer became Lance White, with a mail drop address in Cordova, Tennessee. He used the **print screen** command liberally to capture his sessions. First, he read and printed a message stating that subscribers to AABBS could download GIFs and obtain lists of videos, magazines, and novelty items available for sale by the Sysop. Dirmeyer promptly printed an application form, completed it as Lance White, and sent it to the Thomases' mail drop. His $55 money order bought him a six-month subscription to AABBS with a 90-minute time limit per day.

Dirmeyer also maintained a telephone number and answering machine in the name of Lance White and six days later, he found a message on it from Robert Thomas, welcoming him to AABBS. Later that same day, Dirmeyer was logged onto AABBS when Thomas initiated chat mode and welcomed him to the system as the newest of about 3,500 users. Dirmeyer continued to hit his **print screen** button, capturing all kinds of material for his day in court—such as a list of "nudist" videos advertised as containing "tender young teens caught candid at nudist colony." Such material is legal in all 50 states, but Dirmeyer thought it had prosecutorial merit. The next day, Dirmeyer printed a partial list of the 17,000 GIFs available. Trained to seek out obscenity, he scanned in particular for lewd phrases evidencing underage sex.

Dirmeyer then sent a $41 money order to the Milpitas mailing address, asking Thomas to pick a video for him from those referenced in the AABBS listing as K71 through K74. Thomas had assigned each video a letter and number, and the trial testimony later indicated that the letters were shorthand for the content. For instance, "K", for kinky, was the catch-all category in which Thomas placed everything which did not comfortably fit into a single topic heading, such as one with defecation and bestiality.

In the cover letter in which he had asked Robert Thomas to pick some kinky videos for him, Dirmeyer planted the first seeds of his

4

sting. At trial, he testified, "I also told Thomas, in the letter, that I had some material that he might be interested in. I did not specify the subject matter of my material at that time." Dirmeyer stated at trial that he liked to build up the sting slowly, and thought he might tip his hand if he was too eager at the outset. He was careful not to reveal his kiddie porn mags too quickly. Robert Thomas' recollections of his interactions with Dirmeyer differ greatly from the postal inspector's. Thomas claimed that he was not terribly interested in the magazines, did not remember the chat mode conversations and, in fact, never read the letter in which Dirmeyer finally disclosed the nature of his material.

When Dirmeyer visited AABBS again on August 31, he found E-mail from Thomas waiting, in which, according to Dirmeyer, Thomas expressed a keen interest in his magazine collection. As Dirmeyer was responding to the e-mail, Thomas interrupted him in chat mode; Dirmeyer took the opportunity to express his desire to find some good "teen nudist material." Thomas obligingly showed the postal inspector how to do an automated search of the GIF descriptions using the keywords "teen" and "nudist." A few days later, Dirmeyer E-mailed Thomas, disclosing that his mysterious material consisted of "action mags." Dirmeyer believed that this phrase was a code with special significance in the world of pornography. Thomas later claimed it meant nothing to him.

Around this time, the postal inspector spent hours working on his computer. He searched for and downloaded a wide variety of GIF files described as involving bestiality, kiddie porn, and mutilation. For a while in the fall he visited AABBS' every few days for new GIFs. Soon Dirmeyer found AABBS' master file with descriptions of all its videos—ALLVID.ZIP. When the postal inspector discovered this he skipped his **print screen** button and pulled the file down. It was essentially a grocery list of videos that featured sexually deviant activity.

When video K74 arrived at Lance White's address, Dirmeyer dutifully watched it in its entirety, prepared a written description for later use, and wrote to Thomas again, ordering four more from the K series. In a video described in detail at the trial, a man breaks into a house and brutally rapes the young housewife and her girlfriend at gunpoint. The corresponding text description was "The girls scream with pain throughout the whole video! Excellent Action!" In the same order, Dirmeyer asked Thomas to select two teen nudist videos. In the cover letter, he again alluded to his "action mags." When the new order arrived in the mail, Dirmeyer again watched them and prepared written summaries.

In October, Dirmeyer decided that the time was ripe to proceed to the next step in his sting operation and reveal the contents of his "action mags." Leaving his feigned subtlety aside, he finally specified that he had "hardcore sex magazines featuring young girls having sex with adults and other children." He wrote, "These magazines were hard to come by and are very special to me. I am willing to let you borrow them so you can scan whatever pictures you want for your private collection. All I ask is that you return the mags to me (with a copy of the GIFs) when you are finished." Though the correspondence was later found in his files, Thomas testified at trial that he never saw it.

On November 3, Dirmeyer sent E-mail to Thomas, asking him to respond to the letter sent two weeks earlier about the "action mags." Six days later, Dirmeyer was again on the BBS when Thomas initiated chat mode, and, according to Dirmeyer, indicated he was interested in the magazines. He asked that they be sent two-day air, so he could scan them over the weekend. Dirmeyer wasn't ready to proceed. As he explained at trial, controlled deliveries of contraband must be made in such a way that little chance exists that the material will pass into circulation. If he simply mailed the magazines to Thomas, images placed on AABBS, might be disseminated to other computer systems and pass beyond Dirmeyer's reach before he got his magazines back. He needed to time the delivery to coincide with a trip to California and the obtaining of a search warrant. He therefore sent Thomas what he referred to as a lulling letter, stating that he had been unable to send the magazines due to personal problems and would ship them as soon as he could. At the end of October, Dirmeyer got in touch with the San Jose Police Department, Bureau of Investigations, and spoke to an investigator named Greg Gunsky.

Gunsky told him that AABBS had been seized and searched in January of the prior year, and that no charges had been brought. Investigator Mark McIninch had joined AABBS in an undercover guise in 1991 and over time had made a number of purchases from Thomas. On January 20, 1992, McIninch had gone to the Thomas residence with a search warrant and had seized computers, VCRs, and videotapes. When no child pornography was found, the San Jose police came to the conclusion that the remaining materials—the same ones Dirmeyer had been purchasing—did not violate California community standards. They returned all the equipment, gave Thomas a letter confirming that they had found nothing illegal on the board, and left. What the California police found was crude, pornographic, and perhaps worth the effort of investigating, but it was nothing for which they could reasonably prosecute.

At this point, Thomas was contacted by J. Keith Henson, a self-taught expert in computer law. Henson, a California-based software developer, had wide-ranging interests including planetary exploration, cryogenics, nanotechnology, and freedom on the Internet. Henson has been in the software business since 1972, but it was through his work with Alcor, a cryogenics foundation, that he acquired his expertise in laws pertaining to cyberspace. People sign up with Alcor either to have their entire body frozen in the hope of later revival, or, if they cannot afford the full treatment, have their severed heads preserved instead on the assumption that someday technology will permit the head to be revived and reattached to a body. In 1988, when an Alcor client died at Alcor's facility, she was promptly decapitated and her head frozen. No physician had ever signed a death certificate, and when the San Jose police were investigating a possible murder, they seized Alcor's computer systems. Board member Henson made himself an expert in the Electronic Communications Privacy Act ("ECPA").

This law, which Congress had passed the year before, provides financial penalties for the seizure of computer equipment if it impedes the transmission of electronic mail to the intended recipient. The police who seized Alcor's computers knew nothing about the ECPA and disregarded its constraints on them. Henson effectively backed them off, got the computers returned to Alcor, brought a pro se lawsuit against the authorities, and recovered a settlement of $30,000.

When McIninch seized AABBS, he kept it for five weeks and interrupted the delivery of electronic mail. Five years after the passage of the ECPA, the San Jose police were apparently not any more familiar with the law. Henson discovered what was happening, contacted Robert Thomas, and informally helped him confront the authorities. Henson told McIninch and the prosecutor to contact Don Ingram, the county attorney who had taken a shellacking over the Alcor incident. According to Henson, they did, and after hearing Ingram's tale of woe, they returned the AABBS equipment to Thomas and gave him the written release. Henson contributed the Legal

Issues file, accessible from the main menu of AABBS, which advised putative investigators that AABBS had already been seized and was found to be legal.

An interesting question is whether Dirmeyer really proceeded several months into the AABBS investigation before contacting the San Jose authorities. After reading the Legal Issues file, or certainly no later than his conversation with the San Jose investigator, Dirmeyer must have been aware that, at least under California community standards, the BBS had been cleared. Yet he still pushed forward. He must have either felt certain that Tennessee standards were so much stricter he could get a conviction, or that his controlled delivery of the "action mags" would make up for the lack of child pornography on AABBS. Perhaps the Thomas' text descriptions were so explicit that he simply felt compelled to shut them down.

On November 16, Dirmeyer flew to Milpitas, California and drove by the Thomas residence, observing a handmade "UPS Pickup" sign in one of the windows. One can only imagine the excitement Dirmeyer must have felt to be close to his prey after so many months of E-mail. The following day, he visited the AABBS mail drop, Mail Boxes, Etc., and spoke to Tom Pennybacker, the owner. While Pennybacker was confirming that the Thomases rented mail box #284 from him, Dirmeyer unexpectedly had his first view of one of his suspects, "a white female, approximately 37 years old, 5 feet one inch in height, weighing approximately 100 lbs. with gray streaked black hair, entered the establishment." It was Carleen Thomas. She picked up a package, loaded it into her new sun-roofed Toyota and drove off. Dirmeyer returned to Tennessee and took no further recorded action on the Thomas case until January, when he returned to San Jose. The official purpose of this November surveillance was never revealed.

Dirmeyer applied to federal magistrate Wayne D. Brazil in San Jose for a search warrant, filing a 27-page affidavit which summarized the history of his pursuit of the Thomases. Here he got an unpleasant surprise. The magistrate wouldn't give him a search warrant for the action mags. There were two possible reasons. The federal law Dirmeyer was proceeding under, which governed child pornography, had been held unconstitutional for vagueness by the federal appeals court which had jurisdiction over California. When an appeals court voids a law, its decision is only effective in the states over which it sits, so the same law was still effective in Tennessee. Second, California federal courts will not grant search warrants for a house when the "controlled delivery" is made to a post office box. In any event, Dirmeyer improvised a solution.

On January 9, he returned to Mail Boxes, Etc. and initiated his controlled delivery by stuffing the package into the Thomases mailbox. The package contained three magazines, entitled "Lolita Color Special 6," "Lolita Color Special 18," and "Little Girls Fuck, Too." Dirmeyer confided in Pennybacker that he was setting up a surveillance, then waited outside the building for Robert or Carleen Thomas to pick up the package.

He watched and waited. They never showed that day so he went back to the hotel. He arrived early the next day, set up, and waited again. They still didn't show. Finally, late in the day, he enlisted Pennybacker's help and had him call the Thomas residence. The Thomases later testified that Pennybacker was strange and rather insistent that they get their package, making up an excuse about inventory. Carleen Thomas finally responded to Pennybacker's pressure and came over to the store. Dirmeyer, assisted by San Jose police, followed Carleen back to her house. At five o'clock the same night, he rang the Thomases' doorbell.

After six months, the postal inspector now met his quarry for the first time. He was accompanied by four San Jose police officers, including Officer Jim McMahon (the head of the high tech unit,) an Assistant District Attorney, and two local postal inspectors. Dirmeyer presented Thomas with an unsigned, undated search warrant which noted on its face that it had been issued by Magistrate Brazil. The search warrant listed the tapes that Dirmeyer had purchased, the GIFs he had downloaded, and the description files, and called for the seizure of all computer equipment. The warrant made no mention of the action mags.

Dirmeyer found his magazines in the Thomases' bedroom, but he had no authority to seize them. Instead, it was necessary to get Robert Thomas' consent. According to Thomas, Dirmeyer said that if Thomas didn't cooperate, he would keep them locked up in the house for as many hours as it took him to drive to San Francisco and get a search warrant, and that he and his men would then "rip the house apart." He offered Thomas a "Consent to Search Form." Apparently, Dirmeyer and the San Jose police each carried a stack of these—you never know when you might need to search something. Thomas, who had not yet contacted an attorney, signed the form, but only after making Dirmeyer add some language to it. The form's boilerplate read:

*I,_____, have been informed by _____, who made proper identification as (an) authorized law enforcement officer(s) of the _____, of my CONSTITUTIONAL RIGHT not to have a search made of the premises and property owned by me and under my care, custody and control, without a search warrant.*

The form further acknowledges that the signer knowingly waives this right. In another blank, Dirmeyer hand-wrote a description of the property he was looking for, "namely priority mail package from Lance White addressed to Robert Thomas." Following this was the wording Thomas insisted on as a condition of his signing the consent, "sent without his knowledge." At this point, Thomas had no idea that Dirmeyer and Lance White were one and the same. In fact, he thought that Dirmeyer might really be after this Lance White character, and AABBS had just been caught in the middle.

Around eight o'clock, Thomas thought to call Henson, whom he had never met in person. Henson asked to talk to Dirmeyer. Dirmeyer apparently thought Henson was a lawyer and agreed to speak with him. Henson sternly asked him if he was familiar with the ECPA. According to Henson, Dirmeyer replied that he was in fact aware of the ECPA, and didn't think he had any problem with it because it was their intent to bring the system back within a few days without looking at any of the 2000 E-mail messages stored on the system.

One of the policemen drew a sketch of the house; in addition, every room of the house thought to play a role in the business was photographed. The investigators, not sure where to stop, even got shots of the Atari game computer in one of the Thomas son's bedroom. McMahon, Dirmeyer, and Thomas then headed over to the warehouse. Here they ran into another problem. Dirmeyer was apparently unaware of the warehouse and had failed to include it in the search warrant. They again managed their way around this by asking Thomas to sign two more Consents to Search. This time Dirmeyer used a local form carried by McMahon, as Dirmeyer had no more left. Thomas signed one consenting to the seizure of "three pieces of lined notebook paper with writing by Lance White" and another agreeing to the seizure of the masters of the videotapes Dirmeyer had ordered. The officers photographed the banks of VCRs used for copying, a Ford Mustang, and a boat.

On Tuesday, Dirmeyer again visited the Thomases, taking fingerprints and handwriting samples. As he left, he told Robert Thomas that if he wanted to get any consideration for cooperation, "it might be a good idea to keep the cover of Lance White intact." He was hoping to use AABBS to catch other users, and in fact had engaged in "a couple of transactions [with] one guy from Boston." Robert Thomas still had not put two and two together and apparently thought he was being warned not to talk about user Lance White, the subject of a separate investigation. Copying the electronic files took longer than expected, and it took the San Jose cops the rest of the week to back up AABBS. The system had so much hard drive space, it kept exceeding the capacity of whatever the police tried to download it onto. They, finally went out and borrowed a drive capacious enough.

On Tuesday, Henson wrote up the whole episode and posted it to Usenet's Electronic Frontier Foundation ("EFF") newsgroup. EFF is an organization, founded by Mitch Kapor and John Perry Barlow, which specializes in the freedom of electronic communications. Henson continued to post reports to several newsgroups throughout the trial. Wednesday and Thursday, he spent some time briefing an attorney Thomas retained, Richard Williams of San Jose, on the ECPA and some of the prior cases, including Alcor and a similar, well-publicized government seizure of the computer systems at Steve Jackson Games in Austin, Texas.

On Friday, just as Henson was about to meet Robert Thomas for the first time, Thomas called him. Carleen had found that the original "Lance White" registration form and Lance White's name printed on the "Permission To Search" looked identical. Henson tried dialing the phone number from the registration form: "to my ear, the answering machine's message which says it is Lance White's phone and the person I talked to who said he was Dirmeyer are the same person."

Dirmeyer called Thomas on Friday and told him to come down to a postal facility in San Jose on Saturday morning at 8:30 to retrieve his computer equipment or he wouldn't be able to get it until the following Tuesday. Dirmeyer was leaving that morning to return to Tennessee. Thomas replied that he was sick, that it wasn't convenient for him to come down, and requested the government deliver his stuff back to him. Finally, the Thomases' two sons and a friend went to get the computers, accompanied by Henson. On crutches from an injury, Henson approached Dirmeyer and asked him if he was Lance White. Dirmeyer admitted it.

Dirmeyer reminded Henson of a tall and gangly cousin of his, "given to putting on a hick act." A San Jose police officer, a McMahon subordinate, told Henson to stay out of the Thomas case, and that it was none of his concern. Henson said that "He advised me to butt out of being involved in any way. He asked if I had ever seen the material on that BBS (my answer was no), and expressed the opinion that I would be smeared by it and greatly regret getting involved." Henson testified at trail that the officer told him he would never hold his head up in church again. On Henson's way out of the post office, as he hobbled painfully on his crutches, he said that Dirmeyer and the officer "passed me, opened the doors, went through and let them swing shut in my face. I guess scum like me is below their notice."

## Act II—The Trial

At trial, the jury heard that the Thomases were rich, vulgar, monsters. A Tennessee grand jury had charged them in a twelve-count indictment for distributing obscene pictures and videos, and helping Dirmeyer send them some child pornography.

Count one charged the Thomases with conspiring to break the law. Counts two through eleven were the obscenity charges; two through seven involved the interstate transport of graphic files; eight through ten the shipment of six videocassettes. Count eleven charged them with "aiding and abetting" the shipment of child pornography. They could only be charged with "receiving" Dirmeyer's special action mags in the state where they arrived. Count twelve was a legal extra— it did not charge them with anything, but simply called for forfeiture of all their computer equipment.

The Thomases had retained California attorney Richard D. Williams. Before the trial began, Williams made a flurry of motions. He first brought a motion before the federal court in California, arguing that the Thomases were protected by the Privacy Protection Act, which Congress enacted in 1980 to require law enforcement officials to obtain evidence whenever possible by less intrusive means than search and seizure. But when passing the act, Congress had made it clear that it was geared particularly to prevent the hasty seizure of journalists' and broadcasters' data, which might prove to contain time-sensitive news. It did not apply here.

Williams also asked that the search warrant and the seizure of the computer equipment be invalidated, citing the ECPA. Here, the government denied any wrongdoing and stood by the warrant. The court responded that although it had jurisdiction to decide such a motion, it would rather defer to the Tennessee court, and invited Williams to renew his motion there. When he arrived in Tennessee, Williams had a new set of legal maneuvers for Judge Julia Smith Gibbons.

The first was a motion to transfer the case back to California in the "interests of justice." Williams made a jurisdictional argument that AABBS did not have much to do with Tennessee, claiming "only approximately five of the BBS' 3,500 members reside in Tennessee." In support, he claimed that nothing had been "sent" to Tennessee. "The member pays for the call, reviews a menu, and 'downloads' what they choose. Thus, Defendants don't 'send' anything into Tennessee." Judge Gibbons denied the motion. She pointed out that obscenity cases involving interstate transport can legally be brought either in the district from which the material is sent or the one in which it is received. Because the Thomases' pornography ended up in Tennessee, she was going to try them there.

On April 18, Williams filed a motion to dismiss, alleging that *Miller v. California*, the 1973 Supreme Court decision creating the local community standards test for obscenity, was unconstitutional. However, one cannot ask a district court, or any court other than the Supreme Court itself, to overturn a Supreme Court decision. He renewed his motion that the jurisdiction was not proper in Tennessee, based on a new and strange argument. Some of the Thomases' material was imported and had passed through Customs without objection (the U.S. Customs Service also has the right to seize obscene materials). Williams insisted that the action against his clients was preempted by the North American Free Trade treaty because AABBS was an international business with members in Canada and Mexico. The prosecutor, Dan L. Newsom, an Assistant U.S. Attorney for Memphis, pointed out that *Miller v. California* is "the law of the land" and that NAFTA does not override United States laws. Judge Gibbons denied Williams' motion to dismiss, finding the arguments to be without merit.

On the eve of the trial, Williams made a second motion to dismiss, which Judge Gibbons dismissed just as easily. He claimed that the Thomases' right to a speedy trial had been denied by some government-caused delays between March and July. Judge Gibbons, noting the three motions filed by Williams, held that the case "has moved along as quickly as possible."

Although Williams would, in the end, touch on most of the right issues, unfortunately for the Thomases, they were never presented at the right place or the right time. He came across as bumbling and unprepared and arrived in court without his homework or his pants. The trial began inauspiciously at 11:05 on July 18, with Judge Gibbons asking Williams "where have you and your clients have been since 9:30." Williams was late, without his legal file, and dressed in blue jeans. He explained that his luggage had been mistakenly redirected at Chicago the night before. Gibbons gave him until 2:00, and stated, "you either better find your luggage or take advantage of one of our stores and find something appropriate to wear in court."

Williams arrived at 2:00 with a new suit and a new motion—to dismiss count 11, the action mags/child pornography charge. He based his argument on *X-citement Video*, the 1992 case decided by the Ninth Circuit Court of Appeals, which had held the child pornography law to be unconstitutional because it did not require a defendant to know that an actress or actor in a video he distributed was a minor. The case involved a pornography star who had been acting since age 14 but looked older. Since possession of child pornography could not, at the moment, be a crime in California, to prosecute the Thomases in Tennessee for something that was legal back home was not fair. Judge Gibbons denied the motion.

Williams had one last motion. He wanted all evidence pertaining to chat mode communications excluded. Judge Gibbons said, "I'm going to have to be educated a bit about the whole process and what is involved before I can decide." She warned him that it was very important to her to start on time. "Obviously, we haven't got off to a very good start in that regard."

Williams again stalled the proceedings by discussing something with Robert Thomas. The Judge asked him to pay attention, then finally asked what the problem was. "Your honor, I believe what my client was addressing to me was...he and his wife were discussing that it might be better for her to have separate counsel. I don't know what the Court's position would be at this point. That was what he was trying to get my attention to say, but I think he wanted to say that himself."

Ordinarily, Judge Gibbons would have had prior contact with the defendants and counselled them herself about the potential conflict of being represented by one attorney. A strategy available to Carleen, for example, would have been to accuse Robert of being the mastermind, but using the same lawyer effectively foreclosed this for her. Judge Gibbons had never seen the Thomases before, since the earlier appearance had been before a magistrate, who had assumed that the conflict issue had been handled back in California.

Despite his earlier motion to dismiss on the basis of a slow trial, Williams now requested that the trial be delayed. "I don't know," said Carleen, "I am uncomfortable with him as my attorney." The judge refused to delay the trial, but offered Carleen the assistance of an unprepared legal defender at her own expense. Williams conferred with his clients as the judge looked on. After a few minutes of discussion, Williams announced, "Your honor, I believe they will both accept my representation."

Newsom began his opening statement with an explanation of the indictment, which charged the two defendants with eleven separate crimes. He told the jury it was up to them to determine if the GIFs and tapes were obscene. "If it's obscene, and the proof will show that it is obscene...it's the same as contraband, as machine guns, as drugs or anything else. It's not protected by the First Amendment. It's contraband."

Newsom described the three prongs of the Miller test they would apply to determine obscenity. The first prong was that the average person, applying contemporary community standards, would find that the work, taken as a whole, appeals to a prurient interest in sex. The second prong was that the work depicts or describes sexual conduct in a patently offensive manner. The third prong was that the work lacks substantial literary, artistic, political, or scientific value. After rambling through most of the counts and the obscenity standard, Newsom began describing the on-line chat mode that Dirmeyer had used with Robert Thomas. Williams then made his first objection.

Making an objection during the opening statement is relatively rare, as lawyers have wide latitude in their opening and closing monologues. Williams was jumping the gun, eager to argue that the chat-mode evidence was dubious. The judge overruled him, said Newsom could mention it, and they would get to it when they got to it.

Newsom, without relating them to the counts of the indictment, now spoke of the tapes ordered by Dirmeyer and shipped by Thomas via UPS. He went on to tell the story of the action mags, including Dirmeyer's repeated offers, Thomas' interest, and the result: "The proof will show that in fact the United States government made what we call a controlled delivery. We sent him those magazines, three magazines...involving children engaging in actual sexual conduct with adults...once they are delivered to the defendant, we go in and confiscate those back. We don't let them go out into the public for further circulation or lose control of them. ... Pursuant to the defendant's request, he received the child pornography that he ordered."

Newsom asked the jury to "make that determination if they are obscene or not according to the standards that the judge will give you. If they are, and the government has proven each and every one of the elements in these crimes, we are going to ask you to convict each of these defendants of the crimes with which they are charged. Thank you ladies and gentlemen." He had never told them, specifically, what counts 8 through 11 of the indictment involved. Ironically, these included the sending of the videotapes—the most conventional charges in the case.

In his opening statement, Williams stressed many important issues which are simply beyond the Federal Court's scope. The jury had been instructed to decide if the AABBS material was sexually provocative, offensive, and devoid of artistic merit—according to their community values in Memphis. Rather than try to show that equivalent material existed in their community and that Thomas' pornography was not so bad, Williams raised the larger issue; which community standards should one apply in judging the Thomases? Was it fair to apply the conservative standards of Memphis, Tennessee to a pair of sysops living and working in Milpitas, California? This would later become *the* issue of the case for organizations such as the American Civil Liberties Union and the Electronic Frontier Foundation.

The community standards rule represents an improvisation by the Supreme Court in *Miller v. California*. The First Amendment of the United States Constitution states that "Congress shall make no law... abridging the freedom of speech." Obscenity is one of the few categories of "speech" which falls outside of First Amendment protection.

The evolution of obscenity laws over the decades has followed a more chaotic course than most areas of constitutional law.

Originally, the states were left free to do almost anything they wanted, banning literary and scientific works by Walt Whitman, Theodore Dreiser, and Sigmund Freud, among many others, as obscene. A Walt Disney nature documentary was held obscene in one state because it showed the birth of a buffalo. Another movie was obscene in the South because it showed black and white children playing together. The utter confusion of obscenity law is best summed up in Justice Potter Stewart's famous remark that although he couldn't rightfully define obscenity, "I know it when I see it."

In the 1950s and 1960s, the Supreme Court developed a test somewhat similar to the current three-pronged *Miller* test. Significant differences were that a national community standard was implied, and that the prosecutor had the burden of showing that the work was "utterly without redeeming social value." The Court held during the 1960s that a magazine showing male nudity, without sexual acts, was not obscene, and that it was not a crime merely to possess obscene material in the privacy of one's own home.

The *Miller* standard arose with the arrest of Marvin Miller, who was charged with a violation of a California obscenity law for distributing flyers with explicit sexual depictions. The trial judge had informed the jury that they could apply a local standard on obscenity, and Miller appealed on this issue. The Supreme Court, in promulgating its three-pronged test, did a couple of notable things. First, it rejected the trend of the prior decade by explicitly confirming that a local standard would apply. Chief Justice Burger wrote that "It is neither realistic or constitutionally sound to read the First Amendment as requiring that people of Maine or Missouri accept public depiction of conduct found tolerable in Las Vegas or New York City."

Second, the Court reversed the burden of proof on the third prong of the test. Previously, it had been the prosecutor's job to prove lack of social value. Now, it was up to the defense to show some artistic, literary, political, or scientific value. Interestingly, the court adopted local standards as applicable to the first (appeal to prurient interest) and the second (patently offensive depiction of sexual conduct) prongs, but refused to extend it to the social value criteria of the third prong. It thereby stopped just short of allowing courts to call something art in California, but filth in Tennessee. The standard to be applied on the third prong was a universal "reasonable person" standard. Of the first two prongs, the prurient appeal part of the test has been paraphrased as meaning that it must "turn you on," while the patently offensive prong means that the material must simultaneously "gross you out."

In his opening statement, Williams reintroduced an argument from one of his rejected motions, touching upon the fine distinction between subject and object, sending and taking, with regards to the GIF files. He said that "it's very important that you know that my client is not sending things...the Thomases haven't sent anything anywhere with the exception of the videotapes." Although Williams would continue to argue this technical point that BBS information is not actively sent, but pulled down, he was never able to hammer it home convincingly.

In cross-examining the first witness, Officer MacMahon, whom Newsom established as an expert in computer technology, Williams attempted to show that the Thomases had never transferred anything to the postal inspector; Dirmeyer had logged onto AABBS and downloaded files, in effect transferring files to himself. He asked, "In the event that someone were to contact my computer and downloaded something, would they be taking something, or would I be sending something?" MacMahon answered that they would, of course, be sending.

This was a typical Williams soft-ball question—right concept, not incisively phrased. McMahon was ready for him, walked around the questions, and provided analogies to support the opposite view. Williams was never able to effectively show that the GIFs were not sent. He then discussed the chat mode technology, drawing an admission that the chat mode conversations could have been doctored. He was suggesting to the Tennessee jury that their local postal inspector was a liar who forged evidence. Throughout the trial he was carefree with such implications, while never directly alleging that Dirmeyer forged anything. After McMahon stepped down, Newsom called David Dirmeyer to the stand.

Dirmeyer described his job. "I investigate drug cases, drugs through the mail, and also obscenity cases and child pornography. cases. ... I attended the Postal Inspection Service Training Academy, which was approximately twelve weeks. Of that at least 100 hours were dedicated specifically to child pornography and obscenity investigations." As the jury could see, he was an expert on child pornography, which is governed by stricter laws and standards than other obscene material. Unlike with other obscenity, the government can prosecute for mere possession and artistic or scientific merit is not a defense. Dirmeyer had never found any child pornography in the Thomases' possession, other than that which he sent them. He described how he was first contacted by Earl Crawley, borrowed a computer, logged on for the first time, and was greeted by the slogan "Welcome to AABBS, the nastiest place on earth."

Dirmeyer recounted his undercover search for child pornography, "The main thing that got my interest was the nudist section, as he called it, which he described having GIF files and videotapes of nude teenagers basically is what they were, nude children, ranging from age—any age on up to through their teens." This was the naturist material, which portrayed no sexual acts. Being legal, it wasn't charged in the indictment, but Newsom and Dirmeyer, with no objection by Williams, continued to include it every chance they got. Dirmeyer testified that other GIFs were described as involving bondage, golden showers, and other kinky acts. Newsom quickly circled back around to the nonexistent child pornography, asking Dirmeyer about the term "Lolita." The postal inspector said he was familiar with it as indicating prepubescent girls engaging in sexual activities.

Newsom then instructed Dirmeyer to read from the **ALLVID** text file, which described the available videos and could be downloaded by nonmembers. Williams watched passively as Newsom had several witnesses read from these lewd, explicit, suggestively incestual, but legal, GIF descriptions. As the trial moved on, it became apparent that the Thomases were being largely prosecuted for false advertising. Dirmeyer then related how he had printed out the membership form, completed it, and mailed it to Thomas. The password he requested and received on the system was "Scourge."

The postal inspector then discussed his magazine collection. He said, "In the previous conversation that I had with Mr. Thomas I was complaining about the type of nudist pictures. He had the girls just standing there, and I told him I liked more action in the pictures, so I told him I had action mags." When Newsom sought to introduce a chat mode conversation, Williams objected, on the grounds that the chat mode material can be easily edited. Judge Gibbons said to Williams, "You can certainly make the argument that it could be manipulated. You can make the argument that the witness is not telling the truth. You can make all of those arguments, but, given the witness' testimony, this is sufficient to admit it." She ruled that he could attack Dirmeyer's credibility later, but for now the testimony would continue. Newsom then presented the jury with its first tape—

videotape K74, a kinky video that Thomas had picked for Dirmeyer. Newsom had promised the judge that the tape would run about an hour. She got restless when it seemed to go longer.

Newsom's next pictures were of the Thomases' boat and new Mustang. Williams sat by quietly as the jury was fed this irrelevant information, presented with the implication that these vehicles were ill-gotten spoils of the pornographer's trade. Newsom also continued to mention the naturist material and the pedophilic-sounding GIF descriptions every chance he got. The prosecution's pretense for most of these presentations throughout the trial was to show that Thomas had a predilection for child porn. The argument was that, although he didn't have any on his system, he liked it, he wanted it, and when he was sent some, he gladly accepted it. After Newsom showed a few tapes purported to have young girls, Judge Gibbons remarked, "I think that maybe we should take a short break between each of these."

Seventeen more rape and torture GIFs were shown to the jury and identified by Dirmeyer as originating from previously-shown videos. Williams belatedly asked for a sidebar and stated "It is my understanding that the GIFs were taken from the movie. They have already seen the movie, and I don't see the relevance, unless counsel would like to enlighten me." The judge replied, "I thought about that with the first set, but you didn't object to those."

Dirmeyer read the description of an animal sex video that he ordered in the same letter and then identified some GIFs scanned from the video.

Newsom asked, "According to the defendant, that is a dog in that shot, is that right?"

"That's correct," Dirmeyer answered.

"I think we are done for the day," said Judge Gibbons, despite her previous urging to get through Dirmeyer's testimony.

The next morning, Newsom introduced a film involving children—a legal naturist video. Williams failed to object. Newsom asked, "Your Honor, please, I would ask that about ten or fifteen minutes at least of this tape be played to the court and jury so they can have an idea what the content is." Williams still said nothing. Judge Gibbons, whose usual approach was to let Newsom do anything he wanted so long as Williams didn't object, decided to clue Williams in by asking, "This is not the subject of any of the counts in the indictment, is it?" Williams objected, but the judge cut him off.

"You are admitting it into evidence. There is no objection. If you are going to admit it, the jury can look at it if they need to look at it." Williams had already unwittingly allowed this material into evidence. Two minutes of the nudist video were shown to the jury.

Newsom then sought to introduce the photographs taken of the Thomas residence by the San Jose police. The material was irrelevant, but certainly supported Newsom's implicit attempt to show what kind of toys and wealth these pornographers had amassed. Williams was quicker to object this time. Judge Gibbons asked Newsom, "Why do you want to put them in?" She reminded him, "You haven't charged him with running a pornographic business out of his house. He is being charged with the obscene materials that are listed in this indictment. Furthermore, you have already put in ample material that demonstrates this was the business he was in. ... These are out." On the third day of trial, Williams had finally won an objection.

Williams haplessly began his cross-examination of Dirmeyer by reminding the jurors of his credentials. He had Dirmeyer recount his Postal Inspection Service basic training and numerous subsequent training courses. Williams then elicited some relevant admissions by asking Dirmeyer if he was aware that there was in fact no child pornography on AABBS. "I didn't find any child pornography on the system, no sir." Having established that Dirmeyer had a couple of hundred hours training in combating child pornography and that naturist material had been discussed in that training, he asked, "Now, what did they tell you about the naturist materials? Did they tell you it was legal, or did they tell you it was illegal?" Dirmeyer agreed that as far as he knew, it was legal in all 50 states. Williams inquired weakly into the questionable nature of the search and Thomas' disclosure of knowledge of the consent form. However, he did not really exploit this opportunity to rattle Dirmeyer on entrapment, the chat mode, or anything else.

After Dirmeyer stepped down, Newsom then took another detour to bring in some prejudicial and irrelevant material—without objection by Williams. He called Tom Pennybacker of Mailboxes, Etc. to the stand and asked him about some events which occurred the day after the search. Pennybacker testified that "I was out on a delivery, and I came back from delivery, and my wife, who runs the business with me, was—had been crying and teary eyed and was emotionally shaken. I asked her what the problem was, and she stated she had got a phone call from Mrs. Thomas." Flustered by the search, Carleen had called the Pennybackers to express her displeasure at their involvement—spewing harsh expletives. Pennybacker continued, "I was pretty disturbed by what she had told me, the manner and obscenities used in the phone call directed at us, and I called the Thomases' home." This testimony only served to show that the Thomases were vulgar pornographers with not only new cars and nasty porn, but foul mouths to boot. Williams allowed it to be admitted without objections.

Newsom's next witness was an employee of the Peach Tree Bankcard Corporation. She testified that from January 1 through September 1, 1993, when Peach Tree closed the account for unspecified reasons, the Thomases had processed $238,000 in Visa and Mastercard charges. Williams challenged the relevance of the witness. Newsom claimed that he was just trying to show an overt act, in support of the conspiracy count. Judge Gibbons allowed the testimony. Newsom had just established that the Thomases were *rich* pornographers. Next was the customer service manager from the local Bank of America branch. Williams objected again, but Newsom claimed more proof of overt acts. The Judge finally stopped the testimony: "All the stuff about the bank is not really relevant."

The trial resumed the following morning when Williams introduced Dr. Victor Pascale, Ph.D., licensed psychotherapist, diplomate in human sexuality. "It's the same degree that Dr. Ruth Westheimer holds." Williams asked Pascale "to discuss how a fetish arises, how people get into these things...I think that it is important for them to understand what a fetish is."

Actually, Williams misunderstood the law on this point. The first prong of the *Miller* test has been characterized as whether the works in question are a "turn on" to the jury. Some generally unstimulating material—such as a foot fetish—is often difficult for jurors to find a turn-on. Therefore, a rule had evolved that would allow a jury to ask whether the material was intended to arouse a particular type of person, the fetishist. Williams apparently felt that Dr. Pascale would show the range of human likes and dislikes, thereby making it difficult to convict people for liking what comes naturally. Instead, Pascale's testimony simply made it easier for the jurists to conclude that some people are turned on by fetishism.

Williams then asked whether people who watch these kinds of videos are likely to be offended by them. He was asking the jury to find the videos harmless because they weren't offensive to the intended audience. There would be no obscenity prosecutions at all if this were the standard; obscene material is almost never offensive to its intended audience. Newsom objected and Judge Gibbons sustained the objection.

Williams then asked Pascale whether these fetishes were unusual. He replied, "I would say unusual to the general population, but there is a segment of our population out there that has this as a way of their life....

"We can't confuse disliking something with saying that that's not the way it should be. ... All of us don't like vanilla, and some of us like chocolate better. Some don't even like chocolate. They like pistachio. That is sexuality, too. We have different appetites in our sexuality." Newsom had no questions on cross-examination for Dr. Pascale; he probably felt the doctor already had helped him enough by reinforcing the prosecution on the issue of prurient appeal.

Late in the trial, Williams called his client Carleen Thomas to the stand. She was frightened and ill-prepared. Perhaps being called out of order, when she was expecting another witness to go first, unnerved her. Williams first established her role in the operation. "I took care of all the shipping, and sometimes I would sign the members up, take the credit card information and sign them up."

Under the Fifth Amendment right against self-incrimination, a criminal defendant can never be required to testify at trial. The decision is often a difficult one. One the one hand, everyone knows that a jury is unlikely to acquit a defendant who does not testify—even though the judge instructs them that silence is not an admission of guilt. On the other hand, even an innocent defendant who testifies opens himself up to be trashed by the prosecution on cross-examination. The prosecutor may not be able to establish commission of a crime, but he will do his best to show the jury that the defendant is a bad person. Most defendants choose not to testify. Perhaps Williams thought by putting Carleen on the stand, he would win the jury's sympathy for her and perhaps even for Robert. A wiser approach would have been to keep her off the stand, have Robert testify as to how little involved she was, and ask Dirmeyer on cross-examination whether he had ever had any contact with her—since he hadn't.

Newsom exploited this opening to the fullest, putting on a cruel performance. First, he used her to incriminate Robert further. She insisted that Robert had been responsible for making up all of the titles for the GIFs; but with self-righteousness peculiar to prosecutors, Newsom made her read the title of one GIF after another, asking her whether the description fit the image (e.g., "Blond Lolita Has No Tits. Sucks Huge Cock and Drinks Sperm.")

Remarkably, Williams again failed to object. Newsom was not asking Carleen whether she had seen these GIFs before, or been involved in scanning or distributing them. He was simply asking her to examine them, one by one, and determine whether she agreed with her husband's descriptions. The unstated purpose was to have the jury hear her reading disgusting words—the descriptions of the GIFs were, of course, not charged in the indictment. Whether or not she really did have anything to do with this material, in the eyes and ears of the jury, it and she were one and the same. Gibbons and Williams sat quietly as she read on.

Williams then put Robert Thomas on the stand. Similarly unprepared, he too made a poor impression. Newsom also had Robert read GIF descriptions to the jury. He asked Thomas if he made these up and if he was intending to appeal to pedophiles. Newsom also claimed that Lance White could have been a minor. This was irrelevant. If the materials were obscene, they were illegal for distribution to consenting adults. Elsewhere, Williams had tried to show that the Thomases distributed their tapes and GIFs to a limited, carefully checked adult group before the judge stopped him for irrelevance.

Williams' biggest failure was that he never counterattacked Newsom's conception of Memphis community standards by introducing comparable materials that were available locally. Williams had sent J. Keith Henson out to buy similar videos in stores near the courthouse, but never introduced them into evidence.

In his closing argument, Newsom reiterated much of what he had said in his opening. He told the jury that it was irrelevant whether or not AABBS users were a community of consenting adults, and also irrelevant whether the Thomases thought they were doing anything illegal. The jury only had to believe that the Thomases knew the "general nature and content of the material." He cautioned them that Williams would talk to them of entrapment, and suggested that they think about Robert Thomas' character and reputation. He told them that they must decide whether the GIFs had been transmitted in interstate commerce using the phone lines. Newsom stated, "The transportation of these images, whether its being sent or received, makes no difference. ... [P]lease don't be confused about that as far as whether it was going or coming. ... The question is was the facility used or caused to be used for purposes of transportation of an obscene matter…. I ask you to convict each of these defendants of the crimes charged in this indictment."

In the closing argument for the defense, Williams told the jury that a question existed "as to whether or not they are actually sending it or whether people are reaching out and taking it by way of download. … At any rate though, I think that you will be told by the Court that it's up to you to decide the community standards, and it's up to you to decide what community is the intended recipient…you heard from Inspector Dirmeyer, and you heard from Robert Thomas, and you heard from Carleen Thomas. Now, what did each of these people tell you? Number one, membership only. … This information is not available to the general public, and I guess you can look at that in terms of just the membership curve of the jury and how many of you do have computers and modems." In other words, if the putative victims the jurors were protecting were people like themselves, they had nothing to worry about.

Williams touched on the entrapment issue: "Mr. Thomas had no predisposition to want any of these things. … It was simply sent without his knowledge." On the forfeiture count, he reminded them that the government had only charged a few GIFs—he couldn't remember if it was eleven or thirteen—out of the 17,000 on AABBS. He wanted them to infer from this that everything not charged was legal, and that the computers therefore should not be forfeited, because they were being used largely for legal purposes. He concluded, "[E]ach of you promised in the beginning that you would presume them innocent until they are proven guilty to your satisfaction and I trust that you will do that, and I ask you really to return not guilty verdicts to all counts." A competent defense lawyers stresses the words, "guilty beyond a reasonable doubt," Williams' failure even to use this phrase was another serious omission.

Newsom stood for his rebuttal and reminded the jury that it was not at issue whether a deviant group would find the AABBS materials patently offensive. "It's whether the average person in your community would find that this material is patently offensive."

At 9:45 a.m. on July 28, the jury announced that the defendants, Robert and Carleen Thomas, had been found guilty of all counts except 11, pertaining to the action mags. The jury apparently believed that Dirmeyer had entrapped the Thomases by sending them the magazines. Newsom took the opportunity to add that the

Thomases had just been indicted in the state of Utah. This new indictment was based on non-existent child pornography.

After the trial, the Thomases discharged Williams and hired two lawyers to represent them—Thomas Nolan of Palo Alto for Robert and James Causey of Memphis for Carleen. A major strategy of her new counsel on appeal was to claim that Williams was incompetent. Causey would argue that her interests had been irreparably prejudiced by Williams' representation of Carleen, both because he was incompetent and because she should have had a separate lawyer from the start. Her best strategy would have been to distance herself from Robert and from AABBS, not identify herself with them.

The Thomases also alleged that Williams had never bothered watching the videos for which they were charged; never informed them that their case would be governed by the Federal Sentencing Guidelines; told them they would have to testify but never discussed the risks involved or their right not to testify; and failed to seek a crucial instruction informing the jury that, in the counts charging multiple GIFs, there must be unanimity among the jurors on the obscenity of each GIF.

In a post-trial conference, Judge Gibbons confirmed the forfeiture of all the equipment. She sentenced Robert Thomas "at the upper end of the guideline range, or a sentence of thirty-seven months." She declined to impose a fine, up to $60,000, because the forfeiture of the computers was financial penalty enough. "The Court also recognizes that there will be a need to provide for the Thomases' two children during their incarceration—I don't think they've got the assets that would permit them to adequately take care of them, have the equipment forfeited, and also pay the fine." As for Carleen Thomas, "She is less culpable, and I think that in her case a sentence at the low end of the guideline range is appropriate, or a sentence of thirty months."

The journalistic and legal communities immediately criticized the trial. They generally portrayed Tennessee as the most conservative state in the union and commented on the absurdity of it governing the standards of the on-line world. Judge Gibbons read the disparaging press remarks and was clearly nettled. She remarked that the material was disgusting, repulsive, and would most likely be found obscene everywhere. She was resentful of national publicity that implied that the Thomases could have been convicted only in

Memphis, as if the good people of western Tennessee, not the Thomases, were the outcasts.

Nolan argued that the material was not that bad. Gibbons replied, "What I'm raising my eyebrows at you about is the suggestion that this is a case in which a conviction could only have been obtained in this district or a similar one. This is very, very egregious...this was far at the extreme end of the scale in terms of what might be considered obscenity. ... I haven't seen that many, but of the ones [where] I have seen the material, this was way worse than anything I have seen."

Nolan pressed his argument that the Thomases had not been permitted a fair trial. Judge Gibbons, however, continued to make the point that the AABBS material was extremely disturbing. "Your arguments will sound a whole lot better in the abstract than they will if the appellate court also considers the content of what the jury in fact saw in this case." This statement was remarkable. If Carleen Thomas was denied a fair trial, it is not supposed to matter under our system whether she is accused of speeding or of mass murder. Even an extremely hard-core pornographer is entitled to due process.

Nolan tried to make this point tactfully. "I don't mean to argue with the Court. The Court saw the videotapes, and the jury saw the videotapes, and the jury convicted, and the Court obviously has a belief about those tapes. Those tapes were never subjected to the adversary system. We don't know whether you can buy those tapes down the street, because the lawyer never went and checked." The Judge concluded the conference, "I think you've just about said everything you can say to me today."

Nolan also blamed Newsom for presenting extensive inflammatory evidence not charged in the indictment. The jury had seen 30 irrelevant GIF files had watched the "naturist" video, and had heard numerous descriptions of GIFs and videos when the descriptions themselves had not been charged as obscene. "This evidence," said Nolan "served only to appeal to the juror's emotions and create an atmosphere of disgust toward Mr. Thomas in violation of his right to due process and a fair trial."

Nolan made much of Williams' ineffectiveness, claiming that his performance was inferior to that of "a reasonable attorney" and resulted in prejudice to Robert Thomas' interests. He listed Williams' failure to object to testimony about the Thomases' income and about "bras, panties and dildoes" for sale, and the introduction of the photos of the Mustang and boat, and his failure to move for acquittal when Newsom rested.

In his brief, Nolan cited a Tenth Circuit case, *Carlin Communications*, which said that only "tangible" material sent by conventional means could be determined obscene. This would have eliminated the GIFs from the indictment and transformed the case into a garden variety videotape case. Judge Gibbons conceded he raised some significant issues, but said this point was essentially irrelevant. "They would still be doing the same amount of time even if you prevail on that issue." She had sentenced them concurrently on the video and GIF charges, so even without the latter charge, the sentences for the videos would still have been 37 and 30 months, respectively.

Though Williams did not help the Thomases very much, he did, in fact, raise some of the most important larger issues. In his opening statement at trial he said, "Mr. Thomas will tell you basically that the Amateur Action BBS is an adults-only membership-only bulletin board service.... The menu, of course, would be the only thing, as Mr. Thomas will tell you, that would be available to somebody that is not a member. Why would this be important from our perspective? Because its not like these things are being disseminated to the community generally. You will hear that only the people who look at the menu and decide they want to join the bulletin board would be members and entitled to download anything."

This argument embodies the essential problems with the AABBS case and with obscenity laws in general, pointing out that the Thomases sold their material to an insular community of 3,500 consulting adults, who asked and paid for it.

This argument, however, was ineffective at trial—questioning the validity of applying local, geographical standards on global networks, and the right of government to ban this form of speech could hold no weight in Gibbons' court.

Robert Thomas has been incarcerated in federal prison since February 1995. His wife was allowed some extra time to look after her kids and began serving her thirty month sentence the following July.

# ACT III—THE ISSUES

Soon after the conviction and sentencing, the Internet and the media were both running stories of an unfair trial, based on an outmoded standard. Many mainstream newspapers and magazines, from *The New York Times* to *Playboy*, published pieces on the plight of the Thomases. Several nonprofit civil liberties organizations drafted amicus briefs—third party legal arguments submitted to the court to influence its decision. Jumping into the fray were the Electronic Frontier Foundation, the American Civil Liberties Union ("ACLU"), The Society For Electronic Access, and the Interactive Services Association. In addition, the ACLU brief was joined by other organizations including the National Writer's Union and Feminists for Free Expression. Most of these groups specifically declared that they were not objecting to the Thomases' conviction for mailing videotapes to Dirmeyer in Memphis; they were concerned about the case's certain effect upon free speech on the Internet.

On appeal, Nolan also revisited an important point which Williams had unsuccessfully raised: did the Thomases in fact "send" anything? He tried to persuade the appeals court that a BBS is more like a traditional bookstore than like a mail order operation. He cited *Cubby v. CompuServe*, which held that on-line customers could electronically browse through the available material, pick items, and take these items back home. A higher court would never permit the prosecution of a California bookstore in Memphis if Dirmeyer had travelled to California, bought books there, and carried them home to Memphis.

He maintained that Memphis was not the proper venue because "Mr. Thomas did not send any GIF files to Memphis. ... The acts that did occur in Tennessee, such as the selection and downloading of GIF files, were initiated and performed solely by Inspector Dirmeyer." Nolan argued that, if the standards of any geographical community were to be applied, it should be the standards of northern California, where AABBS was actually located. The EFF concurred, arguing that the Thomases "had no physical contact with the state of Tennessee, they had not advertised in any medium directed primarily at Tennessee, they had not physically visited Tennessee, nor had they any assets or other contacts there." Dirmeyer's actions—logging on and downloading—caused the material to be "transported" into Tennessee. The EFF, like Nolan, used the analogy of Dirmeyer travelling to California, purchasing a computer file, and bringing it back home with him.

Nolan then summed up the central cyberspace issue. "To impose the standards of Memphis, Tennessee on national communications networks would have a chilling effect on the free speech rights of members of other communities. These networks would be compelled to self-censor and impose on the entire nation the standards of the most restrictive community." The EFF centered its argument on this point—Memphis standards should not be used to set the ground rules for all cyberspace. Allowing the conviction to stand would fly in the face of *Miller* by creating a single national, even global, standard based on the law of Tennessee.

In its famous *Butler v. Michigan* decision in 1957, the Supreme Court held a Michigan law unconstitutional which made criminal the sale of books that might have a bad effect on youth. Justice Frankfurter, who traditionally took a hard stance against obscenity, wrote for the majority that the Constitution does not permit a state to reduce its adult population "to reading only what is fit for children." The AABBS case allows *Miller* to reduce the national population to reading only what is fit for Tennessee.

In 1973, when *Miller* was decided, America was already immersed in an age of national television and radio broadcasting and national distribution of books and magazines. Chief Justice Burger's touching fear that New York and Las Vegas—those sinks of vice—would impose their vile standards on Maine or Mississippi, was not balanced by any apprehension that Maine or Mississippi might turn the tables and rule New York or Las Vegas. There is no other area of constitutional law which allows for local variations. A police beating which violates the Fifth Amendment in New York is not acceptable in Memphis because local standards differ. An illegal search violating the Fourth Amendment in California is just as illegal in Maine.

The *Miller* decision presupposed that the material was distributed by a more conventional method, such as the mail, and allowed the distributor a choice of not sending it into any jurisdiction where the local standards might find it obscene. In an age where information located on any server, anywhere in geographical space can be accessed and transmitted anywhere else, and where geographical location is not even mildly relevant in terms of access cost or speed, *Miller* now stands for the opposite of what it did in 1973. By allowing the application of local standards to a vast, instantaneous, worldwide entity like the Internet, *Miller* now allows Memphis, in the heart of the Bible Belt, to apply its conservatism forcibly to the rest of the world.

Many people may agree that the Thomases deserve to sit in prison. The jury found the Thomases guilty of slipping six obscene videos into their state. Perhaps "the nastiest place on earth" would prove illegal in 49 states, and it is not New York or Las Vegas from which the wholesome communities need protection, but Milpitas, California. Judge Gibbons said after the trial that this was the worst stuff she had ever seen, deserving of conviction in any federal district in the country, under any local standards. But even if Judge Gibbons' guess is correct, it does not justify the jailing of these California sysops in Tennessee.

The case stands out because it reveals the glaring shortcomings of the obscenity standard in the face of today's new communications. The fundamental problem was that neither Gibbon's court, nor the Court of Appeals was equipped to handle the real issue. Neither Williams, Nolan, or Causey could rightfully argue the constitutionality of *Miller* before either court. (Although Williams gave it a try.)

On the Internet today, it is not usually possible to determine a user's state of origin from the IP address or domain name. Even if technology is introduced to allow BBS and Internet providers to determine the user's residence, it is unrealistic to expect them to learn the laws and precedents for each community of all 50 states. It is also unrealistic to expect Tennessee to unplug itself from the Internet. The fundamental question is which community has the right to set the standard? Three possible answers to the question are raised by the AABBS case—the status quo (the *Miller* standard), a national standard, or the use of the standards of cybercommunities rather than geographical ones. This third argument added an interesting new element to an old debate.

Nolan argued that "computer bulletin board technology requires the application of a new definition of community." The wording of *Miller* had not required that the standards applied be those of a "geographical" community, and there was precedent in FCC regulations and military law for the proposition that a *Miller* community did not have to be geographically bound. "In defining community standards in the *Miller* case, the Supreme Court neither anticipated nor took into account the rapid advances in computer technology. ... The rapid growth of national and global computer networks have radically altered the nature of communications and have allowed persons to interact without geographic constraints in 'a nonphysical universe called cyberspace."

"The cyberspace community is as much a community as traditional geographic divisions. This community should have the right to articulate its standards on the issue of obscenity. A definition of community based on connections between people rather than one based on geographic location will ensure that all communities have the right to define protected speech."

Though nothing in *Miller* prevented the determination that the standards of a non-geographical, cyberspace community should apply, Judge Gibbons had said at trial that the relevant community could not legally be adult bookstore customers, or pornographic video watchers, or even VCR owners.

Newsom had a brief retort to Nolan's argument. "Computer technology does not require a new definition of community. ... Appellants provide an eloquent essay on the effect of computers on interpersonal communication. While fascinating and well-written, the mini-treatise fails to offer any legal support or any suggestion for how a court is to 'examine the community created by computer technology' and 'adopt a rule that protects and encourages freedom of speech and expression.' The reality is that if the court 'examined the community created by computer technology', it would find that computers essentially create a world community. Computers unite citizens of small midwestern towns with denizens of New York City. For that matter, they unite Memphis residents with computer users in London, Tokyo, Bombay. It would be unrealistic to attempt to define the accepted standards of a 'community' that includes Iowa farmers, Las Vegas casino owners, Icelandic fishermen, and Tibetan monks. Clearly the notion of a 'computer-users community' is unfathomable and should be rejected, just as the United States Supreme Court rejected a 'national' standard in Miller."

Actually, no one was arguing for a global standard. Nolan and the ACLU were really arguing to apply the standards of the AABBS users themselves. The idea is that they are an insular group of 3,500 pornophiles who should be allowed to stew in their own smut if they like.

Such a result—the adoption of the standards of the members of a cyberspace community to judge the obscenity of which they are sympathetic users—would effectively repeal obscenity laws entirely.

Under such a scenario, as long as AABBS did not offend its own members, and disseminated its material only to adults who requested and paid for it, it would never be shut down.

From a broader perspective, the application of obscenity laws to cyberspace is an opportunity to reexamine the legal and moral underpinnings of these laws. Obscenity is held to be a form of speech so degraded that it stands entirely outside the usual First Amendment protections. The problem is that no one seems exactly certain what it is, or how to define it; Justice Potter Stewart's famous but legally weak statement was that he knew it when he saw it.

The meanings of the words pornography and obscenity have evolved over the years. Obscenity is a subset of pornography and it is illegal, because it is prurient, contains patently offensive sexual material, and is devoid of scientific, literary, artistic or political value. Pornography, by contrast, covers much material that appeals to prurient interests but which is either not offensive or which has scientific, literary, artistic or political value. It is almost universally accepted that the written word, even embodied in cheap, transient, anonymous paperbacks intended solely to cause sexual arousal, is not obscene. Most obscenity prosecutions today involve pictures and films.

The "slippery slope" argument posits that regulation slides into censorship, taking other valid forms of speech with it. If we find marginal material to be obscene, soon the courts will be using the precedent to ban literature. This argument is well supported by history; Joyce, Nabokov, Hemingway, and other great authors have all been banned in this country. Critics of this line of reasoning say that those were the dark ages and today's society certainly would not revisit the follies of the past.

The Post Office first became involved in obscenity law after the Civil War. Over the years the post office sought to purge the mail of obscene novels by Ernest Hemingway, John O'Hara, Erskine Caldwell, J.D. Salinger, Alberto Moravia, John Steinbeck, Richard Wright, and Norman Mailer, and nonfiction works by Sigmund Freud, Margaret Mead, and Simone de Beauvoir.

In the 1950s, the Post Office undertook a crusade against a character named Samuel Roth, triggering a major Supreme Court holding in 1957, *Roth v. United States*. Roth, like many of the publishers pursued by the authorities from the 1940s through the 1960s, occasionally published works of genius—he had been prosecuted decades before for a pirated version of *Ulysses*—and sometimes published pure pornography. Roth offended the Post Office because he marketed his works by mailing flyers indiscriminately to huge lists of people, many of whom were offended to receive them. Roth claimed to have sent out ten million circulars during his career.

The work of Roth's that reached the Supreme Court was Volume I, Number 3 of a periodical he published called *American Aphrodite*. The issue contained the illustrator Aubrey Beardsley's last, unfinished prose work, the explicit *Venus and Tannhauser*, which includes a description of Venus masturbating a pet unicorn. The case began when a Post Office inspector, using the name Archie Lovejoy (a fit predecessor of Lance White) ordered *American Aphrodite* through the mails. Roth was convicted in federal court in New York and the case made its way up to the Supreme Court.

Using a tactic worthy of Anthony Comstock, the Justice Department official who argued the Post Office's position in the Supreme Court, Roger Fisher (later a Harvard professor and author of a famous book on negotiation), brought a box of obscene material to the Supreme Court. None of the materials in the box had ever been mailed by Samuel Roth; the sole purpose was to frighten the Court that the mails would be flooded with this kind of trash if it struck down the postal obscenity law. Fisher's box sits in the historical company of Anthony Comstock's sack and Senator Exon's blue book.

The Court affirmed the constitutionality of the postal obscenity law. (An entertaining sidelight to the story: when the box was returned to the Justice Department, half of its contents was missing.) In 1986, the Justice Department under Attorney General Edwin Meese formed a National Obscenity Enforcement Unit which worked closely with the Postal Service to prepare and prosecute obscenity cases. The Unit's efforts reached a nadir with a massive campaign by the Postal Service to entrap individuals into ordering child pornography through the mails. At least one of the resulting convictions, of a sedentary farmer whom the Postal Service solicited for two years before he ordered child porn, was overturned as entrapment. Another targeted farmer committed suicide. To paraphrase the old saw about legislation, obscenity convictions are like sausage: no one who appreciates the result should watch the process by which they are created.

If you look at the *Amateur Action* case in a vacuum, it is hard to comprehend why the ACLU or the Feminists for Free Expression think that there is a slippery slope leading from Robert and Carleen Thomas to more serious purveyors of radical or non-mainstream ideas. After all, the Thomases never sought to argue that the videos or GIFs were artistic expression protected by the First Amendment. (Nolan and Causey didn't even attempt to argue that this was an issue missed by Williams.)

The slippery slope doesn't seem so unreasonable if you think that as recently as 1990, Cincinnati police closed a Robert Mapplethorpe photography show at the Contemporary Arts Center and local authorities indicted the museum's curator for obscenity. Mapplethorpe, whose images included portraits, flowers and sexually explicit homoerotic images, was almost universally recognized in the art world as a major figure. It just does not wash to say, after reading about Post Office vendettas against Hemingway and Steinbeck, that "those were the bad old days; it can't happen again." The slope, starting with Robert and Carleen Thomas, leads to serious artists and the purveyors of radical ideas.

The law of obscenity is so fundamentally confused that, before we bring it into a new technology and a new century, we should tear it down to its foundations, examine it, and determine whether and how to rebuild it to meet modern social needs. After defining the terms, we must determine who this abridgment of the First Amendment is designed to protect. There are four classes of potential victims of obscenity: minors, unsuspecting viewers, women, and users of pornography, who may need to be protected against themselves.

For many, minors form the crux of the obscenity issue. Among consenting adults in a free society, distasteful speech is merely to be avoided. Children, on the other hand, can be drawn by curiosity and corrupted by such ideas. Though the prosecution raised the question of whether Dirmeyer, for all the Thomases knew, could have been underage, they never charged AABBS with distributing to minors. In fact, the Thomases instituted relatively strict measures to keep out children. This becomes more of an issue on the open protocols of newsgroups and the World Wide Web; but AABBS was as secure as any adults-only sex shop on 42nd Street.

Unwilling viewers of obscene material seem to be everyone's second-choice victim. Like secondary smoke, unwanted pornography is a quality of life issue, polluting the lives of people who would rather not be exposed to it. The Supreme Court has dealt with the unwilling viewer issue in two contexts: unsolicited mailings on public policy issues, and non-obscene nudity on drive-in movie screens. The Court said that, with regards to unsolicited mailings, our right not to be bothered does not justify limiting First Amendment rights. The solution is to "escape exposure to the objectionable material simply by transferring [it] from envelope to wastebasket." The Supreme Court also invalidated, on First Amendment grounds, a Florida law that banned nudity on drive-in movie screens to protect innocent passers-by. The Court said that the problem could most easily be cured by turning away after a fleeting glimpse—not by depriving movie-goers of the right to see films.

The cautious AABBS sign-up procedure of credit cards, passwords, and voice verification seems to minimize the possibility that anyone who didn't want to see the GIFs would be exposed to them. Newsom and Dirmeyer tried to raise the specter of the unwanted viewer as victim by describing Earl Crawley's shock at seeing the ALLGIF file without being a member of AABBS, and by the particular attention they paid to the "distribute freely" stamp on many of the GIFs. However, there was no evidence at trial that any unwilling viewer other than Earl Crawley had ever been exposed to AABBS materials, and the only thing Crawley could have seen, the ALLGIF file, probably could not itself legally have been declared obscene, since it consisted of text only. Since Crawley did not appear at trial, the defense never was able to ask him what he was doing logged onto a BBS named "Amateur Action" anyway. (Maybe he thought it had to do with ham radio or local theatricals.)

Even the GIFs marked "distribute freely" were redistributed mainly on other adult bulletin boards and the Internet's alt.sex newsgroups, which require some effort to find and are probably not frequented by too many unwilling viewers. Additionally, a pornographic GIF doesn't just appear on your screen in Usenet; viewing it requires the download of many separate messages (sometimes more than 20) and then the use of special software to reconstitute it as an image.

Although the recent "cyberporn" debate has concentrated on the vulnerability of children in cyberspace, the *Miller* decision and another case, *Paris Adult Theaters v. Slaton*, reveal that the Supreme Court's main concern was with society, perceived as a huge class of "unwilling viewers" whose lives could be polluted by obscene material. The Court expressed extreme skepticism that there was any effective way, short of banning it, to keep obscene speech from intruding on society.

Anti-pornography feminists have recently popularized the idea that pornography causes violence against women and should be banned entirely. Professor Catharine MacKinnon of the University of Michigan Law School is the leading advocate of this view. In 1993, she published a book called *Only Words*, in which she outlined the position that pornography *is* the oppression of women. According to MacKinnon, women in our society try to swim "against the male flood." Pornographic materials contribute to real harassment, objectification, and rape every day. She asks why words degrading to women are protected as speech when other crimes beginning in speech—phrases like "kill him" or "let's fix prices"—cannot hide behind the First Amendment.

MacKinnon wrote, "What pornography does, it does in the real world, not only in the mind. As an initial matter, it should be observed that it is the pornography industry, not the ideas in the materials, that forces, threatens, blackmails, pressures, tricks, and cajoles women into sex for pictures. In pornography, women are gang raped so that they can be filmed. They are not gang raped by the idea of a gang rape. It is for pornography, and not by the ideas in it, that women are hurt and penetrated, tied and gagged, undressed and genitally spread and sprayed with lacquer and water so that sex pictures can be made.... Similarly, on the consumption end, it is not the ideas in pornography that assault women: men do, men who are made, changed and impelled by it." MacKinnon believes that due to female powerlessness and male power, no woman ever really consents to appear in these scenes, any more than children can consent to engage in sexual acts to create child pornography.

She points out that "The law of equality and the law of freedom of speech are on a collision course in this country." Fifteen years ago, MacKinnon was instrumental in getting sexual harassment condemned as illegal, unconstitutional behavior, which denies women their rights of equality under the Fifth and Fourteenth Amendments. Sexual harassment law restricts speech in the workplace, such as sexual epithets or the display of pornography, that creates an environment of inequality for women. Yet, outside the workplace, identical behavior is protected by the First Amendment as speech.

MacKinnon and a colleague, Andrea Dworkin, co-authored a proposed local ordinance outlawing "graphic sexually explicit materials that subordinate women through pictures or words." The law created a private right of action against pornographers and distributors for any woman who had been injured by pornography. The draft law was squarely aimed at the kind of material available on AABBS. It defined as pornography pictures or words in which women are "presented as dehumanized sex objects...sexual objects who enjoy humiliation or pain...sexual objects tied up or cut up or mutilated or bruised or physically hurt...being penetrated by objects or animals."

The law was adopted in a few municipalities, but came under immediate attack. A federal court soon invalidated it as contrary to the First Amendment. This ruling was upheld by the Court of Appeals, which issued a detailed opinion stating that portrayals of the submission of women, no matter how unpleasant, are protected speech, and "The Constitution forbids the state to declare one perspective right and silence opponents."

The court's invalidation of MacKinnon's ordinance was consistent with prior First Amendment caselaw. Over the years, the Supreme Court has overturned a law banning cross-burning as a political statement, and upheld the right of Nazis to march in a Jewish neighborhood. The American philosophy is that speech is to be combated by more speech, not by government censorship.

No exception to the First Amendment was necessary to promote the equality of black people in this country. We didn't pass hate crime laws making KKK-style racism illegal; rather, there was an important change in social attitudes, which fueled, and was fueled by, other types of legal advances under the Constitutional rights of equality. In order to enjoy the full extent of speech and freedom afforded by the First Amendment, we must realize that it protects hateful speech in order to protect good speech. It is hypocritical to carve out exceptions for particular groups. Not every immoral act should be an illegal one and not every social wrong is most effectively addressed by a law; some are best addressed by a change in social attitudes.

The last group potentially protected by the obscenity laws are the pornography users themselves. *Stanley v. Georgia*, the Supreme Court case recognizing a right for individuals to possess obscenity, definitively rejected this view. The First Amendment was intended to protect speech, not protect individuals from speech they willingly hear. John Stuart Mill said that "the only purpose for which power can be rightfully exercised over any member of a civilized community, against his will, is to prevent harm to others. His own good, either physical or moral, is not a sufficient warrant." Mill held that only in an environment of perfect liberty can the individual develop to his or her fullest. The United States, in general, is imperfectly "Millian;" many laws on the books prohibit behavior that is only self-regarding. But the First Amendment is almost completely in accord with Mill's precepts. Mill acknowledged that some of us will go in bad directions; like individuals in a biological evolutionary race, some will succeed, others wither; but, as long as each of us harms only himself and no other, the government must not intervene. The 3,500 users of AABBS, it may be argued, were engaged in such a process of self-development; we may judge it to be a bad one, but as long as they are only harming themselves, we should not intervene.

A free, democratic society should err on the side of speech, not censorship. But, considering that there are children around who should not be exposed to certain ideas and pictures until they are ready to view and handle them, we must build in some safeguards. Although Robert Thomas may very well be, as Newsom argued, a rich, sadistic purveyor of twisted smut, he effectively built in safeguards to prevent his community of 3,500 consumers from being discovered by minors. Then, as the EFF said, "any local territorial community that wants to enforce its own obscenity standards has a duty to use tools to help it stay away from the offending materials."

The AABBS case highlights the 200-year debate between the autonomy of the states and the power of the federal union. The problem is not made any easier in an era of global networks that do not recognize geographic distinctions or any differing value between different streams of ones and zeros running through the wires. This case foreshadows the coming problems that will arise between communities of all shapes and sizes. Will Iran extradite Europeans for posting parts of *Satanic Verses* to a newsgroup? Will China shut down servers in Asia that offer material that sympathizes with Tibet? In December, 1995, CompuServe removed alt.sex newsgroups from it's global service because of a threat by German prosecutors. As difficult as it may be to swallow, speech should be allowed to roam free, just as books are almost entirely uncensored in America.

As for the Thomases, business is booming. Along with a friend, the Thomas sons have pitched in while their parents serve out their prison terms. There is something incongruous about the family life of the Thomases: a seemingly secure, financially comfortable, stable, nuclear American family where the family business, eventually taken over by the sons, trades in images of rape, bondage, and torture. The hype surrounding the case has brought their membership up to 10,000. And though they forfeited all their computers to the government, they have all new machines to better handle the growth of their $300,000+ per year enterprise. The Thomases will be out of prison in a couple of years. But then they may have to stand trial again in Utah (and Nebraska, and Kentucky, and Nevada...?).

# CHAPTER

# II

# THE GOVERNMENT'S KEYS

United States Customs officials were camped out at Dulles International Airport, waiting for Phil Zimmerman to step off his plane from Europe. Zimmerman, an unassuming computer hacker, cryptologist, and American citizen, was returning from a series of speaking engagements about his popular data encryption program, PGP, when the Customs officials halted his reentry and took him aside. They detained Zimmerman for a half an hour as they searched through his luggage and interrogated him about his trip, prior trips, and the exportation of his program. They finally allowed him to pass into the country after informing him that he would be subject to the same searches every time he crossed the border back into America and reminding him that the next detainment could lead to 41-51 months in jail.

It was a year earlier, in the fall of 1993, when Zimmerman first learned that he was the subject of a federal investigation and would likely be indicted for the export of PGP (Pretty Good Privacy). It's a modest name for a powerful piece of software that allows individuals to encrypt and authenticate messages with as much security as anything ever developed. With standard desktop computers complete strangers can easily encipher and send data such that the National Security Agency's top scientists, armed with the world's fastest computers are at a loss. Since the inception of the computer, the government has deemed encryption to be the sole province of the military, not to be used by ordinary citizens. But, until recently, average citizens have simply not had the need or the computing power to employ the necessary algorithms.

41

In 1991, the first version of Zimmerman's program was published on the Internet. In the fall of 1993, Assistant U.S. Attorney William Keane convened a San Jose grand jury and issued a series of subpoenas to determine whether Zimmerman should be charged with violating Title 22, Section 2778 of the Federal Criminal Code, which deals with the "control of arms export and imports" and prohibits the export of munitions without a license. Encryption isn't just frowned upon. The government groups these algorithms with plutonium, napalm, and Tomahawk missiles. They are all deemed munitions and they are all illegal to export. However, the issue is complicated by the fact that mathematical algorithms are somewhat more slippery than two-ton warheads.

Zimmerman never exported PGP; he wrote it, encouraged its use, and distributed it to friends and colleagues—one of whom posted it to a Usenet newsgroup. PGP has since become the de facto worldwide standard for E-mail encryption. By building on the Diffie-Hellman public-key encryption system developed at Stanford University in the late 1970s and the RSA algorithm discovered soon thereafter at MIT, Zimmerman produced a program that is easy to use and, by today's computing standards, essentially uncrackable. He didn't develop any of the algorithms which comprise his program. But by appropriating and combining powerful, patented, academic discoveries, Zimmerman has singularly sent waves of anxiety through the National Security Agency—the once-secret arm of the Defense Department which specializes in developing and cracking codes.

Data encryption, the scrambling of messages so enemies and eavesdroppers cannot listen in, has existed in varying forms for millennia. Some date the first recorded examples of such technology back to the hieroglyphics of the ancient Egyptians. The basic idea is to hopelessly scramble a given set of data according to a mathematical key so that it can be safely stored and sent along insecure channels. Only those with the unique key can reveal the message. Caesar reputedly used the simple substitution cipher when sending messages back to Rome from Gaul. With this method, each letter is replaced with another letter n places further in the alphabet (e.g., in a key where n is two, "a" is replaced with "c", "b" with "d," etc.).

Electronic varieties of encryption arose not long after the development of telegraphs and telephones. Within a year of Morse's introduction of the telegraph in 1845, a commercial coding device was developed. A system such as the one used by Caesar would require only a search of 26 different keys to crack the code. Modern machines, however, measure their power in MIPS (millions of instructions per second) and can be programmed to run exhaustive searches of such keys. To be of any practical use, today's telephone and E-mail cryptographic systems require complex mathematical algorithms and computing power far beyond the unassisted capabilities of the human brain.

Many of the world's earliest computers were developed specifically for cryptoanalysis, or breaking codes. As early as 1943 researchers in England's Government Code and Cypher School had developed a machine that specialized in cipher-breaking. Although the Polish had discovered the key to Hitler's cutting edge encrypting hardware, the Enigma, the Germans were adept at jumbling up their messages by means of complicated algorithms and computers soon became the only possible means of cracking the codes.

In 1943, the most advanced computer of the day was the ASCC Mark1, which was developed at Harvard University with backing from IBM. It was 51 feet long, weighed five tons, and incorporated 750,000 parts. The chairman of IBM, Thomas Watson said at the time, "I think there is a world market for maybe five computers." The government, however, found uses for these machines and spurred their development. In 1952 IBM unveiled the "Defense Calculator"—later renamed the "701"—which could perform 2200 multiplications per second. The NSA, which was in the business of intercepting and deciphering enemy intelligence, found these powerful calculating machines to be just the tools they needed to decode the increasingly difficult ciphers. One of the first major users of computers, the NSA is also arguably the world's largest purchaser of computing hardware.

President Truman created the NSA by Executive Order in 1952. Although the NSA's official charter is still classified, their function has traditionally been to protect United States executive and military communications. In his book, *The Puzzle Palace*, James Bamford describes the agency's birth, which "arrived in silence. No news coverage, no congressional debate, no press announcement, not even the whisper of a rumor.... Equally invisible were the new agency's director, its numerous buildings, and its ten thousand employees.... America's newest and most secret agency, so secret in fact that only a handful in the government would be permitted to know its existence." For many, NSA stood for "No Such Agency."

The NSA's estimated $10 billion budget is unaccounted for and transferred into their coffers under the same language as the charter which provides for the CIA's funding—"without regard to any provisions of the law." Unlike the CIA and FBI, however, the NSA does not need a warrant to tap American communications lines, as long as one of the terminals is outside the United States. Since the NSA openly revealed its existence, it has been widely published that for decades it routinely scanned through every telegram and telex that passed in and out of the United States—that spying on the American people had also become a regular part of its job.

In addition to cracking codes and developing encryption systems, the NSA works hard to keep everyone else from making its task more difficult. Since the development of the computer and the formation of the NSA, encryption has been serious business for the United States government. The NSA continues to adhere to its original policy that America's superior intelligence with regards to powerful encryption has helped win wars; it is a weapon and belongs in the hands of the military, not the masses.

The NSA has played a part in the development and endorsement of all official encryption systems. The latest government-endorsed system to be widely used and rigorously tested is the DES, Data Encryption Standard. This system was developed at IBM before being scrutinized, modified, and approved by the NSA in 1977 for storing and sending classified information. Since it is only through rigorous academic, government, and private testing that any encryption technology can be proven effective, the NSA acquiesced to public pressure and published the algorithm. It knew that by publishing the mathematics, the system would invariably be circulated, but to this day the NSA does not permit DES to be exported. Just to be safe, the NSA insisted upon implementing a weaker version than the original—knowing the government would use it only for basic, classified information.

Still used today, and still considered quite powerful, DES is a symmetric, or secret key, encryption system. The secret key is used to set a complex algorithm into motion that renders a given message incomprehensible to observers. At the time and only until very recent advances in computing power, this provided virtually complete security. But to unlock a given message, the recipient needs either the same key or a duplicate of the one that encrypted it. Thus, in order to successfully pass information across insecure channels, the secret key first has to be run across a secure channel.

For this reason, military officers were often whisked off in government planes to far away places with the secret keys sealed in briefcases handcuffed to their wrists—a time, energy, money, and manpower consuming process. Herein lay the ultimate puzzle for cryptologists for decades...how to encrypt and send data to another party who can decrypt it without ever using a secure channel. Within this mathematical dilemma also stood the most formidable obstacle to the creation of a cryptographic system that could be used by the public at large. In 1977, when DES was approved and accepted, encryption technology was solely in the realm of the military if for no other reason than that microcomputers were not yet a reality. But Apples and PCs were in the wings and academics were devising new algorithms. Computer scientists at the top schools were engaged in the intellectual exercise of developing a encryption system that circumvented the need for a secure channel.

Two researchers in the Stanford University Electrical Engineering Department, Whitfield Diffie and Martin Hellman finally developed the first feasible way to encrypt and exchange secure data over insecure channels in 1976. They knew with this breakthrough that their discovery amounted to more than just an abstract algorithmic eureka. They introduced their discovery of public-key encryption in a groundbreaking paper which began, "We stand on the brink of a revolution in cryptography," realizing that they were on the verge of putting this power into the hands of common people.

Diffie and Hellman had devised a relatively simple technique which permits complete strangers to create a private key over insecure channels, allowing them to freely communicate encrypted data. Each party begins with his own secret key. They then exchange mathematical information about their respective keys to create a new key, called a session key, that they use to encrypt future messages. Though this was the basis for the public-key encryption used by PGP, the Diffie-Hellman system required real-time communication and was thus not possible for data communications, such as E-mail.

Although Diffie and Hellman had indeed come to the brink of a cryptographic revolution, the world was not yet on the brink of really caring. The year was 1976: most people were using rotary phones and you had to speak to a live teller to get your money. IBM still had another four years of work before it would introduce the first PC, and the only people who knew what E-mail was were in the government or academia. By the time the rest of the world was getting on-line, their breakthrough idea would exist in the form of a usable product.

In the Spring of 1976, the Diffie-Hellman paper entitled "New Directions in Cryptography" (which described the public-key method) made its way to the desks of three young professors at MIT's computer lab—Ronald Rivest, Adi Shamir, and Len Adelman. Collectively they set to work on implementing a workable public-key encryption system and by the spring of the following year, they had introduced RSA. Named after the three inventors, RSA employed a powerful algorithm to create a cryptographic system that did not require real-time participation between the sender and the receiver of the message.

With this public encryption method each person has two keys— one secret and one public. These keys have a mathematical relationship, though one cannot be deduced from the other. The "public key" is published in the database equivalent of a phone book. If you want to send, for instance, J.D. Salinger some private data, you look up his public key and encrypt the message with it. When he receives your mail he uses his corresponding private key to unlock the data.

The idea behind the RSA algorithm is that factoring is difficult. When you multiply two large prime numbers you arrive at a very large product. Going backwards, however, and factoring this immense number (in the order of 100 digits long) is nearly impossible—even with today's most powerful computers. So, the properties of the keys generate the product, which is then nearly impossible to trace back to the original key numbers. Until faster computers or more sophisticated mathematics devise new and easier shortcuts to factoring, this method is, barring a short key length, virtually unbreakable.

The power of encryption systems resides in the power of the algorithm and the size of the key. The longer the key the larger the equation. To give an idea of the strength of RSA, consider a challenge the team printed in the August 1977 issue of *Scientific American*. It was an encrypted sentence coded in the form of a 129-digit number. The team offered $100, but the world's cryptographers sat stumped for 17 years. In the Spring of 1994 an international team of 600 cryptographers and computer scientists from 24 countries took 8 months and 1600 workstations to factor the number and crack the code: "The magic words are squeamish ossifrage." (Ossifrage is the name of a large predatory bird.) Phil Zimmerman was a computer science major in college when he received the authors' published hints on how the RSA system had encrypted this message.

Even he couldn't have guessed that this paper would be the seed for his rise to notoriety—though he had enjoyed secret codes in the Boy Scouts. Zimmerman began studying physics at school before switching to computers, but it wasn't until years later that he began to pursue on his own time the study of encryption. Like a kid playing with everyone else's toys, Zimmerman would eventually put the ideas and algorithms together into a shape that finally made sense. RSA alone did not provide the basis for a feasible E-mail program as it required an enormous amount of computational power—the kind only available in places like MIT's computer labs.

Today Zimmerman is a computer consultant in Boulder, Colorado. He doesn't look like a mythical cypherpunk calling for crypto-anarchy. He is a paunchy, bearded man in his 40s. He is married, has two kids, and prefers donning a coat and tie when doing business. Zimmerman ekes out a living as a full-time cryptography consultant, but spends his time lecturing, writing, and giving interviews, mostly about PGP. He spent six months of twelve hour days writing it, gave away most of it for free, and has a pile of debt as he braces for a legal onslaught.

As Zimmerman puts it, PGP is "well featured, fast, with sophisticated key management, digital signatures, data compression, and good ergonomic design." It is essentially an amalgamation of the Diffie-Hellman system, RSA, and a standard secret-key encryption system. PGP solves the RSA problem of heavy computing power requirements by using it only to encrypt the secret key of IDEA, a standard secret-key system which is incorporated into the program and is used to encrypt the bulk of the message. Symmetrical key systems like DES and the Swiss-developed IDEA are about a thousand times faster than the most efficient implementation of RSA.

PGP also contains the most failproof system of authentication yet devised, called a digital signature. Authentication, the assurance that what you got is from whom you think it is, exists in some form or another in all encryption programs. In PGP, the digital signature is accomplished through a reverse signing of the key. After encrypting a message with someone's public key, you place your official stamp by signing your message with your own private key. Then the recipient looks up and uses your public key to verify the signature. With this system, documents cannot be altered and signed documents cannot be disowned. This technology also offers the most promise for anonymous digital cash systems.

The current government investigation of Zimmerman is only the latest installment of the legal difficulties surrounding PGP. For years PGP was outlaw software that infringed upon the RSA patent, which is controlled by a private company, RSA Data Securities, Inc. (RSAD-SI). Zimmerman tried unsuccessfully to persuade the president of RSADI, Jim Bidzos, to give him a free license to the openly published algorithm. When Zimmerman realized he couldn't get the rights, he ignored them. In 1991, with a bill before the Senate that looked like it would ban strong cryptography he issued what he referred to as an emergency release—PGP 1.0. He knew PGP was illegal, but he felt that the Information Age was quickly encroaching upon the individual's right to privacy. Rather than run to the hills in a guerrilla warfare-style fight for privacy, he stayed around the house. It might have been his last moments there, as his all-consuming work set him five payments behind on his mortgage.

Bidzos threatened to sue unless he stopped distributing PGP. Although Zimmerman complied, the rabbit was out and multiplying like mad. It was a great program and received the attention of cryptographers around the world. Zimmerman had released the source code and the next release, 2.0, was created by a combined effort of people from the Netherlands, New Zealand, France, and Spain. That must have really upset the NSA, which was fuming and flustered by the mere fact that foreigners had access to this technology in the first place.

As of September, 1995, the government had not conducted any investigative activity since the previous March, when at least two witnesses were interviewed and one was called before the grand jury. Zimmerman's lead counsel, Philip Dubois, has helped to assemble a stellar team of lawyers—from a Harvard professor to a former counsel for the Justice Department—which could account somewhat for the government's reticence in issuing an indictment. On January 11, 1996, Assistant U.S. Attorney William Keane sent mail to Dubois, informing him that his client "will not be prosecuted in connection with the posting to Usenet in June 1991 of the encryption program Pretty Good Privacy. The investigation is closed." Keane declined to comment further or give any reasons for the government's decision.

In a grander sense, Zimmerman is merely an instrument of the inevitable evolution of technology. In a Promethean gesture, he stole encryption from the government and gave it to the people. Zimmerman bypassed strict patent laws, ignored explicit export laws, and, worst of all, created a market-worthy piece of software. The technology had already been developed and was being carefully regulated and implemented on a controlled scale. It was Zimmerman who ended all that and truly frustrated the NSA by giving the world an easy-to-use product. As he says, "PGP is public key cryptography for the masses."

Although Zimmerman was not formally charged with anything, the investigation has raised many legal issues. The statement on his Web pages pointed out that the government wanted to prosecute him for the export of a munition, a federal felony offense; however, Zimmerman contended he only wrote the software. Another difficult assertion is that posting a munition on a BBS or Internet is an exportation. Even if the U.S. Attorney managed to implicate him with the actual publishing of his program on Usenet, they would still have had to bridge another gap in finding him guilty of exportation. As Zimmerman says, "I think this raises First Amendment issues, because the only way to comply with the law is not to publish at all." But the greatest issue raised by both the case and by Zimmerman himself is whether citizens have the right to powerful cryptology.

Although other agencies and Congress are not all in agreement, the NSA and law enforcement agencies which specialize in surveillance, citing the threat of terrorists, child pornographers, and foreign enemies, share a solid, unequivocal position: "no," we do not have the right. On the other hand there is a powerful grassroots movement afoot which argues that encryption products offer citizens the ability to finally recapture the privacy being stripped away in this age of growing, networked databases of personal information—credit reports, medical histories, police records, etc.

Though the DES has become somewhat of a world standard, U.S. government does not allow it to be exported or built into software products that are exported. Some exceptions are made in the financial areas, such as for the Clearing House Interbank Payment System which moves a trillion dollars a day via wires and satellite. The U.S. considers that a legitimate use of powerful encryption. It otherwise fights to keep the DES within our national borders, prohibiting American software companies from including this technology in their products sold in global markets. When developing programs that require data to be locked by passwords, they must resort to weak alternatives. Ironically, according to a 1994 study by the Software Publisher's Association, 152 DES-based products are being developed and distributed by 33 countries, including Japan, Russia, Germany, France, Austria, UK, Switzerland, the Netherlands, Australia, and Sweden. With superior security functions in their software, these foreign companies have a definite advantage over the U.S. manufacturers of similar products. Software manufacturers argue that the NSA's stance has imposed a chilling effect on the software development industry as the world of networked computers calls for strong security. The issues raised by the cryptology debate, however, extend beyond economics.

When the Founding Fathers incorporated the Bill of Rights into the U.S. Constitution in 1791, they extended the fundamental rights of speech and privacy to the presses, parks, streets, markets, and bedrooms. The advent of recording and transmitting devices, however, inherently shifted the potential amplification and pervasiveness of speech. An idea which could be delivered to a gathered crowd carries more import when instantly broadcast to an audience of 50 million homes. Today, people generate and communicate virtually the same ideologies, plans, and poetry as in previous generations; but the fundamental difference is in the means of transmission. Messages of equal content can now be amplified with bullhorns and billboards and crisscrossed via the world's networks straight into living rooms, kitchens, and bedrooms.

Computers are no longer merely big calculators meant to crack codes, but are quickly evolving into networking, multimedia machines. The recent trend towards distributed computing means that the big proprietary mainframes are being replaced by smaller, interconnected desktops. The Internet consists of millions of networked computers, sharing, manipulating, copying, and sending massive amounts of data, from unimportant junk mail to classified government files. Words that were once whispered in the closet, stayed there. The same words sent in a private E-mail are read, copied, and handled by a hundred computers as they are bounced from node to node en route to their destination.

When the first forms of electronic communication and recording devices were developed, the notion of speech and privacy took on new meaning. In 1791, the First Amendment was conceived to apply to all forms of speech; at the time that only consisted of voice and ink. By the Civil War, the telegraph was in wide use and information could be disseminated more quickly, powerfully, and exactingly. Shortly thereafter, the adjunct art of electronic eavesdropping developed. Information gathering had become a more powerful weapon and within a few years of the first telegraph scrambling device, government intelligence agencies had developed a product which could decrypt these scrambled messages.

The Information Age has made intelligence perhaps the most valuable commodity. Nicholas Negroponte, the founder of MIT's Media Lab, points out that "information about money is probably worth more than the money." No longer is the government the only party passing sensitive, valuable information across far-flung lines. Businesses have been engaged in such practices for years and have consequently spent great sums of time and energy protecting themselves against electronic eavesdroppers. In the 1970s the Soviets routinely listened in on the conversations of IBM executives, who conducted much of their sensitive internal communications along private microwave networks. The French have also recently admitted to having tapped IBM for a few corporate secrets that they then passed on to French government-subsidized competitors. For big business as well as governments, the issue of data security has always been an important one.

These regular users of electronic communication have traditionally employed potent encryption to guard and send their stores of private information. But as individuals begin to generate their own personal databases and regularly communicate by electronic means, it is natural that they need personal implementations of the same technology. The Fourth Amendment explicitly protects the security of our "persons, houses, papers, and effects" against intrusion by the government. Until recently citizens have relied upon postal mail services and face to face contact to convey private information. Now that many of the arenas of human interaction have shifted to an analogous digital sphere, those communications which once passed between people under a reasonable standard of privacy are at far greater risk. History reveals a constant struggle over speech and privacy in the face of new communications media.

In 1918, the federal government introduced the first wiretap law. It came on the heels of the Great War and although it was created to allow law enforcement agencies better means of counterespionage, it soon became very useful to catch criminals running liquor. With this new technology, law enforcement agencies had the ability to surreptitiously listen in on and bring to trial conversations they picked up on the wires.

The government right to wiretap was first challenged in *Olmstead v. United States* in 1928. In a closely divided decision, the court ruled that the Fourth Amendment did not apply to government policies of wiretapping. They reasoned that this amendment applied specifically to material things—"houses, papers," etc.—while electronic communications are obviously intangible and can thus be legally accessed by the government. Justice Brandeis argued in a famous dissent, however, that man has a right "to be let alone."

In 1934, Congress enacted the Federal Communications Act, which was more in line with the dissenting opinion and prohibited the interception of wire and radio transmissions, stating "no person not being authorized by sender shall intercept any communications and divulge...the contents." In ensuing decisions, the Supreme Court upheld the new statute and effectively made information obtained from wiretapping inadmissable in court. The Justice Department, however, disagreed, saying that it did not apply to federal agents. War again turned the tide, and under the threat of espionage, President Roosevelt issued an Executive Order which permitted wiretapping for "national security purposes."

With the development of electronic bugs, the courts again made fine distinctions concerning the interception of information. In *Goldman v. United States*, 1942, the Supreme Court deemed that the FCA did not apply in cases of planted microphones as opposed to tapped phone lines. Barring a physical trespass involved with the planting of a spike mike, the court ruled that the Fourth Amendment did not apply. This was again upheld in 1954, in *Irvine v. California* in which electronic bugs were planted in the walls of the defendants' homes and the evidence was admitted. However, in 1961 in *Silverman v. United States* the courts held similarly obtained information to be inadmissible.

It was not until 1967 in *Katz v. United States* that the Supreme Court erased the distinction between wiretaps and electronic bugs and reversed the 1928 decision. The Court held that there was a "reasonable expectation of privacy" in making a phone call from even so public a place as a phone booth. By extension the decision of the court extended the privacy of the Fourth Amendment to personal communications, rather than solely physical "persons, houses, papers, and effects." The Brandeis voice of reason finally prevailed. Barring reasonable suspicion and a court order, people have the right to keep private dialogue private—be it with others or themselves. As Brandeis said, they have "the right to be let alone—the most comprehensive of rights and the most valued by civilized man."

The courts are faced with new questions concerning the rights to privacy as technology continues to evolve. The penumbra of the law will require refocusing as the changing medium of the Internet seems to defy definition and open new gaps of interpretation. Meanwhile, law enforcement agencies are teaming up, scrambling for position as the digital infrastructure is built. The NSA says encryption is their rightful jurisdiction and it is within their charter to control the codes we use. The FBI says the new telephony technology is tipping the scales of power in favor of the criminals. Now that communications are becoming more digital, the FBI argues it will soon be incapable of performing its current level of wiretapping.

In recent years, these agencies have presented a flurry of legislative proposals to Congress asking for the right to hardwire sophisticated wiretapping systems into the telephony networks themselves. Though the issues inherently concern all forms of electronic communication, the government's arguments have been largely under the guise of straight telephony discussions. With one of these bills on the block in 1991, Zimmerman hastily released PGP, which has helped shift the battle from the realm of wires and telephony and into the world of cryptology.

Proposed by Senator Joseph Biden and devised by the FBI, a measure was buried in the language of a 1991 omnibus anti-crime bill, S.266. The wording clearly paved the way and legislated the right for law enforcement agencies to build federal wiretapping systems into the infrastructure of all electronic systems of communication. "It is the sense of Congress that providers of electronic communications service equipment shall ensure that communications systems permit the Government to obtain the plain text contents of voice, data, and other communications when appropriately authorized by law." With the words "plain text contents," it is evident that secure encryption such as PGP would not be permitted.

As many civil rights groups and industry leaders pointed out, this revamping of the information infrastructure would not simply permit the law agencies to maintain the status quo. With such systems built in, law enforcement agencies would be empowered with a new level of eavesdropping ability. No longer would the FBI need to physically implant devices or even go to the phone companies before they apply for a court order, as the newly envisioned systems would have required only the turning of a switch at command central. The rigorous protests from industry and civil libertarian groups managed to quash the measure.

The FBI did not give up and, in 1992, drafted a Digital Telephony Bill to counter what it said was a growing inability to deal with new, sophisticated communications technology such as call forwarding and digital lines. Although they could not prove that any of the 900 legal wiretaps implemented that year had been thwarted for such technological reasons, the FBI asserted that it was vital that they immediately build powerful wiretapping capabilities into the infrastructure, before they fall behind and lose the eavesdropping capabilities that they currently enjoy. The bill called for the inclusion of wiretap ports that would allow the FBI to remotely tap into all electronic communications that pass along phone lines. Citizen opposition was strong, the bill was unable to find a sponsor in Congress and it subsequently died. After being reworked, however, the FBI resuscitated the bill in 1994.

Passed in the final moments of the 103rd Congress, this version of the Digital Telephony bill was ironically championed by Senator Leahy, a staunch supporter of privacy rights. Reasoning that the FBI was poised to finally push through one of these bills, Leahy worked with industry and civil rights groups to carve out some of the most intrusive parts and work in some safeguards. The Electronic Frontier Foundation (EFF) led a powerful opposition, backed by AT&T, DEC, Lotus, Microsoft, and Sun Microsystems, which was able to effectively remove on-line information providers from the legislation. The final version, which was signed into law October 25 by the President, also required law enforcement agencies to obtain a court order to obtain telephone transactional information—as opposed to a mere subpoena which was previously required. Regardless, this new law will require the phone companies to re-engineer the country's networks to support the FBI's wiretap equipment and most certainly give them a greater technological ability to tap into conversations.

The Clinton Administration was working also on a project which would address the concerns of the NSA and all federal law enforcement agencies which feared the spread of encryption. On April 16, 1993, the White House announced the Escrowed Encryption Initiative. Proposed as "a voluntary program to improve security and privacy of telephone communications while meeting the legitimate needs of law enforcement," this initiative offered a new system of encrypting data in which the copies of the keys to each encrypted conversation are held in escrow by the government. This initiative included its own chip, the Clipper, and an encryption algorithm, SKIPJACK—both of which were developed by the NSA.

Dorothy E. Denning, the chair of Computer Science at Georgetown University and the foremost non-government proponent of the Clipper standard argues that if it is not implemented, the world's networks will become "sanctuaries for criminality wherein Organized Crime leaders, drug dealers, terrorists, and other criminals could conspire and act with impunity." She argues that Clipper strikes a nice balance between the public's need for security and law enforcement's need to wiretap. Denning points out one case in which a child pornographer thwarted police efforts by encrypting his material. At the same time she asserts that as a voluntary product, the Clipper chip can succeed in the marketplace and will be eventually used by criminals, who are for the most part stupid and careless.

Like the opposition to the Digital Telephony proposals, the fight against Clipper has been strong and widespread. Since the chip and the algorithm are classified, critics have been rightfully suspicious—not only of their effectiveness, but also whether there are any built-in trap doors. Traditionally, every accepted system of cryptology has been released for public scrutiny. Academics argue that the only viable way to insure that a system is secure is to subject it to a series of attacks. Others are convinced that the secretive NSA simply hardwired a back-door into the chip (which essentially self-destructs when tampered with). John Perry Barlow, co-founder of the EFF, summed up much of the opposition: "if you're going to initiate a process that might end freedom in America, you probably need an argument that isn't classified."

There has also been criticism concerning the escrow system. Under the proposed system, the session key for each communication would be copied and split, with one half going to the National Institute for Standards and Technology and the other to the Treasury Department's Automated System Division. Both of these agencies are in the Executive branch of the government. Although the FBI would still need to get a warrant to collect the halves before legally reading your mail or listening to your telephone conversations, this arrangement clearly does not provide enough checks and balances.

This issue of obtaining the keys was made even more shady by a clause written into the Clipper proposal outlining the rights of those who have their conversations deciphered. The document explicitly says that if the FBI doesn't play by the rules in obtaining your information, the information still holds up in court: "These procedures do not create, and are not intended to create, any substantive rights for individuals intercepted through electronic surveillance, and noncompliance with these procedures shall not provide the basis for any motion to suppress or any other objection to the introduction of electronic surveillance lawfully acquired."

Far and away the greatest opposition has not been to the specifics of the plan, but to the plan itself—to the idea that the government keeps the keys to all our communications. Barlow, who also wrote the introduction to Zimmerman's *PGP Guide* says, "trusting the government with your privacy is like trusting a Peeping Tom with your window blinds." Ron Rivest, one of the developers of the RSA system, recognizes the legitimate needs of law enforcement, but is skeptical to the extent of this solution. "Given the small number of currently available wiretaps per year (under 1000) and the ease of using alternative encryption technology or superencryption it seems plausible to me that law enforcement could expect at most ten 'successful' Clipper wiretaps per year. This is a pretty marginal basis for claiming that Clipper will 'block crime.'"

The proponents of the Escrowed Encryption Standard repeatedly argue, however, that the proposal is voluntary. Testifying before the Senate Judiciary Subcommittee on May 3, 1994, Assistant Attorney General Jo Ann Harris reinforced this point. "As the Administration has made clear on a number of occasions, the key-escrow encryption initiative is a voluntary one; we have absolutely no intention of mandating private use of a particular kind of cryptography, nor criminalizing the private use of certain kinds of cryptography."

This seems very unlikely considering that criminals would have to be of the highly stupid variety to pick the government-wired Clipper over other equally available, fully secure products. The FBI, the NSA, and the Department of Justice know this. In a "briefing document" that they jointly prepared and sent to the National Security Council, called "Encryption: The Threat, Applications, and Potential Solutions," they clearly state their position that other systems, such as PGP, must be phased out. "Technical solutions, such as they are, will only work if they are incorporated into all encryption products. To ensure that this occurs, legislation mandating the use of government-approved encryption products or adherence to Government encryption criteria is required." Criteria means a set of weak standards sanctioned by the NSA, such as a 40-bit key length (the strength of encryption systems currently permitted for export). Journalist Brock Meeks points out that a 40-bit key is "the digital equivalent of a Captain Crunch decoder ring."

Although the Fourth Amendment permits search and seizure in the event of reasonable suspicion and the issuance of a warrant, the Amendment is a straightforward declaration of our rights to be let alone—not a Constitutional declaration of the FBI's right to wiretap.

If the courts decide that the FBI should search someone's house, it does not mean that this person must make it particularly easy for them. Mike Godwin of the EFF points out that "conspicuously missing from the language of this amendment is the guarantee that the government, with properly obtained warrant in hand, will be successful in finding the right place to be searched or persons or things to be seized." And it certainly does not say that citizens should register the keys to their houses with the government in case they might ever need to search them. "Historically, law enforcement has responded to technological change by adapting. (Indeed, the original wiretaps were an adaptation to the widespread use of the telephone.) Does it make sense for law enforcement suddenly to be able to require that the rest of society adapt to its perceived needs?"

Godwin imagines a situation in which the FBI plants a court-ordered microphone in a restaurant. Suppose the clanging of forks, glasses, dishes, and surrounding conversation foiled their attempts to make out the dialogue they had the right to "seize." "Wouldn't it make sense to have a law requiring everyone to speak more softly and not clatter the dishes so much?" Godwin modestly proposes that "it would make perfect sense to have a law requiring that people speak quietly in public places, so as to guarantee that the government can bug an oral conversation if it needs to." In the same way, citizens should send only plaintext E-mail. And by the same argument, speaking in code should be banned. If the mafia had a lingo in which "shirts" meant "guns" and "pants" meant "heroin," the FBI might cry unfair—the court had authorized a wiretap and what they were able to glean was gibberish.

In World War I the U.S. Army wisely employed the help of the Choctaw Indians to relay messages across insecure lines. This worked so well that in World War II the government expanded the range, using Comanches, Kiowas, Winnebagos, Seminoles, Navajos, Hopis, and Cherokees. The Marine Corps exclusively used the Navajos, who never made transmission errors and never had their language deciphered by the enemy. This presents a good metaphor for the use of encryption devices. In support of one's right to use such technology, Zimmerman argues, "I should be able to speak to you in Navajo if I wanted, even if law enforcement can't understand Navajo." The freedom of expression guaranteed by the First Amendment seems to imply that we can choose our form of speech.

The Fifth Amendment right against self-incrimination can present a significant shield against law enforcement efforts. Consider the hypothetical of the FBI approaching a Navajo with a recorded monologue that they have reason to believe describes his criminal activity. The Fifth Amendment protects this person from being required to translate his words and incriminate himself. However, if the government demanded the key to the same man's encrypted data, would we be dealing with a legal warrant to seize a physical object or an infringement of his Fifth Amendment rights? Meanwhile, the FBI's easy solution to all this is to keep our keys on file, so they can have a look if there is ever a question.

The public, however, did not care for that idea. In July of 1994, Brock Meeks reported that the Clipper coalition had cracked "after the Administration and the agencies most responsible for the Clipper program...withered under a blistering fire of a nationwide anti-Clipper grassroots campaign waged by the U.S. software companies, Crypto-rebels, privacy and civil liberties groups." The White House received a petition signed by 47,000 denizens of cyberspace calling for an alternative to the Escrowed Encryption Standard. The final nail was driven in with the discovery of a flaw by Matt Blaze of Bell Labs, who found a way to confuse the SKIPJACK algorithm, thereby disabling the function that sends the keys to the government's escrow repositories. Without the keys, it no longer served the government's purpose.

In a letter to Representative Maria Cantwell (D., Washington), who represents the district which is the home to Microsoft and has been a staunch opponent of Clipper, Vice President Gore conceded that "the Clipper chip is an approved federal standard for telephone communication and not for computer networks and video networks. For that reason, we are working with industry to...design a more versatile, less expensive system [that]...would not rely on a classified algorithm, would be voluntary, and would be exportable." Gore also suggests that the government may explore the option of "private sector key escrow agents."

Now that the Digital Telephony Act is law the FBI is itching to build in its wiretaps. Never mind that Congress has not really figured out where it's going to find the necessary $500 million. Never mind that FBI has not been able to prove that any of the less than 1000 wiretaps last year were thwarted for technological reasons. They want their high-tech surveillance system and Congress said they could have it. The New York Times ran a front page article on November 2, 1995, describing what they want: "the FBI has proposed a national wiretapping system of unprecedented size and scope that would give law enforcement officials the capacity to monitor simultaneously as many as one out of every 100 phone lines in some high crime areas of the country." The proposal reportedly "contends that in such places, the demands of digital wiretapping may make it necessary to intercept tens of thousands of phone calls at once."

In the Corrections section of the paper the next day, the *Times* said "the new approach would allow monitoring of one of every 1,000 phone lines, not one of every 100; the system would let the FBI monitor as many as one of every 100 phone calls." And in a letter to the editor, FBI director Louis J. Freeh wrote "we have not and are not asking for the ability to monitor 1 out of every 100 telephone lines or any other ridiculous number like that." Why? "To obtain that many court orders and conduct that extent of wiretapping would be nearly impossible." Perhaps if we gave them broader authority and more agents...

In a recent article in *Wired*, Brock Meeks refers to "the government's not-so-new 'Clipper II': a trainwreck waiting to happen." He refers skeptically to the Clinton Administration's new approach to cryptography. They are still apparently married to the idea of key escrow, but now would like to explore the option of placing the keys to our E-mail and phone conversations with trusted third parties, "provided they adhere to a yet-undefined set of guidelines that will render them 'government certified.'" Meeks then predicts that "down the road, our government will push for outlawing encryption. Only the FBI won't call it that. The new law will most likely prohibit the use of non-government-certified encryption."

In a paper hailing the Clipper as a perfect solution, Denning had unwittingly revealed the extent of the government's policy: "The government decided that it would not be responsible to use its own expertise and resources to pursue encryption standards that fundamentally subvert law enforcement and threaten public safety and national security." So they half-baked a plan, called it a compromise, and convinced people like Denning to espouse it. The Executive branch is fumbling around for a constitutional solution as it tries to grasp the import of the Internet. The NSA and the FBI, on the other hand, know exactly what they want.

Mark Rotenberg, the director of the Electronic Privacy Information Center, says "the wiretap bill is cut from the same cloth as the Clipper proposal. Both proposals were developed by the same federal agencies with the same goal. Both seek the holy grail of absolute surveillance, an aim the U.S. government has never previously pursued." Godwin disputes the law enforcement agencies' claims that they are simply trying to maintain their current level of power as technology shifts the current communications landscape. "It seems clear to me that Digital Telephony, together with the Clipper initiative, prefigure a government strategy to set up an information regime that precludes truly private communications between individuals who are speaking in any way other than face-to-face. This I think is an expansion of government authority by almost any analysis."

In 1928, Justice Brandeis conjured images of force and violence in discussing the new powers made available to the government by technological advances. "Discovery and invention have made it possible for government, by means far more effective than stretching upon the rack, to obtain disclosure in court of what is whispered in the closet." Brandeis referred often to the concept of private things which are whispered in the closet and the violation of having them disclosed, or proclaimed from the rooftops. In the 1920s, when a relatively insignificant amount of sensitive information was passed along wires, his colleagues decided that the Fourth Amendment did not preclude the government's right to listen in. Brandeis dissented: "As a means of espionage, writs of assistance and general warrants are but puny instruments of tyranny when compared with wiretapping."

If the government insists that cryptography be considered a weapon, perhaps it should be treated like a gun or a car. For the most part, anyone can own a gun or car; in most states it is easy to keep tabs on who has them and where they have been. But these rights are not absolute—gun-slinging and car driving privileges can be revoked in the interest of public safety. Just as big, powerful companies can apply for licenses to employ strong data protection, so too should individuals be allowed the option.

The FBI can tell when a line they have tapped is passing encrypted messages—they just can't read them. It is not until someone proves to be suspect that law enforcement can tap into his or her personal communications. If we expand the technological capabilities of the FBI, the FBI will expand to fill the role. By giving them the right to tap 10,000 lines and run keyword searches on this flow of digital data, they gleefully come one step closer to the potential criminal. With access to private mail and phone conversations, the FBI has the ability to get up close and make judgments concerning intentions.

Jake Baker would never have encrypted his work. Foolish criminals find ways to let you know what they are up to. The smart ones do not. Will the government be placing bugs in rental trucks so that bombers cannot discuss their plans in those increasingly suspect vehicles? The government has no place in our trucks, our mail, or in out personal affairs unless our persons—real or cyber—are reasonably suspected of a crime. That, after all, is the only basis allowed by the Fourth Amendment for the issuance of a warrant.

The debate over cryptography, which essentially concerns our right to privacy weighed against the eavesdropping rights of the government, has come to a head in the case of Phil Zimmerman. Zimmerman believes in the strength as well as the social good of PGP, but remarks that wiretapping is not the only police enforcement tool. FBI director Freeh asserts that "court-ordered wiretapping is the single most effective investigative technique used by law enforcement to combat illegal drugs, terrorism, violent crime, espionage, and organized crime." Zimmerman cites the fact that over the past decade the FBI has conducted less than a thousand wiretaps per year. And without it, "they may work a little harder in some cases, but good old fashioned police work is still effective. These crimes leave footprints in the real world."

A recent *Newsweek* article on Zimmerman mentioned the case of hacker Kevin Mitnick, who broke into high security systems and stole thousands of credit card numbers. "Cybersleuth" Tsutomu Shinomura, who finally tracked him down, was later asked how we can better protect ourselves against such crime. His terse reply: "strong cryptography."

# CHAPTER

# III

# A STALKER IN CYBERSPACE

J ake Baker liked to write savage, pornographic snuff stories and post them to the Internet. Always written in the first person and tinged with an eerie realism, his tales were simple, explicit, and gruesome. In January of 1995, a sixteen-year-old girl in Moscow was reading through the **alt.sex.stories** newsgroup when she came upon a particularly violent and misogynistic Baker original, which was named "Doe" and prefaced with a few words for the lighthearted: "The following story contains a lot of sick stuff. You have been warned."

The sixteen-year-old was horrified by its violence, and she showed it to her father. He read the story and showed it to a friend, Richard DuVal, a fifty-year-old American attorney and University of Michigan alumnus working in Moscow. DuVal was disturbed by Baker's twisted tale and wondered why it bore the **umich.edu** stamp of his alma mater. "When I saw the story I thought, 'There's something here that crosses the line from bad taste to pathological,'" said DuVal, who called the University of Michigan's President's office to ask why the school's account was disseminating such material.

"Doe" was a vicious abduction narrative that reads like an actual account. It follows the footsteps of the storyteller and his friend who have broken into a girl's apartment and prepare to violate her.

She's shaking with terror as Jerry and I circle her...

She says in a little, terrified voice, "Why are you doing this...I've never hurt you...p-please stop!" I pause in front of her. Jerry smiles at her terror. He laughs at her pitiful pleas. I say, "Shut the fuck up, stupid whore!" and hit the side of her head, hard. She collapses on the ground, crying, curling up into a little ball."

"Alright. Let's have some fun!"

They proceed to tie the girl's hair to a ceiling fan and tear into her as she dangles and spins. Baker's hero then rapes and mutilates her. For the denouement, they pour gasoline on her and say good-bye with a lit match. Baker, a twenty-year-old sophomore at Michigan majoring in linguistics, posted this piece to Usenet under his own name.

Born Abraham Jacob Alkhabaz, Baker is a quiet sort, with glasses, a slight build, and mild manners. His on-line persona, however, had a somewhat different flair. In October of 1994, Jake posted his first submission to **alt.sex.stories**, an original sexual fantasy, "Gone Fishin," which contained, in his words, "nonconsensual rape, torture, and snuff of a teenager by her brother and his friend. Consider yourself warned." The story is told from the first-person perspective of a youth who conspires with his friend to rape the friend's sister. After tossing around the idea, they build up their courage and, armed with a pliers, a paring knife, a power drill with all the tip attachments, a box of needles, and a lighter, they go to the lake to find the girl. When the protagonist comes upon the sister's "wimpy boyfriend" he quickly drowns him. Together the boys have fun raping and murdering her with all their tools.

For a small, nerdy kid weighing about 120 pounds, Baker surely had a monstrous imagination. In the text-based world of alt.sex.stories this harmless looking student morphed into a rapist of quasi-heroic stature—a cross between Charles Manson, Hannibal Lecter, and your run-of-the-mill pedophilic rapist. Baker infused his female characters with innocent, harmless qualities, while his first-person protagonist always delights in surprising them with guns or sudden punches, making them strip, and then laughing at their reaction.

Lost in this realistic role-play, Baker naively and ingenuously laid out the darkest part of himself in the electronic hangout of weirdoes and wannabe murderers. In earlier, unpublished writings, Baker's fantasy characters would sometimes laugh and walk away when they were finished. However, the stories became progressively more graphic and began to regularly culminate in violent death.

Baker's second original piece was called "A Day at Work" and again involved the abduction, rape, and murder of an unsuspecting girl. The main character picks a spot, lies in wait, then leads a little "Asian girl" into a room and slams her on the head with a paperweight. The character never flinches, but rather smiles maliciously.

This story was particularly popular among wannabe sex offenders, who came out of the woodwork to compliment Jake's writing ability. "Yea, I just caught your new one. Great stuff!" remarked one. "You, sir, are sick. And I love it! Keep posting these great stories," wrote another. One man compared Baker to Hemingway and asked him to write a special piece about his ten-year-old neighbor—a little girl who was the secret object of his rape fantasies. The man offered to send Baker a home video that captures a few seconds of her dancing. "You are a Master!…really savage rape really gets me off." Jake relished the feedback and said he would think about it.

His next submission to the on-line club again employed the irony of a mundane title. In "Going for a Walk," a young man forcefully abducts, rapes, and murders a young girl who happens to be jogging by him. Leaving the scene, he happily muses that her corpse will be eaten by worms and never found.

The world of **alt.sex.stories** is not like a church or a courtroom. Frequented by social misfits, sexual deviants, and the simply curious, this place has no imposed boundaries—just a loose culture of sex-talk in which almost anything goes. The **alt.sex** newsgroup had been created as a sort of rebellious joke in 1988. Due to a perception that there was too much volume on Usenet, and too little of value, an informal and self-appointed group of system administrators began in 1987 to take control, deciding which newsgroups would continue and which new ones might be added. One of their first acts was to reject a request for a drug-related newsgroup. An Internet pioneer, John Gilmore, responded by creating the **alt** hierarchy, in which anyone could create a newsgroup without the permission of the governing cabal. **Alt.drugs** was the first newsgroup in the hierarchy. The following year, Brian Reid added **alt.sex** and **alt.rock-n-roll**. "I have no idea what sort of traffic it will carry," he wrote. Usually it is your standard smut. Occasionally, however, the group is joined by someone like Baker, who likes to play psychopath. A sexual neophyte who was moving dangerously toward the edge, Baker drove up the level of violence, and predictably incited reaction.

The real-world Baker was a quiet kid who played with computers and didn't draw much notice; but on the Net he excited, offended, and garnered attention. In the preface to one of his stories, he stated that he wrote his fantasies to turn some people on and to annoy others. "Either way, have an opinion," he added. "The greatest insult to a writer is not to have any feelings for his work." In the introduction to his final contribution, Baker wrote, "Responses to my last posts have been good. As long as people give me feedback (positive or negative), I'll post on a regular basis. As always, comments and criticisms welcome."

That last contribution, "Doe," was posted January 9, 1995, and again included a simple plot, sadistic torture, and murder. The difference, however, was that "Jane Doe" (a pseudonym used by the press) was a real girl who sat in his Japanese class the previous fall semester and on whom he had had a secret crush. Ten days after the posting, the young Russian girl happened upon this story and it eventually came to the attention of the University of Michigan.

Baker was contacted by officers from the University of Michigan Department of Public Safety (DPS). Although he was surprised by the contact, he readily admitted to writing the stories. Baker waived his *Miranda* rights, and let them search his room and E-mail account. There they found an unpublished story about Doe and a number of E-mail conversations with a fellow rape fantasizer, Arthur Gonda. One of the officers interviewed Baker, who grinned at the kind of reaction his fiction was generating. Baker said he wrote to exorcise his "demons" and had no interest in counseling, which was conducted by the "shamans of our age." He spoke bitterly of his mother and about two failed suicide attempts as a teenager. Baker stated he wrote to relieve the tensions caused by a student loan he feared he would lose. He also told the officers that he wrote to impress certain others of the **alt.sex** milieu.

Baker's roommate Jesse Jannetta later remarked, "He never realized how serious this was until it was too late. He thought if he cooperated and gave the university what they wanted—told the truth—it would all work out." The university's sudden involvement prompted Baker to mention his writing pastime to a couple of his friends in the real world. Jannetta urged his roommate to seek counsel and the university authorities strongly suggested that he seek "help." Baker, however, was more concerned with his computer privileges and keeping his mother from finding out.

A few days later, Baker was approached by a plainclothes DPS officer and two Housing Department officers who were waiting for him outside of class. They notified Baker that he was suspended and the officers escorted him back to his dorm room to quickly collect a few of his belongings and took him to the edge of campus with strict instructions not to re-enter university grounds. The day before, University of Michigan President James J. Duderstadt had side-stepped the student court system and suspended Baker without a hearing, citing the little-used Regents Bylaw 2.01, which gave him such authority in the name of maintaining "health, diligence, and order among the students." Baker stayed in a local hotel room until a meeting with his lawyer the following day.

David Cahill, the attorney who defended Baker in the university's proceeding, remarked that "the university has taken on the job of literary critic and decided it's a campus emergency. I think they've overreacted to something that's constitutionally protected." In following President Duderstadt's edict, the campus authorities assumed Baker was dangerous. As Captain James Smiley of the DPS put it, "We think it's a very serious matter. When he named a student, that put a different light on it—he's not just fantasizing any more."

Cahill pressed for a formal hearing. He remarked that the university had taken the emergency action because they did not have a strong enough case to show a violation of the Statement of Student Rights and Responsibilities, the University of Michigan's code of nonacademic conduct. Cahill also pointed out that Baker had already undergone a psychological evaluation before the suspension, which determined that he was not dangerous. In an attempt to work out a temporary compromise that would get Baker back to class, Cahill met with university officials and made an offer: his client would follow a university-proscribed therapy program, live off campus, and enter the campus grounds only for classes. The offer was rejected.

Baker's violently misogynistic stories set off powder kegs of controversy in other parts of the university. Unfortunately for him, University of Michigan law professor and scholar on sex equality, Catharine MacKinnon—the world's foremost proponent of the idea that pornography *is* violence—was concurrently leading an attack against this kind of speech. MacKinnon believes that pornography undermines and marginalizes women, both in public life and private relationships; that it promotes violence and hostility; and that it should be illegal.

In the preface to his "Doe" story, Baker offered a philosophical disclaimer: "The following is just words. Words have no inherent meaning. Plato is dead." In her most recent book, *Only Words*, MacKinnon argues that "a society is made of language" and pornographic words are effectively acts of violence. MacKinnon specifically commented on the Baker case: "What he wrote constitutes libel, sexual harassment, and is a violation of privacy." Baker's story made "pornography of someone's name. In addition, it targets an individual for assault, not only by the individual who may be thinking to carry it out, but by other people who consume it. ... [Jane Doe] has been pimped out to the world to masturbate over." MacKinnon pressed her point that pornography affects not only the women who are unwillingly exposed to it, but also those who are affected by the behavior of the men who create and consume it. At the same time, she began to counsel Jane Doe.

University officials alerted the FBI to see if Baker had, in fact, broken any laws. FBI Special Agent Stejskal read the collection of stories and E-mail and prepared to mount a case. Although the stories were all prefaced by warnings and disclaimers avowing they were fiction, Special Agent Stejskal became determined to prosecute the author of this perverted writing and posited that a charge could be found: "We're looking into the possibility of charging him with the distribution of obscene material." In consulting with the U.S. Attorney's office, he would later learn that under the *United States v. Miller* standard, writings, as opposed to pictures, have never been found obscene by the courts.

University officials already had contacted and shown Doe the stories. When asked if she felt threatened by the story bearing her name, Doe was visibly shaken. Although she had only vague recollections of Baker, had never been contacted by him, and realized she was never meant to see the story, reading a fantasy about her being raped and murdered offended her. Yes, she felt threatened. There are laws against making threats, and it seemed the government had the basis for a case.

The university arranged to hold a closed suspension hearing. Meanwhile, the FBI had been orchestrating its case with the U.S. Attorney's office in Detroit to see if they could bring Baker to trial. After looking at the student's writing, Assistant U.S. Attorney Ken Chadwell felt that Baker was dangerous and likely to actualize his fantasies. Chadwell realized that with the stories and E-mail alone, it would be difficult to charge Baker with conspiracy, which requires another conspirator and proof of an overt act. Perhaps they could yet discover such evidence. However, since Baker had named a girl in his story, who said that she felt threatened, the government could try charging Baker with issuing a threat. "We're still assuming it has prosecuting merit," Stejskal reported.

Meanwhile, Baker commented to reporters, "I regret posting all the stories in general and I deeply regret any harm I've done to her or anyone else. I'm more than willing to make up whatever harm I've done, but not to leave the university." The university proceedings, however, would soon become the least of Baker's problems.

On February 9, 1995, the day the school hearings were to start, the FBI knocked on the door of Cahill's blue-framed house (which also served as his office). They arrested Baker, citing a federal statute against using interstate communications to transmit a threat. Stejskal insisted later in court papers that the basis for the arrest stemmed not only from Baker's latest story on the Internet, but also from the E-mail found on his computer. The E-mail contained correspondence with a Canadian identified as Arthur Gonda and, in the words of Stejskal, represented a "desire to commit acts of abduction, bondage, torture, mutilation, sodomy, rape, and murder of young women."

Baker and Gonda had swapped snuff stories and expressed their desire to meet. At one point, Baker discussed the logistics of finding a secluded spot in Ann Arbor, writing, "I don't want any blood in my room, though." Baker also revealed that he had figured out an excellent way to abduct a fellow student: "As I said before, my room is right across from the girl's bathroom. Wait until late at night, grab her when she goes to unlock the door. Knock her unconscious, and put her into one of those portable lockers (forgot the word for it), or even a duffel bag. Then hurry her out to the car and take her away." The next day Gonda replied, "I have been out tonight and I can tell you that I am thinking more about 'doing' a girl. I can picture it so well...and I can think of no better use for their flesh. I HAVE to make a bitch suffer!" In the course of their correspondence, they made tentative plans to meet the following summer and commit some rapes and murders together.

Baker had only had one girlfriend in his life and was still a virgin. He had never had sex—so he made some up. His stories revealed a writer with at least a few psycho-sexual hangups and openly exposed a kind of adolescent exhibitionism. In psychological evaluations, and even in the interview with the DPS officer, he admitted to loathing his mother. Baker's parents divorced when he was a teenager and he did not have any contact with his father. In his spare time between a full course load and a part-time job in the computer lab, he said he liked to unwind by role-playing. In real life he didn't have much luck with girls. So he would assault them, rape them, and kill them—all in the anonymous hangouts of cyberspace. Baker insisted, however, that he would never hurt anyone in real life. In response to one angry **alt.sex.stories** reader, who castigated him for the explicit violence, Jake wrote back, "I have never hurt anyone, and never plan on hurting anybody."

Vilma Baker, Jake's mother, was outraged by the authorities' treatment of her son and blamed the campus administrators whom she described as Femi-Nazis, full of hatred toward men. She said that when her son heard that officials had shown a copy of his story to Jane Doe, "he couldn't eat for a week. He cried and cried and cried." On the charges against her son, "I can't believe this is happening in America." On the snuff stories, "I thought it just sounded like a couple of boys trying to outdo each other. I didn't take it very seriously." And on Jake, "He thinks he hasn't done anything wrong. [He thinks] a mistake has been made, and it's all going to work out fine."

The FBI had told Cahill that they were taking Baker to Detroit for a routine arraignment and that he would be brought directly back to Ann Arbor. Instead, Federal Magistrate Judge Thomas Carlson refused to set bail and ordered him detained until a hearing the next day: "The allegations, if true, represent a profoundly disturbed individual."

Baker, not accompanied by counsel, was argumentative with the magistrate. He protested the detention order and told reporters that he had acted within his rights. "I have been a free man for four months. I wrote this story four months ago. I haven't harmed anyone. I think it's a violation of my First Amendment rights and probably several other rights."

Since Cahill only practiced in state court, Baker retained Douglas R. Mulkoff, a criminal lawyer with federal court experience to defend him against the government's charges. The next day, at the detention hearing in Detroit, Assistant U.S. Attorney Chadwell sought an unsecured $100,000 bond, with the restrictions that Baker not travel outside of his hometown of Boardman, Ohio, that he not contact the victim of his story, and that he turn in his passport.

The media began to hover over the action surrounding this first-of-its-kind Internet case. The university suspension hearings attracted Detroit television and radio stations, the *Detroit Free Press*, local papers, and CNN. A crowd of reporters and camera crews camped out at the Michigan Union offices where the hearings were held while another group of reporters surrounded Baker at the Federal Building in downtown Detroit as he arrived for his arraignment. Cahill told the press that "This guy has never, ever threatened or contacted this woman in any way. We think it's unwarranted punishment for pure speech. A rather violent and pornographic story, yes, but we don't think he has a problem. We think he has an active imagination."

Mulkoff arrived at the detention hearing with two recent psychological evaluations affirming that his client was not dangerous. He argued that the Internet stories were violent, but nonetheless were simply fiction, and that his client had simply written fantasies. Judge Carlson did not agree with these contentions. He described Baker as a "ticking bomb waiting to go off" and dismissed Mulkoff's First Amendment argument by saying that he had made threats against a specific woman and that the E-mail evidence pointed to a more "in-depth plan" to abduct the woman.

Judge Carlson stated, "If we only had a story of rape and torture, we would have the issue of the First Amendment here but there are at least two additional elements to the case. Mr. Baker named an individual at the University of Michigan as a subject of his story and had discussion with another person about where and how the actual assault could be carried out. This is more than just writing a story." Carlson ordered Baker to be held without bail. Assistant U.S. Attorney Chadwell had originally only sought to have Baker held on bond, but he now altered his recommendation and supported the magistrate's assessment. The once attenuated charges now seemed to have merit.

Carlson's decision seemed to be largely based on Stejskal's testimony that the woman mentioned in the story was extremely upset and felt threatened by Baker's freedom. Stejskal presented the unfinished "Doe" story found by DPS officers in Baker's dorm room. "I plan it well. It will be my first kidnapping; my first real rape of a pretty young girl. My first experimentation with all the devices of pain I had thought up before. I obsessed about my target more than any other girl on campus—Jane Doe."

Mulkoff made it clear that Baker had no history of violence and commented that the court simply did not like the content of the stories. Judge Carlson had remarked, "I fully recognize that the defendant doesn't have a prior record and he comes from a good family. But after reading the works, the court is persuaded that there is another side to Mr. Baker that the psychiatrist and his family don't know." Mulkoff pressed for an immediate appeal and later that afternoon, Baker's case went before United States District Court Judge Bernard Friedman.

Mulkoff again presented the psychological evaluation made by Dr. Steven L. Gotlib, who concluded that Baker "presented no clear and present danger to [Doe] or anyone, at the time of the interview." Mulkoff also quoted psychologist Robert Loiselle, PhD who stated, "Although Mr. Baker may, because of his poor judgment, continue to get into difficulty with authority, there is no evidence that he is a danger to others or himself." Mulkoff attempted to draw a distinction between the protagonist in Baker's stories and Baker himself. If this distinction cannot be made, he argued, we risk "locking up every writer of prurient fiction because of his thoughts. Mr. Chadwell said that if you read what's in [Baker's] mind, you should know he's dangerous. That sounds like 'thought police' to me."

Judge Friedman, however, chose not to make a distinction: "the key to almost every story that he has written is the element of surprise; that each of the victims are in his story are taken by surprise." Friedman recognized the import of the evaluations, which said that "there is no evidence that he is a danger to others or himself. And, again the court disagrees with that conclusion." Disregarding the advice of the psychological evaluations and First Amendment argument, he deemed Baker "too dangerous for society" and a threat to the woman named in his story. Friedman therefore upheld Judge Carlson's decision to deny bail in the charge of transmitting a threat to injure or kidnap Doe. Judge Friedman said, "I sit here and I think, I certainly wouldn't want my daughter to be on the streets in Ann Arbor or Ohio, or anywhere else, with him in the condition I believe he's in at this point."

Mulkoff had to restrain Vilma, who rushed up to her son to give him a kiss as he was being cuffed by federal marshals. She later remarked that "the judge must have woken up this morning and thought he was a psychiatrist." Baker was sent to Wayne County jail pending a probable cause hearing set for February 17, 1995.

Mulkoff immediately filed for appeal to the United States Circuit Court of Appeals for the Sixth Circuit in Cincinnati. He asserted that

Baker's "messages were taken out of context, and he is no threat to society. It's not right that he's locked up without a bond." Barring serious charges of treason, murder, or terrorism, Mulkoff argued, it is rare for someone with no criminal record and no previous history of violence to be refused bond in federal charges.

Mulkoff had offered some conditions to Carlson and Friedman in his request for Baker's release: his client would live with his mother in Boardman, Ohio, would have a curfew, would be monitored regularly by the court, and would undergo psychological evaluations. "We will present the court with the same release conditions we suggested in the detainment hearing," Mulkoff said. "I don't expect to lose in the Sixth Circuit."

Cyberspace was flush with discussion concerning the case. **Alt.sex** groups were filled with postings concerning its progress. Other newsgroups, such as **soc.culture.usa**, **misc.legal**, and **alt.internet.media-coverage** were also highly interested, and several groups were set up to discuss it, such as **alt.jake-baker.d**. Although the general consensus was that Baker's stories were crude and violent, most people on-line were afraid of government overreaction. The **alt.sex.stories** newsgroup was particularly flooded with postings about the case. Most of them denounced the government action as a blatant violation of free speech and a harbinger of things to come. Of the university action, one subscriber wrote, "this incident has laid to rest any lingering illusion that a university encourages free thought, articulate expression or principled behavior." However, other eroticists found the debate tiresome and intrusive. "Write your congressman! Blow up a fed! Whatever!" wrote one subscriber, "but no more messages here, OK?"

The University of Michigan maintained Baker's suspension and it appeared as though he would not be returning. On February 15, two days before the probable cause hearing, a Wayne County grand jury indicted Baker on one federal count that he "knowingly transmitted communications in interstate and foreign commerce containing a threat to injure the person of another, in violation of Title 18, United States Code, Section 875(c)."

Media coverage of the case raised the question of whether the Internet was a medium out of control—teeming with offensive and dangerous ideas and images and flooded with Baker-like characters plotting horrific rapes and murders. Cahill continued to emphasize that Baker's crimes were simply fiction. "Jake doesn't drool. He doesn't have a manic gleam in his eye. Nor does he have any sexual expe-rience," Cahill says. "He's a virgin. He just has an active imagination."

Jannetta, Baker's former roommate, told reporters that Baker "has a good sense of humor. He is definitely not the monster the FBI makes him out to be. It has all been blown way out of proportion... I want to help him because I have read the papers and it is not looking good for him. It has gotten to the point where it doesn't matter what happens in his trial. These kinds of things have a way of destroying people's lives."

Mulkoff said he was preparing a motion to dismiss and asserted that the case would never come to trial. He wrote that Baker's Internet story was "in reality nothing more than words floating in space. Absent showing of a tangible threat to another person, these words cannot form the basis of a legitimate prosecution." He attempted to dispel any theories that Baker, who had posted his name in conjunction with the stories and had willingly handed over all of his E-mail correspondence, was involved in a criminal plot to actually harm anyone. "We have a fantasy writer's workshop going on here," Mulkoff said. "That's what this Internet really is."

Vilma Baker concurred, saying the idea that her son was danger-ous was "pure fantasy." She taught creative writing in Boardman, Ohio, and had been an English teacher for thirty-two years. When asked about her son's explicit stories of rape and murder, she admitted, "it is not a genre that I would read. But I don't like Stephen King or MTV either." She insisted that the stories were pure fiction, or creative writing as it were, and she claimed that her son used the victim's name in the "Doe" story only because it coincidentally served as a sexual play on words. (The woman's actual name included a syllable used as a synonym for the male phallus.)

As Baker sat in jail, the Internet buzzed, the media swirled around the case, and the government stepped up its search for the elusive Gonda, with whom Baker had corresponded. Authorities hoped that finding Gonda would provide the missing connection needed to prove the suspicion of conspiracy. The FBI was convinced that the man going by this name was a university student in Ontario; but as Staff Sergeant Bob Matthews of the Ontario Provincial Police reported, "it's a fictitious name. The only Arthur Gonda we can find is an eighty-year-old man who doesn't know anything about com-puters." Cahill had remarked that "'Arthur Gonda' could be two fifty-year-old women for all we know." Gonda's Internet account was already terminated and had not been used since February 6, 1995. The Toronto-based Internet Access provider that held his account refused to give authorities any further information.

Assistant U.S. Attorney Chadwell continued to push the argument that Baker was a dangerous man and that his words constituted actual threats. "There is a natural progression in these cases," he said, quoting some mail in which Baker writes, "just thinking about it anymore doesn't do the trick. I need to DO IT." Chadwell concentrated on certain correspondence that in his opinion appeared to indicate a legal threat. In a December E-mail to Gonda, Baker wrote, "I want to do it to a really young girl first, 13 or 14. Their innocence makes them so much more fun—and they'll be easier to control. What do you think?" Gonda agreed, adding that "you can control any bitch with a rope and a gag." Later, Baker wrote to Gonda, "Sometimes, I'll see a pretty one alone in the quad and think 'Go on Jake, it'd be easy.' But the fear of getting caught always stays my hand."

The prosecution's case gained another stamp of legitimacy when the Sixth Circuit Court of Appeals denied Mulkoff's appeal, thereby upholding Baker's detention. On March 9, 1995, Baker turned twenty-one years old in jail and, at Judge Avern Cohn's behest, Baker was evaluated the next day by a court-appointed psychiatrist, Dr. Harold Sommerschield. In spite of the Sixth Circuit's recent reinforcement of Friedman's decision to hold Baker without bond, Judge Cohn scheduled another bond hearing for that day.

Cohn, to whom the case was now assigned, is a federal judge, appointed by President Carter, with a warm, gracious air about him that can put a court at ease. When pressed, however, his congeniality shifts to a penetrating glare and an intimidating bellow. At the hearing, Judge Cohn calmly received the doctor's report and announced that Dr. Sommerschield "did not perceive (Baker) as having any mental illness and did not think he would act out any of his fantasies." Baker was released that day, after twenty-nine days in jail, on a $10,000 bond.

On the steps of the U.S. District Court in Detroit, Baker was approached by reporters. "I am sorry to have used a real person's name in any of the stories," he said. "It was a stupid thing to do and I have paid for it over the last few weeks." Jake's stepfather, David Hutchinson, said, "It was hell for him and hell for us. He didn't have any paper or pen to write with, and he had nothing to read." At the end of the hearing, Cohn issued a restriction concerning Baker's freedom to write while free on bond. Judge Cohn half-humorously stated that Baker could download whatever he wanted but could not post any more of his material—the court rippled with laughter. Chadwell, who made no objections to the court's decision to release Baker, stated, "The government has agreed to be bound by the letter of these recommendations." Baker hugged and kissed his mother.

After further examination, Assistant U.S. Attorneys Saul Green and Chadwell worried that the current charge of a threat to injure might not succeed. They realized it would be difficult to construe a story as a threat, particularly when it was clearly labeled as fiction; widely published; and about a woman that the author never met, nor expected to read his "threat." From the beginning, however, the government seemed to be intoxicated by the brutality of the stories and felt they provided a clear look into the mind of a latent murderer.

On March 15, 1995, at the U.S. Attorney's request, the grand jury dropped the existing count only to replace it with five more, based entirely on the E-mail with the pseudonymous Gonda. Baker was charged with five separate counts that he "knowingly transmitted communications in interstate and foreign commerce containing a threat to injure another person." Each count carried a maximum penalty of five years in prison and a $250,000 fine. The prosecution abandoned the attempt to prosecute Baker for threatening Ms. Doe and instead attempted to establish a threat against a class of people, such as the young women of Ann Arbor.

Each of the five counts was based upon a particular message or exchange between the two fantasy rapists. The elusive Gonda was also indicted on three of them, including the fifth count, which was based on E-mail in which Gonda references a well-known Canadian murderer, Paul Bernando. Gonda's E-mail read, "speaking of torture, I have got this great full-length picture of the Mahaffy girl Paul Bernando killed. She's wearing this very short skirt!" Bernando was on trial for raping, murdering, and dismembering two teenage girls. He was charged with encasing parts of fourteen-year-old Mahaffy in concrete. It was to this message that Baker responded with the oft cited, "just thinking about it anymore doesn't do the trick. ... I need TO DO IT."

Mulkoff prepared a motion to dismiss the charges against Baker. He insisted that Baker's stories and E-mail were largely misrepresented by the prosecution and the media and nothing showed the stories and E-mail to be anything more than fantasies. The government, he wrote, "views Jake Baker as a threat because of what he has written. While Jake's writings are disturbing to many, they cannot accurately predict his future conduct."

Mulkoff submitted the motion to Judge Cohn along with an appendix of the complete correspondence between Baker and Gonda. He recognized that although the statute under which Baker was charged had previously been used to punish "pure speech," it had "withstood constitutional challenges only because the courts have limited its reach to 'true threats.'" Mulkoff, in asserting that Baker never published a true threat, said, "Instead, he expressed ideas that the government's agents found dangerous and offensive."

In a controversial case in 1989, Judge Cohn had struck down a University of Michigan hate speech code on the grounds that it was too broad and too vague. He held the code's anti-harassment policy infringed upon the students' rights of free speech. Mulkoff hoped that Judge Cohn would take a similar stance toward the Baker case and view it as a classic First Amendment issue.

Chadwell and Green prepared a response to Mulkoff's motion that stated, "Contrary to the Court's suggestion at argument, Jake Baker was not indicted for lusting after women or for fantasizing. He is the subject of a criminal prosecution because he discussed kidnapping women in Ann Arbor, Michigan, and Boardman, Ohio, he cultivated a relationship with a willing accomplice, and he used international electronic transmissions to devise plans to meet the accomplice and carry out violent acts. These facts, coupled with Baker's emphatic statement that I NEED TO DO IT, left the United States Attorney no choice."

The government stressed that the charges were filed "in order to prevent physical harm to women in Ann Arbor." In response to Mulkoff's assertion that this was a classic case of free speech, the government argued that "This case is a classic threat prosecution undertaken to prevent violence before it occurs. The alternative—waiting for people in Baker's position to act on their stated intentions—is simply not acceptable in a civilized society."

On March 22, 1995, Judge Cohn granted Mulkoff's motion and dismissed the charges, ruling that the prosecution failed to show the required intent to carry out a threat. In his decision Judge Cohn wrote, "The government's enthusiastic beginning petered out to a salvage effort once it recognized that the communication which so much alarmed the University of Michigan was only a rather savage and tasteless piece of fiction." Judge Cohn prefaced his opinion by quoting a case from 1886 that stated, "there is so much opportunity for magnifying or misunderstanding undefined menaces that probably as much mischief would be caused by letting them be prosecuted as by refraining from it."

In his decision, Cohn cited *United States vs. Kelner*, in which the court ruled that in order for a statement to be a true threat it must be "on its face and in the circumstances in which it is made is so unequivocal, unconditional, immediate and specific as to the person threatened, as to convey a gravity of purpose and imminent prospect of execution." At the core of this case was whether or not Baker's words were a true threat or simply fantasies and role play. Judge Cohn avoided the tremendous hype surrounding the involvement of the Internet and the offensive nature of the stories; instead he focused solely on the government's charges and the key issue became whether Baker in fact issued a true threat or was he acting within the bounds of constitutionally protected speech.

Cohn rejected the government's assertion that the private E-mail between Baker and Gonda reflected "the evolution of their activity from shared fantasies to a firm plan of action." Cohn recognized that a threat does not necessarily need to point to a single person and can refer to a group, such as workers at a post office. However, a firm plan of action is still only words; and Baker never meant for his words to reach the ears or eyes of his "intended victims," whoever they were. Had Baker written a letter to Jane Doe or sent an open letter to a newsgroup that he knew included her, his behavior would have been easier to construe as a threat. Because he included Jane Doe as a character in one of a series of stories he posted to an **alt.sex** newsgroup—the rest of which apparently dealt only with fictional characters—and because it was not clearly foreseeable that the story would come to Ms. Doe's attention, it is hard to characterize Baker's actions as a threat.

Had the government attempted to pursue a charge of conspiracy between Gonda and Baker to commit a crime more in line with prosecuting him explicitly for devising a firm plan of action, it would have been required to demonstrate "an overt act in furtherance of the conspiracy." Had Baker run out to buy some rope and tools or started to make his way to Canada, the government may have had a basis for a conspiracy charge. Perhaps the authorities acted prematurely; if they had established surveillance until Gonda arrived, a more solid case would have existed. But the Canadian may never have showed up—there is a lot of talk, but little action, on Usenet. Meanwhile, fictional acts (i.e., those of Baker's twisted characters) could not be submitted as evidence of a nonfictional crime.

The brutality and vulgarity of the writings were also not on trial—Baker was not charged with obscenity. This would not have been a valid charge, because the courts have held that only pictures and film can be obscene, not text. The CDA was not yet law, or it might have been used as a basis to prosecute Baker. Currently, judges must abide by the laws that govern physical publications in the everyday world. In that context, in America no restrictions exist governing the adult exchange of pornographic text.

The government's and society's fears about Baker being a latent murderer were reasonable; however, the U.S. Attorney's heavy-handed approach did nothing more than reveal an ignorance of the applicability of the First Amendment. Judge Cohn stated that Baker's behavior was a fit subject for the university, not the U.S. Attorney's office. "Why the government became involved in the matter is not really explained in the record," Judge Cohn said. He continued, "Musings, considerations of what it would be like to kidnap or injure someone, or desires to kidnap or injure someone" are simply not grounds enough to bring someone to trial. Judge Cohn also criticized the decisions of the Federal Magistrate Judge and the U.S. District Judge who sent Baker to jail for twenty-nine days for writing what was, in the final analysis, tasteless fiction.

Few would disagree that Jake Baker is one disturbed individual. Obviously, he found fantasizing about rape, torture, and murder to be rewarding, and he enjoyed discussing these fantasies with other people. His E-mail to his Canadian friend suggested that he was either quite serious, or at least half serious, about getting together to turn fantasy into action—perhaps if the two had met, they would have worked each other up to it. Perhaps Baker will act on his own, but being a latent murderer is not a crime in this country. People are always shocked that the law punishes far more than it prevents, but there is no way to prevent the first murder by the incipiently murderous, without rounding up and incarcerating many innocent people in the process.

Professor MacKinnon would most likely ask, "Do you mean that a Jake Baker can walk around saying that he hates women; regards them as objects for his use; plans to rape, torture, and kill them—and nothing can be done until he actually kills someone?" On certain levels, the answer is yes: nothing should be done in federal court; nothing should be done on Congress's floor. But something can be done in the schools and in the community. As Judge Cohn pointed out, this was a fit case for the university to take action. Some community action is also possible. Perhaps individuals such as Jane Doe might obtain civil protective orders against Baker, keeping him away from the campus or even out of town. The University of Michigan has, in fact, maintained its suspension of Baker, who has apparently given up his fight to return and has willfully withdrawn. Baker is now living with his mother in Boardman, Ohio, and he attends community college there.

Mike Godwin of the Electronic Frontier Foundation put the case in simple perspective by saying the issues "have nothing to do with the question of whether Baker is a nice person, or even a healthy one. Instead, the case spotlights the question of whether what he transmitted is a crime—or should be." Judge Cohn held that Baker's stories and E-mail did not constitute a threat and he was therefore not guilty of the charges. In the final analysis, most lawyers, writers, and journalists familiar with the case agree that Baker's stories and E-mail were protected by the First Amendment and current laws. But should the laws be changed to punish his behavior? Would the First Amendment permit such a change?

Under Senator Exon's CDA, Baker would be likely be guilty of indecency and subject to both heavy fines and imprisonment. Some point out that "the freedom of the press belongs to those who have one." With the Internet, half-baked ideologies, dangerous ideas, and sordid fantasies can be posted, published, and circulated with virtually no restrictions. The First Amendment allows this. The government's case against Baker collapsed when real-world standards were applied. Without the CDA or equivalent legislation creating different rules for cyberspace, Baker's posting to Usenet was no different than if he had distributed his stories as leaflets on street corners.

In his opinion, Judge Cohn took a swipe at the CDA, which had just cleared the Senate, by saying, "The Senate's recent passage of a telecommunications bill including Senator Exon's measure criminalizing the distribution of 'filthy' material over computer networks suggests that the First Amendment's applicability to on-line communications has not been well considered."

Paul Denenfeld, Legal Director of the ACLU in Michigan, applauded Judge Cohn's decision. "The language was offensive but not an imminent threat to anyone. People should not have to stand trial for private thoughts and fantasies." An ACLU brief prepared in support of the motion to dismiss cited *Whitney v. California*, which said: "Fear of serious injury cannot alone justify suppression of free speech.... To justify suppression of free speech there must be reasonable ground to fear that serious evil will result if free speech is practiced. There must be reasonable ground to believe that the danger apprehended is imminent."

The government apparently does not agree. After Judge Cohn's dismissal, U.S. Attorney Green said, "we strongly disagree with the court's reasoning in the decision." On November 21, 1995, his office submitted an appeal to the Sixth Circuit Court of Appeals in Cincinnati, arguing that Cohn had erred. If the appellate court decides to send the case to trial, it will then come back to the U.S. District Court in Detroit. The entire process could take months.

In Mulkoff's motion to dismiss Baker's case, he asserted that "Allowing the government to use the statute to suppress might have the effect of censoring explicit stories on the Internet. But it will not have any effect in eliminating violence against women." He asked, "Do we let people with dangerous ideas speak freely, though we fear the dangerous ideas may take root? Or do we silence those people now, to ensure that those dangerous ideas never turn into conduct?"

As Justice Oliver Wendell Holmes said in 1919 in *Abrams v. United States*, "The ultimate good desired is better reached by free trade in ideas...the best test of truth is the power of the thought to get itself accepted in the competition of the market." To allow extremely vile speech to enter into this market is to allow the competition to take place. May truth and beauty drown out violence and smut.

# CHAPTER

# IV

## THE UNRULY BOOKSTORE

On October 23, 1994, a hacker using someone else's account posted a series of angry statements on Prodigy's Money Talk bulletin board about a stockbrokerage named Stratton Oakmont ("Stratton").

Stratton, according to this individual, (whose name has never become known), was a "cult of brokers who either lie for a living or get fired"; a public offering that Stratton conducted for Solomon Page Ltd. was "major criminal fraud"; and Daniki Porush, Stratton's president, was "seen to be proven criminal." The anonymous poster struck again two days later, leaving more venomous accusations.

The Prodigy service, a joint venture between IBM and Sears with more than two million subscribers and 60,000 to 75,000 messages posted every day, was unaware of the messages until Stratton sued Prodigy and "John Doe," the anonymous poster, for libel.

Libel is similar to slander, and the words are often used interchangeably; in fact, *slander* involves spoken words, while *libel* pertains to published material. On-line speech is considered published rather than spoken; sensibly, the law treats a printed word on-screen the same as a printed word on paper. Generally, libel involves the making of a knowingly false statement to someone else's detriment.

In its first few years, Prodigy had to combat a perception that it was just another overfinanced, underplanned IBM joint venture, premiering at a time when IBM was announcing numerous others that didn't seem to go anywhere quickly. Prodigy attempted to solve this problem by positioning itself against its competition as a more "family-oriented" service. Ironically, Judge Stuart Ain, sitting in the

New York State Supreme Court in Mineola, Long Island, found this to be Prodigy's downfall. (Despite its name, the New York Supreme Court is the state's trial court.) On Stratton's motion for partial summary judgment, Judge Ain ruled that Prodigy was more responsible for false postings than other online services because of its statement that it screened the content of its bulletin boards.

According to Jennifer Ambrozek, Prodigy's Manager of Bulletin Board Communications, Prodigy hadn't planned to be in the bulletin board business. "[A]s the on-line service industry developed, it became clear that bulletin boards were a factor of on-line life and [Prodigy] launched into having bulletin boards trepidaciously because it is new and people get up there and say what they think and initially every note that was posted was reviewed.

"It certainly became clear over time that that wasn't going to work, if we were going to be a provider of bulletin board[s], because it wasn't the way the industry worked. It didn't work for the members." Ambrozek's account reminds one that Prodigy is part of IBM. Only Big Blue would get into the bulletin board business and try to read all the messages. Right idea, wrong implementation. According to Prodigy spokesman Brian Ek, when Prodigy stopped monitoring board messages, the time it took for a newly posted message to become public decreased from twenty-four hours to ten minutes.

Unfortunately, much of this information was not brought to Judge Ain's attention before he made his decision. Prodigy's original attorney submitted sketchy papers, failing to attach relevant material that might have affected the judge's decision.

Judge Ain was particularly impressed by a statement made by Geoffrey Moore, Prodigy's Director of Market Programs and Communications, in a February 1993 article called to his attention by Stratton. "We make no apology for pursuing a value system that reflects the culture of the millions of American families we aspire to serve. Certainly no responsible newspaper does less when it carries the type of advertising it publishes, the letters it prints, the degree of nudity and unsupported gossip its editors tolerate." Judge Ain read the Moore comment to mean that Prodigy acknowledged that it is more like a newspaper than a bookstore.

Courts must choose the correct analogy to apply to a new technology. The legal debate regarding on-line services has centered on whether they are publishers or distributors of the information they carry.

The difference is that a publisher is presumed to know what it publishes, while the law recognizes that a distributor cannot possibly be aware of the contents of everything that passes through its hands. A magazine or a book publisher has editors who review and modify content and attorneys looking for libelous material and other legal problems. A newsstand or bookstore sells many publications that its owner has not even read, and can only be held responsible for illegal material, such as libel or obscenity, if its owner can be shown to know what he was selling. (In the *Amateur Action* case, the government was eager to prove that the sysop, Robert Thomas, was quite familiar with the contents of the GIFs and videos that he sold.)

In every new field of law, there is a groundbreaking case that applies common sense and that is quoted by nearly every case that comes after it. On the question of the liability of on-line services for libel, the seminal case is *Cubby v. CompuServe.*

CompuServe, like all commercial on-line services, contains a number of bulletin boards, which it calls *forums.* One of these was the Journalism Forum, a service for journalists operated for CompuServe by Cameron Communications Inc. In addition to message boards, CompuServe forums have libraries from which text and picture files and programs can be downloaded. Posted daily to one of the Journalism Forum's libraries was a newsletter called "Rumorville USA," published by Don Fitzpatrick Associates of San Francisco. Don Fitzpatrick signed a contract with Cameron to provide "Rumorville" and had no direct relationship with CompuServe.

In 1990, Cubby Inc. began publishing "Skuttlebut," a competing on-line newsletter. "Rumorville," perhaps concerned with the competition, called "Skuttlebut" a "start-up scam," implied that it was stealing information, and claimed that the publisher of "Skuttlebut" had been fired from his previous job at WABC. Cubby sued CompuServe and Don Fitzpatrick Associates for libel; CompuServe had no notice of a problem with "Rumorville" until Cubby brought the suit.

CompuServe moved for summary judgment, arguing that as a distributor, it should not remain a party to the case absent proof that it knew the libelous content of "Rumorville."

Cases begin with the serving of a complaint by the plaintiff. When drafting the complaint, the plaintiff's lawyer's job is to include every cause of action he can and to sue everyone who may possibly be responsible (what we call the "kill 'em all and let God sort 'em out" theory of litigation). He may be accused of malpractice if he doesn't do this thoroughly. Thus cases often begin in a sort of fog of war.

Just as having a gun pointed at one's head clears the mind marvelously, a *summary judgment motion* made by the adversary forces an attorney to determine the merits of the case. A summary judgment motion is an attack on the other party's theory of the case. Since American law disfavors disposing of claims without a full hearing, the thrust of a summary judgment motion is not to establish that a party's claim or defense is true—this kind of factual determination is usually made by a jury after hearing testimony of witnesses. Instead, a party making a summary judgment motion is arguing that his adversary has failed to raise any material issue of fact that deserves to be heard by a jury.

For example, assume John Doe sues you, claiming that you agreed to buy his house. You make a motion for summary judgment to which you attach a sworn affidavit that you have never heard of John Doe, never saw his house, and never agreed to buy it. You have placed a burden on John to show the court that he has evidence worthy of being evaluated by the jury. Therefore, he must show what he is holding in his hand to beat your summary judgment motion. A letter or contract signed by you, an affidavit by a broker stating that she showed you John's house, or even John's allegation that he met with you and accepted an offer would be sufficient to defeat your motion. If John fails to give any evidence, however, summary judgment will be granted and the case thrown out. A judge does not evaluate the quality or credibility of evidence on a summary judgment motion, but simply determines whether any evidence exists.

Both the *CompuServe* and *Prodigy* cases were decided on summary judgment motions, but with opposite results. Federal Judge Leisure granted summary judgment to CompuServe on the grounds that CompuServe was a distributor that was unaware of the libel. Judge Ain, on the other hand, granted partial summary judgment against Prodigy, finding it to be a publisher.

Judge Leisure based his decision on *Smith v. California*, a landmark Supreme Court case striking down a law which imposed liability on a bookseller for possession of an obscene book, regardless of whether the bookseller had knowledge of the book's contents. The Court ruled that a distributor must have knowledge of the contents of a publication before liability can be imposed.

The Supreme Court reasoned that under this law, "Every book-seller would be placed under an obligation to make himself aware of the contents of every book in his shop. It would be altogether unreasonable to demand so near an approach to omniscience. ... And the bookseller's burden would become the public's burden, for by restricting him, the public's access to reading matter would be restricted."

Judge Leisure held that CompuServe was entitled to the same protection as the bookstore in *Smith*. "CompuServe's CIS product is in essence an electronic, for-profit library that carries a vast number of publications and collects usage and membership fees from its subscribers in return for access to the publications. ... While CompuServe may decline to carry a given publication altogether, in reality, once it does decide to carry a publication, it will have little or no editorial control over that publication's contents. This is especially so when CompuServe carries the publication as part of a forum that is managed by a company unrelated to CompuServe."

Judge Leisure concluded that CompuServe had no more control over the content of the messages and files it carries than a "public library, bookstore, or newsstand," and that it would be no more feasible for CompuServe to examine the contents of every file it carries "than it would be for any other distributor to do so."

While Supreme Court decisions are the law of the land and cannot be disputed by any other court, Judges Leisure and Ain are trial judges in the federal and state systems respectively. Judge Ain was not bound by Judge Leisure's decision. Nevertheless, Judge Ain went out of his way to make clear, in holding Prodigy to be a publisher, that he did not disagree with Judge Leisure. "Let it be clear that this Court is in full agreement with [*CompuServe*]. ... Computer bulletin boards should generally be regarded in the same context as bookstores, libraries, and network affiliates. ... It is Prodigy's own policies, technology and staffing decisions which have altered the scenario and mandated the finding that it is a publisher."

Judge Ain found that by holding itself out to the public as a family-oriented service and by putting specific controls in place to deliver on this promise, Prodigy elevated itself from a distributor to a publisher. First, the judge found, Prodigy announced to the public that it screened the content of bulletin boards such as Money Talk. Second, Prodigy had screening software that scanned all messages for dirty words. Third, Prodigy had a set of guidelines that its sysops, known as *Board Leaders*, were expected to follow.

Judge Ain concluded, "By actively utilizing technology and man-power to delete notes from its computer bulletin boards on the basis of offensiveness and 'bad taste,' for example, Prodigy is clearly mak-ing decisions as to content...and such decisions constitute editorial control. That such control is not complete and is enforced both as early as the notes arrive and as late as a complaint is made does not minimize or eviscerate the simple fact that Prodigy has uniquely arrogated to itself the role of determining what is proper for its mem-bers to post and read on its bulletin boards. Based on the foregoing, this Court is compelled to conclude that for the purposes of Plaintiff's claims in the action, Prodigy is a publisher rather than a distributor."

Judge Ain's reasoning is strange. Following his line of reasoning, a Times Square newsstand would have no responsibility for the materials it sold, while a small-town newsstand might be in trouble if it put up a sign that read, "Your friendly family store." Prodigy's vague statements to the public about maintaining a family-friendly service were nothing more than a promise that it would quickly delete inappropriate materials once they are called to its attention.

In its papers on the summary judgment motion, Prodigy acknowledged that it had once tried to read all messages posted to its boards, but it had ended this approach long before the October 1994 attack on Stratton. But Judge Ain wasn't satisfied with Prodigy's response on this issue. Courts typically will not deny summary judg-ment if the other party's sole response is a conclusory, self-serving statement unsupported by any evidence. In the John Doe hypothet-ical given above, Doe might avoid summary judgment by saying that you met him at his house on October 15, 1995, but he would not win with a mere statement that you agreed to buy the house. Judge Ain determined that "[N]o documentation or detailed explanation of such a change [in Prodigy's policy], and the dissemination of news of such a change, has been submitted."

Judge Ain stumbled in dealing with this issue, however. Prodigy had pointed out that an eighteen-month gap existed between the last Prodigy statement relied on by Stratton (the Geoffrey Moore article from February 1993) and the October 1994 date of the supposedly libelous posting. Prodigy asserted that a lot had changed in the inter-im. Judge Ain disagreed and said: "Although the eighteen-month lapse of time between the last article and the aforementioned state-ments is not insignificant, and the court is wary of interpreting state-ments and admissions out of context, these considerations go solely to the weight of this evidence."

But the weight of evidence is a question for the jury. On a summary judgment motion, the question is, "Is there any evidence?" and no evaluation of its weight is made. Judge Ain's off-handed statement, "these considerations go solely to the weight of the evidence," would be appropriate only if he were denying summary judgment. Then, his answer would mean, "There is evidence, so I cannot grant summary judgment; the considerations you are raising impact the weight of the evidence, rather than contradicting that it exists." In granting summary judgment, Judge Ain seems to say that Prodigy's evidence has little weight. But, to support a grant of summary judgment, evidence must be nonexistent, not light. Judge Ain weighed the evidence himself—something he had no authority to do.

Prodigy's Content Guidelines, heavily relied on by Stratton, asked users (and the Board Leaders) to avoid "insulting" messages, harassment, "bad taste," matters "repugnant to community standards", and, as an additional catch-all, anything "harmful to maintaining a harmonious on-line community." The wording of the "penalties" section of the guidelines, significant but ignored by Judge Ain, stated that offensive matter "will be removed when brought to Prodigy's attention." The allegedly libelous messages were never called to Prodigy's attention until the lawsuit began.

Money Talk's Board Leader, Charles Epstein, testified at his pretrial deposition that Prodigy provided its Board Leaders with a software tool called the "emergency delete function." This allowed a Board Leader to remove an offending message and send a prepared message explaining the offense—"solicitation, bad advice, insulting, wrong topic, off topic, bad taste, etcetera."

In the early 1980s, before any specific legal precedent pertaining to bulletin boards existed, sysops, lawyers, and other interested parties avidly searched for the analogy that would lead to a common-sense set of rules. A popular idea at the time, and one borne out by the *CompuServe* case, was that BBSs are like grocery stores. A line of cases going back many decades deals with the situation in which a shopper slips on something, such as baby food from a broken jar, spilled in the aisle of the grocery store. The grocery store is liable only if it was aware of the spill and failed to clean it or if enough time had passed since the spill that the store's employees should have discovered it. Similarly, it was argued, a BBS sysop should only be responsible for any illegal material—obscenity, libel, pirated software—if he knew it was on his board or should have reasonably discovered it.

Texts on the law of the on-line world, such as Lance Rose's *Netlaw*, counsel sysops to take reasonable measures to ensure that their boards are not used for illegal purposes. Recommended measures included: posting warning messages visible at logon, saying that illegal files will not be tolerated; deleting illegal materials when found; and locking out users after a warning and second offense. No one involved in this debate ever believed that it was possible, let alone necessary, for a sysop to read every message or examine every file on a heavily used BBS.

The first known case of the arrest of a sysop for illegal material on a BBS happened in 1984, and it involved a California sysop named Tom Tcimpidis. The police were concerned about a stolen credit card number that had been posted in a message on Tcimpidis's BBS while he was on vacation. He didn't know about it, didn't encourage this kind of posting, and would have deleted it if he had discovered it. The charges against Tcimpidis were dismissed after a storm of public opinion educated the police and prosecutors that Tcimpidis's policy disapproving illegal materials on the BBS should have been enough to shield him from liability. Judge Ain's ruling, by contrast, discourages Tcimpidis from having a policy or reviewing the contents of the BBS at all.

Judge Ain's opinion implies that you are damned whatever you do. If you do nothing at all, most lawyers agree that you are taking a risk. If you take some measures to avoid harmful material on your board, Judge Ain confirms that the law may hold you liable if the measures are not effective. "Prodigy's conscious choice, to gain the benefits of editorial control, has opened it up to a greater liability than CompuServe and other computer networks that make no such choice. For the record, the fear that this court's finding of publisher status for Prodigy will compel all computer networks to abdicate control of their bulletin boards incorrectly presumes that the market will refuse to compensate a network for its increased control and the resulting increased exposure. ... Presumably Prodigy's decision to regulate the content of its bulletin boards was in part influenced by its desire to attract a market it perceived to exist consisting of users seeking a 'family-oriented' computer service. This decision simply required that to the extent computer networks provide such services, they must also accept the concomitant legal consequences." Judge Ain's economic analysis is decidedly bizarre. He asserts that his decision will not deter on-line services from exercising care, because those that do will be able to cover their risk by charging more.

Contrary to Judge Ain's assertion, it is unlikely that most adults would pay enough of a premium for a "family-oriented" on-line service to justify the additional risks of litigation. On-line services, which not many years ago charged as much as $12 an hour, are running scared because Internet access services like Netcom and Interramp charge as little as $1.50 an hour. The downward pressure on prices has not stopped there; some access providers, especially the smaller ones, are now charging fixed fees of approximately $20 a month for almost unlimited hours on-line.

The reason CompuServe, Prodigy, and America Online are concerned is that many users perceive that the resources available on these services are available more cheaply on the Internet. The on-line services themselves are accordingly trying to compete in the low end of the Internet access marketplace.

Prodigy, shocked by the judgment, dismissed its attorney and retained a famous First Amendment specialist, Martin Garbus. Garbus is one of the elite group of attorneys who defended comedian Lenny Bruce in the 1960s when law enforcement officials were hounding him nationwide. As soon as he was retained, Garbus filed a motion asking Judge Ain for "reargument" of his decision.

A motion for reargument is a way of giving a judge an opportunity to reconsider a decision before taking it up on appeal. It is rare, but not unheard of, for a judge to overrule his or her own prior opinion; fair-minded judges may be persuaded that they misunderstood the law or missed an important fact in making their decision. In his affidavit in support of the motion, Garbus reminded Judge Ain of a famous aphorism of former Supreme Court Justice Felix Frankfurter: "Wisdom too often never comes, and so one ought not to reject it merely because it comes late."

In his brief, Garbus struck the balance appropriate for a newly-hired attorney, delicately blaming his predecessor for some of the problems in the case and the judge for others. He started by admitting that Prodigy had failed to provide the judge with enough information on the original motion, and he promised to remedy that problem with the materials attached to the motion to reargue. Then, Garbus staked out his territory: "Prodigy is not materially different from any other provider of bulletin boards. All on-line providers, in some form or another, take steps to prevent illegal conduct such as obscenity, fighting words or hate speech, harassment, or obstruction of communication on their bulletin boards."

Oddly for a First Amendment expert, Garbus made some misstatements. Hate speech, no matter how awful, is First Amendment–protected in this country, and therefore is not "illegal conduct." Harassment may or may not be illegal, depending on the context; similarly, the phrase "obstruction of communication" is too vague to be meaningful. Breaking into a computer system to delete an adversary's message is illegal; drowning out an opponent's voice with 1000 strongly worded messages may be obnoxious and may "obstruct" communications but is First Amendment–protected speech. Garbus certainly knows the difference; he may have thought that Judge Ain wouldn't.

Garbus went on to warn Judge Ain that his decision had already "generated widespread concern" in the press and in the publishing and on-line communities. This reflected an unusual strategy: impress upon the judge that his decision had met widespread social and legal criticism. Judges are supposed to adhere to the law; trials are not intended to be popularity contests where the judge enforces the will of the majority. But judges are human beings, and they are sensitive to the way their decisions are received. Judge Gibbons, in the *Amateur Action* case, was nettled by the press coverage suggesting she had erred. Garbus hoped that Judge Ain would be affected by the outpouring of criticism his decision had generated in the media.

"The libel law," said Garbus, "should not be extended to someone who—as here—merely rejects obscenity, fighting words, harassing and obstructing conduct." He complained that Stratton had misled the judge, marshaling fragmented evidence from the depositions, Prodigy's guidelines, and other sources to give Judge Ain a "false impression." Garbus argued persuasively that there was no real-world difference between CompuServe and Prodigy.

Garbus concluded that on-line providers of bulletin boards "have no control or practical ability to edit the contents of postings or to refuse to distribute someone else's words. For example, unlike a book publisher or newspaper, Prodigy has virtually no relationship with the authors of the notes that are posted on the boards. Prodigy cannot require that the authors of the notes justify the content. Prodigy cannot require that the authors provide sources or explain the basis for the assertions they make. Prodigy has no ability to require an author to change any note. For these reasons, on-line providers cannot be deemed to 'publish,' or assume as their own, the words that they distribute."

Garbus explained that minimal measures taken to discourage illegal or obstructive behavior should not be construed to hold on-line services to an impossible standard. "On-line providers must be entitled to monitor obscenity and racial epithets and messages that harass other members or obstruct the bulletin boards without fear that they will be subject to liability for the actual *content* of everything that is posted." He compared Prodigy to a newsstand that refuses to carry sexually explicit magazines. If such a refusal subjects the newsstand to liability for anything that slips by, the law's message will be that distributors are only safe if they take no measures at all.

Attached to Garbus's affidavit were hundreds of pages of other affidavits, newspaper articles, and other materials. One affidavit was from Ross Glatzer, former Chief Executive Officer of Prodigy. He said: "[B]y January 1994, Prodigy had abandoned its policy of manually prescreening communications on the bulletin boards. This change came as a result of the increase in the number of Prodigy subscribers, the volume of messages posted each day on the boards, and the speed at which messages could be posted. Monitoring messages for content—as Prodigy once tried to do—simply became impossible." The screening software, still in use, involved no editorial discretion. "The mechanism automatically returns messages that contain foul language without regard to the substantive content of the statement."

Even the notorious guidelines are not content-based, Glatzer claimed, but are merely intended to be a mechanism for dealing with messages that "obstruct the operation of the bulletin boards." However, the excerpts from the guidelines quoted by Judge Ain— banning "insulting" messages, harassment, "bad taste," matters "repugnant to community standards," and anything "harmful to maintaining a harmonious on-line community"—contradict this claim and make it clear that Prodigy's restrictions were very much content-based.

It shouldn't matter, though. Prodigy's guidelines are no different than a BBS sysop's message at logon that pirated software will not be tolerated on the board. The guidelines warn the users that the sysop will deal strictly with certain conduct when it is discovered. They do not guarantee that illegal materials will not appear on the BBS unbeknownst to the sysop.

Glatzer claimed that it had never been Prodigy's policy to screen its bulletin boards for false statements. "Prodigy advised its members that they bear full responsibility for the content of the messages they post. If a member posts a defamatory statement, the guidelines make clear that the member can be held legally liable."

Glatzer concluded by arguing that in the absence of "minimal policing" not only would "obscenity and pornography" flood on-line services, but complete chaos would result because "it would be impossible for on-line providers to deal with those individuals that would disrupt the services. Prodigy and every other on-line provider would probably close down most boards. The court could not possibly have intended this result."

Although his statement is exaggerated, there is an element of truth in Glatzer's fears. Unmoderated Usenet newsgroups—everyone's favorite speech sewer—illustrate that "bad" speech drives out "good." For example, a feminist newsgroup, flooded with hateful misogynist messages, was forced to transform itself into a moderated list to avoid the problem.

Garbus submitted to Judge Ain a July 1995 column by *Boardwatch Magazine* editor Jack Ricard, which discusses the problem in entertaining language. "You join a discussion group on-line who are pleasantly conversing on a mutual topic of passion—butterfly census methodologies and the upcoming July 4th count. Suddenly, a brief message appears in the thread: 'butterflies suck.' Technically, this may be accurate, but it is inevitably followed by increasingly lengthy and tortuous posts from a new participant who not only is intent on abusing the innocent butterfly, but Lepidopterists in general. Who knows, he may have been misclassified during his caterpillar days and has obsessively resented the field since then. For whatever reason, no message can be posted in the conference without a scathing and often abusively obscene response from the Jackass at the Trough. Within days, the other participants begin resigning from this now less than useful and enlightening conversation and a peaceful community is destroyed—wrecked by a single individual with too much time and too well-connected a keyboard. He has slobbered into the trough, and no one now wants to drink from it."

Ricard concludes that "if [the *Prodigy*] decision stands, the only way to survive as an on-line service is to simply not levy any controls on message areas. And the result will be that everything everywhere will enjoy the same level of chaos as Usenet."

The next affidavit was from another former Prodigy employee, Member Security Officer Willard McDowell. Stratton had relied, in its summary judgment motion, on statements McDowell had made at his deposition, which he now claimed were taken out of context. At the deposition, McDowell, unfortunately for Prodigy, had said that he "assumed that Prodigy performed a management function over the Board Leaders."

McDowell explained that his responsibilities had been to investigate fraud and other related problems and that his job never involved "any significant interaction with the Board Leaders." His understanding of the Board Leaders' functions and of their interaction with Prodigy was based "only upon hearsay. ... I explained this to plaintiff's counsel at my deposition." In other words, he was now asking the judge not to pay attention to anything he had said before.

The lengthiest affidavit was filed by Jennifer Ambrozek, Prodigy's Manager of Bulletin Board Communications. Bulletin boards, she said, are "simply the conduit through which [Prodigy's] members may communicate with each other." Howard Rheingold echoed this in *The Virtual Community*, explaining that the on-line services' big discovery was that there is more money to be made selling the users to one another than there is in selling them information.

According to Ambrozek, Prodigy's Executive VP, Scott Kurnit, had publicly announced in January 1994 that Prodigy had abandoned its effort to monitor message content because, as she put it, "Notes on our bulletin boards are uploaded in such volume and with such speed that Prodigy could not—even if it wanted to—edit, monitor, or otherwise control the content of the notes that its members post." Unfortunately, Prodigy's former attorney had not called this to Judge Ain's attention. Ambrozek attached a copy of the guidelines, which apparently had not previously been submitted to Judge Ain in their entirety. She noted that "Prodigy *does not* affirmatively undertake to prescreen or censor notes based on content, as the court seemed to believe. Enforcement of the guidelines is a reactive process." The guidelines make clear that members bear exclusive responsibility for their comments. "Prodigy is not responsible for any note unless posted by us. ... You can be held legally liable for what you say on the board."

In her affidavit, Ambrozek said that if someone contacts Prodigy to complain of a defamatory posting (which Stratton never did), "our policy is to provide the complainant access to the board for a response."

Ambrozek acknowledged that the Board Leaders were sometimes referred to as "editors." The original programmers of the Prodigy software had coined the phrase and named parts of the system "editor's tools" and "editorial department." Ambrozek stated that "These phrases have stuck and may appear in documents from time to time...[but] should not be given any meaning," because Board Leaders "perform no editorial functions."

At her deposition, Ambrozek had testified that the messages about Stratton did not violate the guidelines, because "it is a member's expression of opinion." When asked what a Board Leader does "if he sees a note he believes is not truthful in its content," she had replied, "Well, Board Leaders aren't out there looking for notes and whether or not they are truthful; that's not their main mission in life. As I've been trying to explain, the way the boards work are the notes are posted and unless somebody alerts us to something, we don't take any action on them."

This in itself raised a material issue of fact that should have gone to the jury. Ain held Prodigy accountable to prevent libel, even though its guidelines, according to Ambrozek, did not make Prodigy or its Board Leaders responsible for ascertaining the truth of messages.

However, in making his decision, Ain did not have the entire deposition transcripts available to him, only those portions attached by the parties to their motion papers. Prodigy had indeed done a very poor job of mining the transcripts for material showing that unresolved factual issues existed.

In September 1995, Prodigy settled with Stratton Oakmont, issuing a written apology but claiming that no money had changed hands. Garbus had announced his intention to inquire into the terms of a confidential settlement of securities fraud charges between Stratton Oakmont and the Justice Department. Stratton Oakmont may simply have concluded that a face-saving settlement was better than a protracted battle over the truth of the anonymous allegations made on Prodigy. The parties announced that they would ask Judge Ain to vacate his decision, effectively erasing it from the law books and declaring it of no value as a legal precedent. Two months later, Ain denied Garbus's motion to reargue and declined to cancel his prior discussion. He declared that the world of cyberspace needed a precedent.

While the *Prodigy* case was being decided, another opinion regarding on-line services was issued by New York Supreme Court Judge Emily Jane Goodman.

In the spring of 1994, radio talk show celebrity Howard Stern announced his candidacy for the governorship of New York. Delphi, a commercial on-line service, opened a bulletin board on Stern's candidacy and ran full-page ads in *New York Magazine* and the *New York Post* asking "Should this man be the next governor of New York?" The ads featured a photograph of Stern in leather pants with his buttocks exposed, which was used without Stern's permission.

Stern sued under a New York State law that protects people whose "name, portrait, or picture" are used in advertising without their consent. "Stern," said Judge Goodman, "does not deny that it is his picture and buttocks that appear in the advertisement. " Judge Goodman considered whether Delphi was protected by an "incidental use" exception to the law. This exception was first adopted in a 1919 case. The defendant in that case, a movie distributor, had used the name and photograph of a woman to advertise his newsreel about her. The court observed that if the law prevented the defendant from using the woman's likeness in the ad, he would be unable to advertise at all. In this case, use of a name and likeness without permission was "incidental to the exhibition of the film itself."

Judge Goodman granted summary judgment in favor of Delphi—with the result that all three of the major cases dealing with the responsibility of on-line services have ended in summary judgments. She found that Delphi was a "news disseminator" entitled to the incidental use exception.

Relying on *Cubby v. CompuServe*, Judge Goodman observed, "This service is analogous to that of a news vendor or bookstore or a letters-to-the-editor column of a newspaper, [all of] which require purchase of their materials for the public to actually gain access to the information carried. ... Affording protection to on-line computer services when they are engaged in traditional news dissemination, such as in this case, is the desirable and required result. ... Delphi used Stern's photograph to communicate to the public the nature and style of its service, which in this case was the promotion of a news event in which plaintiff was a principal. To restrict Delphi from informing the public of the nature and subject of its service would constitute an impermissible restriction."

She added this acerbic aside: "Indeed, it is ironic that Stern, a radio talk show host (as well as author and would-be politician) seeks to silence the electronic equivalent of a talk show, an on-line computer bulletin board service."

Judges Leisure and Goodman were clearly correct, and Judge Ain was wrong. An on-line service is analogous to a bookstore or newsstand and should not be held responsible for illegal material of which the service is not aware. An on-line service must be able to take reasonable measures to discourage illegal material and to protect the service's culture and environment, without being held responsible for any illegal material that evades its detection.

If you think the issue is settled simply by finding the right analogy, consider the following recent Maryland case. Seven FBI agents entered Kathleen Eckstein's bookstore and showed her a search warrant that contained a section so vague that it allowed them to seize First Amendment–protected novels from the bookshelf, including one by John Updike. Although Mrs. Eckstein was not arrested, shortly after the search she received a letter from the Assistant U.S. Attorney assigned to the case, warning her that she would be prosecuted if "obscene" material were found in her shop again.

No one had ever made it clear to Eckstein what, if anything, seized from her shop was obscene. She attempted to seek guidance from the U.S. Attorney's office, from the police, and from numerous other government officials, none of whom would help her. Finally, she brought suit in federal court, claiming that the government's action was infringing upon her First Amendment rights.

After her case was dismissed by a Federal District Court, she appealed to the Fourth Circuit Court of Appeals, which said, "While laws such as the one at issue indeed may chill the expression of protected speech in certain instances, such secondary effects seem unavoidable if the federal anti-obscenity statute is to be enforced."

In other words, getting rid of obscenity is worth a few violations of the Bill of Rights. In *Smith v. California*, quoted above, the Supreme Court struck down a California law that imposed liability on booksellers for carrying obscene books even if they did not know the books' contents. The FBI and the U.S. Attorney's office in Maryland found what they thought was a loophole: they'll put you on notice of obscene materials in your shop, but—Catch 22—they'll refuse to tell you what they are. Whatever today's courts say, the 1959 Supreme Court would not have permitted this. The authorities effectively put Eckstein in the position of having to read every book and magazine in her shop.

Telephone and cable companies have also been put on notice by the authorities that they will be liable if they do not act as censors. In 1987, an Arizona district attorney wrote a letter to Mountain Bell, the local telephone company, threatening prosecution if it continued supplying 976-line service to Carlin Communications, a supplier of indecent recorded messages. Mountain Bell originally resisted, but it finally adopted a policy excluding all "adult entertainment" messages from the 976 network.

The First Amendment only protects individuals against state action (i.e., government intervention). The Court of Appeals held that, even though the state could not legally ban indecent communications, Mountain Bell's decision to do so was not state action and therefore could not be a violation of the First Amendment.

From this perspective, Judge Leisure's *CompuServe* decision and Judge Goodman's *Delphi* ruling, though important to the health of on-line services, don't really offer much comfort. The decisions, after all, protect the rights of on-line services, not of the users whose speech may be chilled by the threat of litigation.

Cubby and Stratton failed to give CompuServe and Prodigy any notice that they objected to the messages. If they had, each of the services would almost certainly have deleted the offending posts, and a lot of legal fees would have been saved—but censorship would have occurred. CompuServe or Prodigy might have deeper pockets than the people suing them, but it would not have been worth their while to take a costly stand to protect user's rights.

Moreover, the *Eckstein* and *Mountain Bell* cases encourage legislators and law enforcement officials to pressure on-line services into banning what the government itself cannot. Courts will then find that this is a private act of censorship, not a First Amendment violation.

The chilling effects of cases like *Stratton Oakmont v. Prodigy* are evident in the following quote from Peter DeNigris. A Money Talk user, he was sued in 1992 by a company named Medphone for disparaging its stock on the board. Though DeNigris only paid token damages, the message was clear. "I learned that the electronic bulletin board is a wonderful thing," DeNigris said, "because it gives the little person the opportunity to speak his opinions to other people. But now when I'm on Prodigy, I'm very careful."

# CHAPTER

# V

## INQUISITION ON THE NET

"The purpose of the suit is to harass and discourage rather than win. The law can be used very easily to harass, and enough harassment on somebody who is simply on the thin edge anyway, well knowing that he is not authorized, will generally be sufficient to cause his professional decease. If possible, of course, ruin him utterly." These words were written by L. Ron Hubbard, the founder of Scientology, in a 1965 campaign against the unauthorized usage of his scriptures. Although his followers may argue that this statement is taken out of context and can never be fully understood by uninitiates, it seems to speak for itself. This directive appears to be the guiding policy of the Church of Scientology ("CoS"), which over the last few decades, has filed numerous suits against ex-members, critics, and even journalists. The church, however, is now having a very difficult time with its latest target—free speech on the Internet.

In 1991, Scott Goehring, a 26-year-old college student in Bloomington, Indiana, founded the **alt.religion.scientology** newsgroup for discussion and criticism of Hubbard's expensive religion. His wife's first husband was a CoS member and he hoped this new forum would help debunk what he considered to be a bogus cult. But it was an obscure newsgroup, ranking, in the spring of 1993, somewhere in the last 50 (of over 10,000) groups in popularity. That is, until the Scientologists found out that people were talking about them.

In December of 1994, some computer-savvy members of the church began canceling messages intended for the newsgroup. The church never openly admitted to the censoring, but the canceled messages themselves began to state what would soon become the official position of the CoS: the deleted postings had contained copyrighted material. This attracted the attention of both the Internet provider for the "robocanceler" account, Netcom, and Netizens at large who saw this as a blatant violation of etiquette on the global networks. It is acceptable to use the **cancel** function to recall a message that you mistakenly sent out. It is not to be used to censor others' speech.

Netcom finally disabled the accounts of the cancelers, who appeared again elsewhere and were then tracked by a group that called themselves the "Rabbit Hunters." This name arose after Ron Newman, one of the most outspoken on-line voices against the CoS, labeled the canceler the "cancelbunny," because like a character in a famous battery commercial, it kept going, and going, and going. The cancelers accepted this name and soon began signing their messages "Cancel Wabbit." The rabbits were chased around the globe and flushed out of most of their hiding places until, in January 1995, the CoS's "Counsel for Trademarks," Helena Kobrin, decided it would be more effective to just shut down the newsgroup entirely.

Kobrin attempted to do so by sending out what is called a "rmgroup message," which instructs systems administrators to remove a given group from their directories. Kobrin said **alt.religion.scientology** was never properly created, illegally used a trademarked name, and serves only to carry blatant copyright and trade secret violations. The "rmgroup message" cannot, however, automatically cancel a newsgroup from Usenet servers, which collectively represent an excellent example of Net democracy.

Newsgroups are not grounded in any central location, but are instead distributed across thousands of computers around the world. These servers are maintained by the community of systems administrators, who decide which of the thousands of newsgroups to accept for their clients. When a message is sent to **alt.religion.scientology**, it bounces from node to node, leaving a copy in all the computers which ask for it, eventually finding its way to most subscribers around the world. To dismantle an established newsgroup would take a concerted effort by the entire cyberspace community.

Kobrin's "rmgroup" letter amused the Internet community, which largely ignored her demand. She tried again, citing recent legal precedents regarding copyrights. "Our request is not made for the purpose of stopping the discussions on a.r.s. ... We are trying to deal with an anarchy created by some Net users who callously trample on the intellectual property rights of organizations and individuals under the guise of the First Amendment." Again her request was ignored.

Newman fired back a letter in which he announced the obvious problems CoS would have in trying to cancel a newsgroup or even suppress information, "What makes you think you can shut down a newsgroup whose existence is controlled by tens of thousands of separate system administrators throughout the world. And if you did manage to do this, what makes you think this action would actually stop the copyright infringements that you are complaining about? The offending messages would obviously move to a different Usenet group."

Around the same time, another church attorney, Thomas Small, went after several anonymous remailers—services that strip-mail messages of their addresses, thereby allowing users to remain anonymous. CoS saw that many critics were routing their postings through these remailers, so Small sent a letter threatening legal action. If the remailers did not prevent certain messages from reaching both **alt.religion.scientology** and **alt.clearing.technology** (another newsgroup formed to discuss the church), CoS would initiate litigation.

The Electronic Frontier Foundation (EFF) issued a response to the CoS threats against systems administrators and remailers operators, urging the church to find solutions other than litigation. The EFF argued that continuing this course would have an adverse effect on free speech on the Internet, as small providers, without the resources or the stamina to stand up to such requests, would eventually be forced to discontinue all contentious forums. The EFF press release quoted Justice Brandeis who, in 1927, said that in the face of fallacies and falsehoods, "the remedy to be applied is more speech, not enforced silence." In a certain sense, CoS explored this option. At the urging of one Scientologist, church members instituted a concerted policy of flooding the newsgroups with short messages. This was equally offensive to Netizens, who refer to unsolicited mailings as "spamming" and consider them the only legitimate reason to cancel another user's messages.

By the summer of 1995, the once-obscure **alt.religion.scientology** had become one of the most popular forums on the Net, with tens of thousands of monthly visitors. Although most netizens had previously never heard of this religion, they now saw it as the greatest non-government threat to freedom on the world's networks. The Internet reacted to the attack by spreading CoS documents and criticisms to the corners of the earth. Soon the hype made the information popular. In China FTP servers carrying Scientology information were forced to restrict their access, as demand was slowing the entire Internet feed into the country. The church discovered that it was impossible to shut down the criticisms and remove the discussion groups, so it shifted its approach to tracking down the people responsible.

On February 2, 1995, CoS approached Julf Helsingius, the operator of an anonymous remailer in Finland, and demanded the real name of a person who had used his service to post allegedly confidential information. Helsingius refused and the CoS said they would be back with a warrant. Created in 1992, Helsingius's **anon.penet.fi** is one of the world's most famous remailers, retransmitting nearly 7000 messages a day and residing in a country renowned for its strong policies with regards to human rights and freedom of expression. Helsingius is considered a scrupulous computer specialist who selflessly offers his service to the Internet community.

On February 8, the Finnish police arrived at Helsingius's door with a warrant of search and seizure. CoS had contacted Interpol via the police in Los Angeles, where they claimed data was stolen from their computers. The Finnish police came prepared to copy his entire user list, but Helsingius managed to persuade them to take only the single name they came for. Within an hour, they had given the information not only to the Los Angeles Police Department ("LAPD"), but also directly to CoS. An uproar followed in the Internet community, which realized how easily anonymity could be circumvented with just a few lawyers.

CoS now had an address that led to an alumnus account at the California Institute of Technology ("Caltech") at Pasadena. CoS sent three private investigators to the school who approached the Caltech Security Office and Campus Computing Organization and demanded the name of the person corresponding to the address. When Campus Computing said it would need more information, the CoS lawyers jumped in. Finally the LAPD began to investigate the church's claims. After finding no supporting evidence of computer theft, the LAPD, despite repeated pressure, finally advised the CoS to drop its claims. CoS would not, however, abandon the policy of using the law to seek out on-line critics.

A few days later, the doorbell rang at the home of Dennis Erlich, a former member and now vocal critic of CoS. Standing outside were a group of twelve strangers, including three with guns. Erlich refused to open the door and called 911. The voice on the phone told him he had to open the door—it was the law outside.

Erlich walked out on the porch and discovered that he was facing a CoS contingent, led by attorney Thomas Small. Small was accompanied by one on-duty Glendale, California, police officer, and two off-duty officers that Small had "rented" for the occasion. Also along were a private detective, an officer of the Religious Technology Center (a CoS affiliate and Small's client), and a computer expert. Erlich questioned Glendale police officer Steve Leggett, who told him that the group had been authorized by federal judge Ron Whyte to enter his house and search for copyrighted material. "I objected," Erlich says, "but was told that they would use force if I resisted."

Small served Erlich with a sheaf of legal papers and the group entered his home, where they searched his computer, looked in every desk and dresser drawer, and photographed everything—including his closets. The computer expert examined every file on Erlich's hard disk; whenever he found something Small determined was relevant, he copied it and deleted the original from Erlich's disk. They finally left almost seven hours later, taking three hundred floppy disks and two back-up tapes they had made, along with Erlich's copies of CoS materials he had received while a member of the church, and others he had bought from bookstores or been given by other ex-Scientologists. "Potentially they copied all my personal correspondence, mailing lists, financial records and personal notes. Anyone who has sent me anything in confidence must assume that it has been compromised," Erlich wrote that night. When he asked to examine the materials Small was taking, he was refused, even though a Fox TV camera crew was filming the encounter. "I hope this at least shows what type of fascist organization I am attempting to expose," Erlich said.

Erlich had joined CoS in 1968, and, over the next 15 years, had become a minister admitted to its inner circle, the Sea Organization. After leaving, he had made it his goal "to reform Scientology and to expose the crimes I saw committed" during his time in the Church. Starting in 1994, he took his campaign to the Internet, using a server operated by Tom Klemesrud as his base for the posting of messages to **alt.religion.scientology**.

In a 1986 case, a federal appeals court had summarized CoS's teachings, "The Church teaches that a person's behavior and well-being are improved by removing 'engrams' from the unconscious mind. Engrams are impressions recorded by the unconscious mind in times of trauma in this life or in previous lives." CoS's most secret texts, referred to as "the Advanced Technology," describe an incident 75 million years ago in which an intergalactic being called "Xenu" eliminated a race called the Thetans. "He trapped selected beings and flew them to volcanoes on Earth, then called Teegeeach. He then dropped powerful H-bombs on the volcanoes." Before founding his church, L. Ron Hubbard was a science fiction writer.

CoS's complaint, filed with Judge Whyte on February 8, named not only Erlich as a defendant, but also Klemesrud and Netcom, the company that provided Klemesrud with access to the Internet. CoS had written to Erlich before, ordering him to desist quoting the Advanced Technology; when he failed to comply, CoS had instructed Klemesrud and Netcom to stop passing Erlich's messages to the Internet. Each had asked CoS to produce the originals of the copied works, for comparison purposes but CoS refused. When they failed to fall into line, CoS sued them as well.

CoS claimed that Erlich had violated its copyrights in the Advanced Technology documents, which were to be revealed only to adherents of the Church. These documents were mainly short memoranda pertaining to CoS procedures and doctrine. Erlich had quoted some of these in Usenet posts, but claimed that what he had done was a "fair use." "Fair use" is a copyright doctrine which says that reasonable excerpts from copyrighted works may be used for purposes of criticism and discussion.

CoS also claimed that other unpublished Advanced Technology texts were "trade secrets," such as the Coca Cola formula, and that Erlich was wrongfully appropriating these for his own use. In order to prove a trade secrecy violation, a party must show that it had non-public, valuable information that it took pains to protect. In its complaint, CoS described the lengths to which it had gone to protect the Advanced Technology, "These measures include, *inter alia*, the numbering of all copies of the materials containing Advanced Technology; locking all such materials in locked cabinets or safes when not in use; logging of the materials upon each use; electronically connecting the materials to the cabinets in which they are stored and to the tables on which they are used and monitoring of those connections by security computers and alarm systems."

CoS had followed what would prove to be its usual tactics in pursuing Erlich: it appeared before a federal judge and requested an "ex parte" temporary restraining order and order of seizure. Ex parte means that the other party to the case—the one CoS wants to seize things from—is not given advance notice. Since the Fifth Amendment to the Constitution guarantees due process, any proceeding to which an affected party is not invited is heavily disfavored under the law. In copyright cases, ex parte orders of seizure are sought when the defendant is thought to be a really bad character—someone who will illegally dispose of the evidence or flee if he is notified in advance that he is being sued. Orders of seizure in such cases are intended to allow the plaintiff to take all the evidence away so that it cannot be tampered with or destroyed by the defendant. An accompanying temporary restraining order prohibits the defendant from committing any more infringements.

The court, after issuing a seizure or temporary restraining order, must then hold an immediate hearing to determine that the ex parte order is necessary. If a judge concludes that it was "improvidently" requested, he will revoke the restraining order, order the seized materials to be returned, and possibly fine the plaintiff. If, on the other hand, the hearing shows that the ex parte order was justified, the judge may confirm the temporary restraining order by transforming it into a preliminary injunction pending the trial's outcome.

CoS's actions in obtaining an order and coming to Erlich's house were similar to Postal Inspector Dirmeyer's execution of the search warrant at Robert and Carleen Thomas's house the previous year. The difference was that Dirmeyer was initiating a criminal prosecution, and he took the Thomas's computers away for copying. CoS was beginning a civil copyright lawsuit, and left Erlich his computers. Judge Whyte held a hearing on February 21, just eight days after CoS carried out the seizure. Attorneys appeared on behalf of Klemesrud and Netcom. Erlich appeared in Judge Whyte's court on his own behalf, not having retained counsel yet, and gave the Judge a letter he had prepared explaining that he had quoted only small excerpts from the published Advanced Technology texts, which he said were available in many bookstores in California. "To the best of my recollection, I quoted only a few sentences from each of those policies. I believe that fair use and my status as a minister trained on these materials while within my ministry in Scientology allows me to quote small segments to make a point, for public service, or for use in my religious sermons on the Internet."

As for the unpublished excerpts, these had been entered into public court records in a Los Angeles case, and Erlich believed them to be in the public domain. Someone else had posted them to Usenet and Erlich had quoted excerpts from the posts. Erlich asked Judge Whyte to find that CoS was acting in bad faith against him and to dismiss the temporary restraining order.

Judge Whyte began by expressing concern about CoS's tactics. He had the opportunity to read the submissions from Netcom's attorneys and affidavits from CoS, which included copies of the materials that had been seized. He had been led to believe, by CoS's original ex parte application, that Erlich was engaged in wholesale copying of CoS's works. Instead, some of the seized copies presented to him appeared to be essays containing excerpts of CoS's texts. Judge Whyte said, "[H]e has a right, it seems to me, to do satires or articles or criticisms or anything he wants to with respect to publicly available information pertaining to Scientology. And looking through the list of items seized, it may be that it includes some items that are articles by him that he would have a right to do. I want to make sure that any injunction, if one is issued, is issued in terms of making sure that his right to comment and criticize...if he wishes to do so, is protected."

Judge Whyte was also concerned that CoS had named Klemesrud and Netcom, since they had merely served as a conduit for Erlich's postings to **alt.religion.scientology**. He said, "It's probably a practical impossibility for them to be expected to do any kind of censoring or checking what's published through their services. So I have some real concern as to whether or not they're appropriate defendants, but perhaps more immediately whether or not any type of injunction would be appropriate as to them."

Attorney Small spoke for the plaintiff, Religious Technology Center—the division of the church which controlled the trade secrets and copyrighted material. First, he reassured the judge that Erlich had been engaged in wholesale copyright infringement by saying, "The seizure netted approximately 200 unauthorized copies of those works, about 160 that had been downloaded from the Internet, about 30 that had been posted on the Internet by Mr. Erlich and stored in his hard drive, one that was on a floppy disk beside his computer, and about 30 other works that were stored in the hard drive."

He then did what litigators often do; he made his adversary out to be a bad human being. He said, "Mr. Erlich attempted to conceal his computer containing the hard drive, set up a decoy computer in his computer room and attempted to divert our attention from it." Small criticized Netcom's position that it could not possibly police

Erlich's posts to Usenet. Judge Whyte interrupted him, "How would they possibly police? How would they do it?" Small replied that, using the IP address, it was technically possible to write software that would archive all Erlich's messages for Netcom's review before forwarding. He noted that CoS had developed software that used the IP address to determine when Erlich was on-line, and he volunteered the services of CoS programmers to help Netcom develop its own censorship software.

Small had made an inventory of the materials seized; the judge, thumbing through it, was further troubled that some of the seized messages were described as containing only one paragraph of CoS material. Small was also somewhat ill-prepared and was not able to tell the judge which of the seized materials CoS considered "unpublished" or "published" works, and he acknowledged that copyrights might never have been filed on some of the materials. This would bar their inclusion in the copyright infringement claim of the lawsuit, though not in the trade secrecy claim.

Judge Whyte asked Erlich if he had been making wholesale copies of CoS works for redistribution. Erlich replied, "The most that I would ever post out of a book of 400 pages," Erlich replied, "would be maybe two pages excerpted with comments about how this shows that these are the activities and real beliefs of the Church of Scientology."

A peculiarity of the case—which Erlich now described to the judge—was that CoS had deleted from his computer all of the files they had copied. Erlich claimed that two of his computers wouldn't boot after Small left. Of course, in a traditional case, in which the plaintiff is seizing books, or recordings, or videotapes, the plaintiff carts everything away and the defendant retains nothing. But in a case involving electronic records, there is simply no precedent for deleting what is taken. There was no reason why Small could not have copied files from Erlich's hard drive, without deleting anything. Dirmeyer, in a far more serious criminal case, had returned the Thomases' hard drive with the contents intact. CoS's deletion of Erlich's files had left him without copies of his own work—he could not even defend himself effectively in the hearing without them. Erlich stated, "[T]hey sat at my computer...and deleted and copied files wholesale without permitting me to make an inventory of what they were actually deleting or copying. So I have nothing even to defend myself to say, okay, these were the original postings that I made."

Richard Horning, Klemesrud's attorney, addressed Judge Whyte and said, "What the plaintiffs seek in this case is an order from this court compelling my client to keep Mr. Erlich off the air entirely, whether he's engaged in legitimate criticism or wholesale copyright violations or something in between. ... I don't think this court should permit its processes to be used for those purposes." He quoted *Smith v. California*, a Supreme Court bookstore content regulation case, for the proposition that Klemesrud wasn't responsible for policing all the communications that passed across his server. In *Smith*, the Court held that a bookstore owner was not responsible for the contents of every book in the store.

Attorney Randolf Rice, speaking for Netcom, insisted that his client wasn't even a "bookstore." He said, "It's a fair analogy to say that if you looked at this as a pollution case what the plaintiffs are doing is pointing to a polluted river and suing the river along with the polluter. That is exactly the position of Netcom here. We are simply a means of transmission." He pointed out that Netcom, if forced to police Erlich's behavior, would have no option but to disconnect Klemesrud's server, cutting off 500 other subscribers along with Erlich.

Small took one more swipe at Erlich in his closing statement, claiming that Erlich cooperated nicely in the seizure "until he got the press on the premises and began drinking beer and got a little unruly."

Judge Whyte decided to dissolve the temporary restraining order against Klemesrud and Netcom. As far as Erlich was concerned, the temporary restraining order would stay in force for three more days in order to give Small a chance to return to court with a revised inventory, establishing which materials were copyrighted and which were considered trade secrets. Erlich asked for clarification from the judge because he intended to post messages to **alt.religion.scientology** describing the week's events; if he did so, and included, for example, a paragraph from a CoS document, would he be raided again? Judge Whyte replied that Erlich was entitled to "fair use" of CoS material but should be careful to avoid any wholesale copying.

In addition to letting the world know he was being sued by CoS, Erlich promptly posted another document to **alt.religion.scientology** and CoS moved to hold him in contempt. Months later, Judge Whyte would deny the contempt motion, holding that a confused Erlich, unrepresented by counsel, had relied on the Judge's words about "fair use" and would not be held in contempt of court for publishing the document.

The preliminary injunction hearing was not held until June. By the time of the hearing, Erlich was represented by a volunteer counsel from one of San Francisco's largest law firms, Morrison and Foerster. Judge Whyte indicated an eager interest in the case, and knowledge of the workings of the Internet and of Klemesrud's bulletin board system. Riding the parties hard to make sure that they kept within the time limits he had established, Judge Whyte patiently heard tales of volcanoes and Thetans and accusations that CoS religious doctrine was gibberish.

In September, the judge ruled that Erlich's posting of CoS texts to **alt.religion.scientology** was not a fair use. Accordingly, he granted a preliminary injunction against Erlich pending trial. The standard to determine whether copyright infringement occurred is that the defendant must have had access to the copyrighted work and that the infringing work has "substantial similarity" to the original. Since copyright protects expressions, not ideas, it is not enough to show that a claimed infringement treats similar topics; a significant borrowing must be shown, which, in the case of a document such as a novel, essay or story, generally means that the words themselves must have been copied. Access and similarity were not in issue here, as Erlich acknowledged from the start that he was posting excerpts from CoS documents to the Net. Instead, he relied on a "fair use" defense. The copyright laws explicitly allow the use of portions of a copyrighted work for purposes such as criticism, comment, news reporting, teaching, scholarship, or research.

The court balances four factors: "(1) the purpose and character of the use, including whether such use is of a commercial nature or is for nonprofit educational purposes; (2) the nature of the copyrighted work; (3) the amount and substantiality of the portion used in relation to the copyrighted work as a whole; and (4) the effect of the use upon the potential market for or value of the copyrighted work." Though Erlich had not sought any financial gain from his use of the CoS materials, Judge Whyte felt that Erlich had fallen afoul of the third leg of the test by posting entire short CoS documents to Usenet, many of them with minimal comments of his own. It seems clear that Erlich would have escaped liability if he had used shorter excerpts, interspersed with more of his own critical interpretations. "Although criticism is a favored use, where that 'criticism' consists of copying large portions of plaintiffs' works—and sometimes all of those works—with often no more than one line of criticism, the fair use defense is inappropriate," Whyte said. Accordingly, he prohibited Erlich from posting more CoS materials to Usenet.

Whyte's remarkable order betrayed some continuing sympathy for Erlich. Most preliminary injunctions merely state that a defendant may not continue making copies. Whyte added to this that Erlich was not prohibited from "fair use", so long as the excerpts were brief and the criticism long. "Fair use of the copyrighted material for the purposes of this order includes use of the copyrighted work for the purpose of criticism, news reporting, teaching, scholarship, and research...no more of a work may be taken than is necessary to make any accompanying comment understandable." Rarely does a judge provide a defendant with a blueprint for avoiding the terms of an injunction.

Judge Whyte also held that CoS was ill-advised in seeking the ex parte order. Like many other judges over the years, Whyte had initially been misled by the fact that some copyright regulations adopted in 1909 were still on the books. These regulations, upon which CoS had relied, give a court wide power to seize copyright infringements; however, they contradict the more recently adopted Federal Rules of Civil Procedure and the Fifth Amendment due process cases, which disfavor ex parte orders. Whyte held that CoS had not presented any evidence to establish that Erlich would destroy evidence or flee, if he had been given prior notice of the seizure. Furthermore, Whyte acknowledged that he had been led to sign an overbroad order—by its terms, it had permitted Small and his cohorts to seize Scientology books legally owned by Erlich. Finally, Small's behavior in taking a backup of Erlich's entire disk, and of deleting files from Erlich's computer, were of great concern to the judge. He canceled the writ of seizure and ordered all the seized materials returned to Erlich within ten days.

In November, Whyte issued a further order partially granting summary judgment in favor of Netcom and Klemesrud, while denying CoS's preliminary injunction against them. He declined to let the parties out of the case entirely, though. CoS had advanced two theories under which both Netcom and Klemesrud might be held responsible for Erlich's infringements. Each of the theories relied on the fact that their servers had stored and forwarded Erlich's posts. They might be considered direct infringers, meaning that by making copies of the offending mail, they made themselves as guilty as Erlich. Or they might be contributory infringers, who contributed the means to make illegal copies without doing so themselves. The contributory infringement theory had been used for many years to pursue BBS sysops who promoted the trading of pirated software on their boards. For example, a sysop naming his BBS "Pirate's Lair" and placing a log-on message which said "Contribute something juicy for access to the Inner Sanctum" might be considered to be facilitating illegal software copying, though it could not be proven he had made copies himself. CoS's theory was that once it put Netcom and Klemesrud on notice that Erlich was infringing its copyrights, they had a responsibility to shut him down.

The parallel to the *CompuServe* case is exact. The judge in the *CompuServe* case had held that an on-line service, like the bookstore in the *Smith* case, was not responsible to know the content of everything it distributed. Once put on notice of illegal material, though, the distributor has an obligation to do something about it. While the plaintiff in *CompuServe* had failed to notify the on-line services of the allegedly libelous messages before bringing suit, CoS had done exactly what the *CompuServe* case requires, putting Klemesrud and Netcom on notice. Both had declined to take any action against Erlich.

Netcom's attorney was diffident in the June hearing when Judge Whyte asked about the legal standard defining Netcom's responsibility to CoS. "If you clearly know that a copyright has been violated," Judge Whyte asked, "do you agree you have some obligation?" "I don't know the answer to that, Your Honor," Randolf Rice said. "I'm not sure whether Netcom is liable simply because the matter has appeared in copied form on its system." Klemesrud's lawyer similarly evaded defining his client's responsibility. CoS was able to establish that Netcom had, on occasion, deleted materials or disconnected users when notified of illegal activities. CoS made a persuasive plea to Judge Whyte that Netcom had willfully disregarded its rights. It introduced a Netcom rules manual which said that illegal material should not be posted to the system, and that offending users might have their service terminated.

During depositions, a Netcom representative had testified about instances in which Netcom had deleted offending newsgroup messages and prevented the copying of a developer's software based on his verbal complaint. If this developer had not been required to jump through hoops to prove that he owned the software being copied, why was CoS not given the same courtesy? CoS claimed that Netcom had admitted to deleting infringing materials on 1180 occasions, but had refused to do the same for CoS. "And under the same circumstances we should have that protection, particularly I think if Your

Honor has been reading about the problems of pseudonymity and anonymity that prevail on the Internet. It may very well be that one's only remedy, if that is not ameliorated in some way, is to deal directly with the access procedure." Netcom's counsel admitted that Netcom, in looking into the situation, had concluded that it was being asked to resolve a theological or political dispute, rather than a legal one: "It's very clear, as Scientology says in their papers, that Mr. Erlich is a, quote, 'renegade,' that he's someone who they have a dispute with and that there is a controversy going back and forth between the two. Thus it doesn't take a genius to realize that in California, there are free speech issues that apply here."

Netcom's attorney clearly wanted his client treated as a common carrier, like the telephone or telegraph, obligated to carry everything and with no responsibility—or even right—to censor any message. Earle Cooley, speaking for CoS, scoffed at this. "These are not passive infringers. This is not the telephone company. These are people that copy it, store it, and thereby immediately infringe." Judge Whyte, however, found the common carrier analogy persuasive. "In a sense, a Usenet server that forwards all messages acts like a common carrier, passively retransmitting every message that gets sent through it. Netcom would seem no more liable than the phone company for carrying an infringing facsimile transmission or storing an infringing audio recording on its voice mail." In the end, however, he refused to declare Netcom a common carrier; this status cannot be awarded by a judge, but is granted by the legislature, usually as part of the award of a monopoly.

A distinction can be made between services like Netcom and those like CompuServe and Prodigy. The latter attempt to create an entire environment, even a community, with a consistent identity and vocabulary. They have the right to censor, to ensure that users abide by the standards of the community. Prodigy presents itself as a family-oriented service, for example, and automatically scans messages looking for words that violate its guidelines. Netcom solely provides a wire to the Internet, and as its attorney explained to Judge Whyte, it was no more than a conduit.

CoS attorney Helena Kobrin argued that Netcom should be considered a direct infringer and pointed out that the copyright law does not include any requirement that the defendant know it is copying a copyrighted work. Judge Whyte, whose questions were consistently well-informed and intelligent, asked, "What would Netcom do to try and protect itself from infringement if it could be held liable for direct infringement without any knowledge that it was publishing something that was copyright[ed]?" He was troubled by the thought that, despite the *CompuServe* and *Smith* cases, a distributor of on-line information would have to review everything passing through its hands in order to be safe. Kobrin replied that, if she knew the answer, she would be testifying before Congress. She explained, "We are simply trying to fashion a realistic remedy for ourselves here."

Cooley commented on Netcom's and Klemesrud's attempt to paint themselves as passive conduits, owners of servers that automatically stored and forwarded Erlich's posts without any human intervention. He said, "We're confronted with a sort of devil-made-me-do-it concept where the-computer-made-me-do-it. There's no human agency involved here? I don't understand any argument that permits the owner of hardware and software to store, in equipment that he owns, a bootleg copy, an infringing copy, of a copyrighted work."

Judge Whyte was confronted with a mismatch between copyright law and the reality of the Internet. The doctrine of contributory infringement, which requires knowledge of a misdeed, was intended to apply to one who provides the means to make an illegal copy but does not actually do so himself. But Netcom and Klemesrud, unlike a BBS sysop who merely maintains a server to which other people upload software, actually were responsible for making copies of Erlich's posts. This did in fact happen automatically, without human involvement; Klemesrud's system copied Erlich's messages for the purpose of transmitting them to Netcom, and the Netcom server replicated them to transmit them to numerous other servers as part of the arcane process by which Usenet newsgroups are distributed. Direct infringement actually requires no knowledge—you can be held responsible for making an illegal copy even if you had no idea the material is copyrighted. Judge Whyte wrestled with the fact that Netcom and Klemesrud, because they made copies, looked more like direct infringers than contributory ones; but Judge Whyte understood that if they were direct infringers, so was every other Usenet server, and in fact every user who read a copy of Erlich's messages.

In his November opinion, Judge Whyte wrote, "Although the Internet consists of many different computers networked together, some of which may contain infringing files, it does not make sense to hold the operator of each computer liable as an infringer merely because his or her computer is linked to a computer with an infringing file. It would be especially inappropriate to hold liable a service that acts more like a conduit, in other words, one that does not itself keep an archive of files for more than a short duration." Judge Whyte commendably held that neither Klemesrud or Netcom could be considered a direct infringer. He wrote, "The court does not find workable a theory of infringement that would hold the entire Internet liable for activities that cannot reasonably be deterred."

However, Judge Whyte declined to grant summary judgment for Netcom on the contributory infringement claim because he held that an issue of fact existed that must be decided at trial. If CoS could prove that Netcom knew that Erlich's postings were infringements, "Netcom will be liable for contributory infringement since its failure to simply cancel Erlich's infringing message and thereby stop an infringing copy from being distributed worldwide constitutes substantial participation in Erlich's public distribution of the message." Netcom's arguments that it could not judge whether the works were copyrighted was not persuasive, given that Erlich had posted certain CoS memoranda with the copyright notice intact. However, Netcom's argument that it thought Erlich might be entitled to a "fair use" defense had more merit. "Where a BBS operator cannot reasonably verify a claim of infringement, either because of a possible fair use defense, the lack of copyright notices on the copies, or the copyright holder's failure to provide the necessary documentation to show that there is a likely infringement, the operator's lack of knowledge will be found reasonable and there will be no liability for contributory infringement for allowing the continued distribution of the works on its system." In any event, Judge Whyte deferred determination of this issue until the trial, scheduled for early 1996.

He gave a possible forecast of the trial's outcome, however, by denying a preliminary injunction against Netcom and Klemesrud. One of the standards for the grant of a preliminary injunction is that the party seeking it must be likely to prevail at trial. "The only viable theory of infringement is contributory infringement," Judge Whyte wrote, "and there is little evidence that Netcom or Klemesrud knew or should have known that Erlich was engaged in copyright infringement of plaintiff's works and was not entitled to a fair use defense. ... Further, their participation in the infringement was not substantial."

On the whole, Whyte, unlike Judge Ain in the *Prodigy* case, revealed himself to be knowledgeable, thoughtful, and adept at balancing the needs of injured parties against the public interest in the growth of a new mass medium. judge Whyte wrote, "Netcom and Klemesrud play a vital role in the speech of their users. Requiring them to prescreen postings for possible infringement would chill their users' speech."

Since the initial volley against Erlich, CoS has brought several more lawsuits against opponents both in the United States and abroad, alleging the posting of copyrighted material to the Internet. Another of these defendants is Arnaldo Lerma, who left the church in 1978 after 15 years as a low-level staffer. But, according to CoS, he signed a "billion-year contract." Lerma is a 44-year-old audio-video technician from Arlington, Virginia, with an Internet connection and a lot of deep hostility for the church. In September of 1994, he started posting church criticism on America Online. The following summer he started distributing high-level training documents. Included within these were restricted "OT," or "Operating Thetan," courses. CoS claims that the OT documents are high-level holy scriptures, and are reserved for only a few eyes only, unlike the bestseller *Dianetics*, which was first published in the magazine *Astounding Science Fiction*.

A few weeks later, Lerma answered a knock on his door. He was drinking his Saturday morning coffee, when, he opened up to find lawyers and federal marshals, brandishing warrants. They stayed for three hours and inventoried all of his computer hardware and software—before carting it off. CoS lawyer Earl Cooley had convinced the court, as in the Erlich case, to issue a temporary restraining order prohibiting any further publication of documents and a writ of seizure for the computer equipment.

Lerma probably should have seen this coming. One day in November of the previous year, there had been a similar knock on the door, but the men outside were not bearing a warrant. "We represent the Church of Scientology," announced one of the two men in dark suits. Lerma quickly shut the door. In a three page letter that he found wedged inside the screen door, Lerma read the draft of a confession they wanted him to sign. It read, in part, "I engaged in taking illegal drugs and eventually left the Church entirely because I could not maintain a high enough ethical standard. ... I wish to make it known that I have been involved in trying to denigrate the name of Scientology and some of its leading members. ... I wish to recant these statements in full." Lerma never signed the letter and ignored the faxes sent a few hours later, which demanded that he "cease and desist" speaking against his billion-year master.

After Lerma posted the documents to Usenet in August 1995, he had a strong feeling that the church would come for him again, so he sent a hard copy of the documents to a reporter, Richard Leiby, at *The Washington Post*. The CoS investigators quickly discovered the disclosure and visited Leiby the evening of the raid and requested that he hand over the secret documents. Leiby consented.

These particular documents are collectively called the Fishman Affidavit and are in fact court papers from an earlier case involving Scientology and an ex-member. Fishman had testified that the Church was guilty of threatening and brainwashing practices and submitted the Advanced Technology teachings (which include some of the OT courses) to support his claim. The Church, on the other hand, said that these documents were irrelevant to the case and Fishman inserted them solely so that they might leak into the public domain. Ever since the affidavit became part of the public court file in Los Angeles, CoS has been fighting to have it sealed. Since these attempts were unsuccessful it did the next best thing; it established a rotating guard whereby someone would arrive in the morning at the opening and check out the affidavit for the entire day—every day. After the CoS seized the Lerma copy, the *Post* became curious and sent a reporter to make a copy of the legally available court records. The day after the *Post* obtained another copy, CoS applied for a sealing order, which was granted by a trial judge.

Five days later the *Post* published an article by staff reporter Marc Fisher, who used a few excerpts from the sacred texts. His article was entitled, "Church in Cyberspace: Its Sacred Writ is on the Net. Its Lawyers are on the Case." Fisher reported that the current cost of enlightenment—the price to obtain the training in CoS's highest scriptures—could amount to hundreds of thousands of dollars. On August 22, CoS amended its Lerma complaint to include *The Washington Post* and its two reporters, Fisher and Leiby. In the end, CoS would also include Lerma's Internet access provider, Digital Gateway Systems. As in the Erlich case, the Church would charge that these parties illegally used material that was protected by copyright and trade secret law.

On September 15, federal judge Leonie Brinkema refused the request for a preliminary injunction and ordered the church to return everything it had confiscated from Lerma. The judge believed that CoS had misrepresented the urgency in requesting the warrant, and abused the rights that it had been granted. "This case is somewhat out of control," said Brinkema. "It was not the court's intention to give wholesale license to go through Mr. Lerma's possessions willy-nilly." In a written opinion issued September 28, Brinkema dismissed the charges against the *Post*, denying the charges that they overstepped the doctrine of fair use and rejecting the claim that any of the documents in question represented trade secrets.

"When the RTC first approached the Court with its ex parte request for the seizure warrant and Temporary Restraining Order, the dispute was presented as a straight-forward one under copyright and trade secret law. However, the Court is now convinced that the primary motivation of RTC in suing Lerma, DGS and the *Post* is to stifle criticism of Scientology in general and to harass its critics." The judge ordered that CoS pay the *Post*'s legal fees. As for Lerma, Brinkema conceded that his "use of the AT documents is more extensive than the *Post*'s and may not constitute fair use...they appear to have been copied without any comment or criticism whatsoever."

Several days after having brought the *Post* into the Lerma suit, CoS decided to try to shut down another on-line critic, FACTNet. Fight Against Coercive Tactics is a nonprofit group that opposes CoS and other organizations that it regards as coercive cults. FACTNet created a Web page with links to public documents it gathered regarding CoS. In March 1995, Lawrence Wollersheim, an ex-Scientologist and director of FACTNet, issued the following statement: "Scientology has responded to our collecting and electronic making available of these public records by threatening our organization with four lawsuits using three different law firms covering everything from copyright infringement to libel and slander. They have followed and intimidated our staff, attempted to infiltrate to possibly sabotage our organization, threatened our Internet Web page provider with a lawsuit, and they have even threatened to sue our secure mail and offices services provider (Mail Boxes Etc.) if they even send out another fax out for us."

Wollersheim warned that the organization's archives might soon become unavailable; he was expecting a seizure any day, similar to the one carried out against Erlich the previous month. "We believe Scientology is preparing to do a search and seizure of our premises based on false affidavits and illegal applications of copyright law as it applies to religious freedom." He called for interested parties around the world to copy his CoS archives to other servers, so that the anticipated attack would not succeed in censoring FACTNet's archives. "For those faint hearted who have heard what Scientology does to its critics, take heart. It is not generally known, but if you can last the harassment Scientology is horribly unsuccessful in the courts. It really has NO victories other than intimidating critics by spending or scaring them into silence. Like cowards, Scientology usually only attacks those who have no insurance or whom they believe are weak or they can intimidate or wear down."

FACTNet's nightmare came true on August 22, when CoS representatives showed up at Wollersheim's home and that of a co-worker with a court order, taking away all FACTNet's computers and numerous other materials. Unlike the Erlich case, which dragged on for months before a hearing took place, FACTNet's directors got their day in court on September 8 before Judge John L. Kane, Jr. At the end of three days of hearings, Judge Kane denied the preliminary injunction and ordered the return of all the equipment.

Unlike Judge Whyte or Judge Brinkema, Judge Kane found that the defendants had made a fair use of CoS materials. There were some significant differences in the cases. FACTNet maintained a bulletin board system that was not connected to the Internet. Wollersheim testified that almost all of the unpublished CoS documents, which CoS claimed were copyrighted and also trade secrets, were stored in a private archive on the same server, but were not generally available to users of the BBS. All of the materials stored on the FACTNet server had been legally obtained from ex-Scientologists.

Judge Kane held that CoS had failed to show that FACTNet's use of the materials affected CoS's business in any way. "The evidence showed the works are esoteric in nature and are delivered to certain followers by advanced Scientologists known as 'auditors' as part of an elaborate system of instruction. The only financial harm RTC would suffer would be if followers were to forsake the Church's didactic methodology in favor of self instruction through the works copied by Defendants. There was no suggestion, let alone evidence, of this potential for financial loss to the Church." Similarly, Judge Kane denied the trade secrecy claim, on the grounds that CoS itself (represented once again by Cooley and Kobrin) had contradicted itself in court, claiming at first that all of the documents were trade secrets, then that only portions were. The judge noted that the documents were in the public record as a result of the lawsuit in California, and that numerous others were available worldwide on the Internet. Considering the public interest, the judge held that: "Public interest lies with the free exchange of dialogue on matters of public concern. The injunction sought would silence the Defendants as participants in an ongoing debate involving matters of significant public controversy. Relief of this kind does not serve the public interest." He ordered the immediate return of the computers and materials.

CoS defied Judge Kane by deleting its "secret scriptures," the Thetan documents, from the disk before returning the computers to Wollersheim. "We are not...returning our sacred, confidential, unpublished and copyrighted scriptures," Warren McShane, a church leader in Los Angeles, wrote to FACTNet's counsel. CoS said in a press release, "In many respects, the judge's decision is wrong, both on the law and the facts, which shows he bought the bogus and dishonest defense of copyright criminals hook, line and sinker."

One of the people who had answered Wollersheim's call for help the prior March was a resident of Holland, who had copied the contents of the FACTNet server to a machine owned by a local Internet access provider, XS4ALL. CoS, an international organization, now targeted its Dutch critics. On September 5, two American representatives of CoS visited the offices of XS4ALL with a court officer to threaten a seizure and to perform an inventory of the access provider's computer equipment. Dutch law is stricter than U.S. law about seizures; CoS was required to hold a hearing before being able to take equipment. CoS's local lawyer indicated the organization had two bones to pick with XS4ALL. An anonymous remailer it operated had been used to transmit CoS files to Usenet. An issue apparently more upsetting to CoS, however, was the XS4ALL user whose home page was a mirror of the now-defunct FACTNet site. CoS offered to drop the case if XS4ALL agreed to delete the Fishman affidavit from the user's Web page. In a press release issued later that day, XS4ALL said, "XS4ALL categorically denies any responsibility for contents of users' homepages. The users decide for themselves what is on their homepage. Since XS4ALL does not edit the homepages and has no mechanism of control over the contents we strongly feel that the users themselves are responsible for what they say on their homepage."

The Fishman affidavit included lengthy excerpts from CoS's secret scriptures pertaining to the "Operating Thetans", the same documents in question in the Lerma and FACTNet cases. Because the Fishman affidavit had been placed in public court files in California, CoS was considered to have lost its trade secret rights in these scriptures. Generally, court records are public and can be freely reproduced. By the time CoS had the file sealed, it was already on the Internet.

On November 8, CoS brought suit in Amsterdam against XS4ALL, three other access providers, and the proprietor of another CoS-related home page, newspaper columnist Karin Spaink. The lawsuit contained a novel legal theory (also espoused by Senator Exon in the indecency debate in June 1995): a Web hyperlink to an illegal document, even though it is on someone else's server, constitutes an illegal republication of that document. CoS's complaint said that "When the infringing documents are made available to others by a so-called 'hyperlink', e.g., a 'built-in' reference to another document (whether or not on a different system) that, when activated, causes the publication and/or duplication, this must also be regarded as publication and/or duplication by the user and the provider."

Publicity about CoS's visit to XS4ALL in September caused the FACTNet documents, particularly the Fishman affidavit that was a particular thorn in CoS's side, to proliferate to 80 other servers in Holland—an illustration of the statement that "the Net interprets censorship as damage and routes around it." CoS apparently went after the access providers because it was unable to determine the identities of any of the individuals who reposted the Fishman affidavit, other than Spaink. In a column for a newspaper, *Het Parool*, she wrote scathingly that "All across the planet, Scientology is hunting down copies of a court document that contains a part of their material. This document, the so-called Fishman Affidavit, is considered...proof of the fact that Scientology brainwashes its adepts, intimidates its critics, commits fraud, plans to murder people, abuses the legal system, etcetera. This particular court-document is different from all the others, in that 'Fishman' contains quotes from the expensive lessons that Scientology sells to their high-leveled adepts. It is a ridiculous scrap of a space-opera, with all the galactic federations and overlords that come with the genre. The most elevated lessons teach how to communicate with plants and animals." She wrote that CoS had probably been reluctant to take the Dutch cases to court, because the prospects were not very good, but had likely felt it had no choice. However, a loss in the Netherlands would have worldwide implications, due to the global nature of the Net. "After all, that would mean that the document that the cult so desperately tries to remove from the public eye, is declared officially free in the Netherlands. And as far as Internet is concerned, any document that is available in the Netherlands can be downloaded all over the world."

Despite their science fiction plots, the recent CoS cases do raise some important issues concerning intellectual property in the Digital

Age. First, CoS makes the valid point that copyrighted material on the Internet is still subject to the same laws as in the physical world. Fair use gives a right of comment, but not the right to copy and disseminate the texts wholesale. With a computer and an Internet connection, one can effortlessly post huge tracts of text to the world. Erlich and Lerma both seem to have crossed the line of fair use.

These cases have also invoked the central issue of the *Prodigy* case—who is responsible for illegal material sent across the Internet? Among those attacked or threatened by CoS are Internet providers, electronic bulletin boards, anonymous remailer operators, and the thousands of systems administrators who take it upon themselves to help maintain the globally distributed Usenet. Although CoS has ultimately been unsuccessful in its attempts to shut down speech on the Net, it has set a disturbing precedent by going after access providers, declaring that they are conduits of crime and threatening them with aiding in the transfer of illegal information.

CoS's problem is that its scriptures are not protected under American law quite as stringently as it would like. In a country that abides by a doctrine of free speech, certain aspects of privacy are bound to suffer. The First Amendment implies that large organizations, including the government, can be subjected to any form of criticism as long as it doesn't cross the line into libel or an imminent threat of harm. CoS, on the other hand, seeks extra protection. Criminals, CoS rightfully argues, must realize that new technologies cannot avoid the standard application of copyright laws; on the other hand, it implicitly asserts that its new religion of technology should be granted exceptional levels of secrecy, because it is a church. However, CoS also presents itself as a business, a publisher, and a science. By seeking the protection afforded to each of these categories, CoS has attempted to establish the kind of secrecy only available to governments.

Judge Brinkema observed that CoS files suits under the pretense of copyright infringement, then tries to hide behind claims of religious persecution. As she noted in her November 29 opinion, CoS argued that the exposure of their sacred texts wreaks havoc "upon the free exercise of the Scientology religion. RTC asserts that maintenance of the secrecy and confidentiality of the documents in question…represent a fundamental and inviolate tenet of the Scientology religion." The judge points out that, although this country is founded upon a conception of religious freedom, these personal beliefs may not supersede the laws of the land. "In their effort to enjoin the

*Post,* the RTC is essentially urging that we permit their religious belief in the secrecy of the AT documents to 'trump' significant conflicting constitutional rights. In particular, they ask us to dismiss the equally valid First Amendment protections of freedom of the press."

Although the church's practice of harassment may work well to suppress criticism in the real world, the Internet effortlessly routes around it. Before applying L. Ron Hubbard's policies of attack and censorship on the Net, CoS should have studied the battleground. The once obscure rantings of disgruntled ex-Scientologists have now gained center stage in a medium that naturally thwarts attempts to ban information. CoS will never be able to suppress open discussion on the world's networks. Governments, groups, and religions who are afraid of opposing ideas and criticism should avoid the Internet. Though particular chunks of code and words can be monitored and regulated, ideas cannot.

# CHAPTER

# VI

# THE BARNUM OF CYBERPORN

An astonished child with perfectly round eyes and mouth, staring directly at you, looking like no child on earth. Child pornography? Not quite: the image appeared on the cover of *Time* magazine's July 3, 1995 issue, above the headline, "On a Screen Near You: Cyberporn."

The illustrations inside the issue were no better than the cover; two showed what can only be described as a man having sex with a computer. Senior *Time* writer Philip Elmer-Dewitt, who wrote the story, acknowledged later that the art for this issue was "over the top" and "sort of spoiled the story."

Elmer-Dewitt's cover story began with "Sex is everywhere these days. ... Something about the combination of sex and computers, however, seems to make otherwise worldly-wise adults a little crazy. ... Yet suddenly the press is on alert, parents and teachers are up in arms, and lawmakers in Washington are rushing to ban the smut from cyberspace with new legislation—sometimes with little regard to either its effectiveness or its constitutionality. If you think things are crazy now, though, wait until the politicians get hold of a report coming out this week."

Elmer-Dewitt then introduced the public to the Marty Rimm cyberporn study, which was being published that week in the *Georgetown Law Journal*, and for which he had an exclusive. He wrote that "A research team at Carnegie Mellon University in Pittsburgh, Pennsylvania, has conducted an exhaustive study of on-line porn—what's available, who is downloading it, what turns them on—and the findings (to be published in the *Georgetown Law Journal*) are sure to pour fuel on an already explosive debate."

According to Elmer-Dewitt, Marty Rimm, "the study's principal investigator," had announced the first accurate look at computer porn in America. "We now know what the consumers of computer pornography really look at in the privacy of their own homes. ... And we're finding a fundamental shift in the kinds of images they demand."

The main finding of the Carnegie Mellon study, as reported by *Time*, was that porn was not only prevalent on the Internet, but that there was a decided shading towards kinky and violent material not easily available elsewhere. The article summarized the study's conclusions as follows: "There's an awful lot of porn on-line. ... It is immensely popular. ... It is a big moneymaker. ... It is ubiquitous. ... It is a guy thing. ... It is not just naked women."

Elmer-Dewitt opined that the pervasiveness and availability of computer porn raised issues too important to ignore. "Parents have legitimate concerns about what their kids are being exposed to and, conversely, what those children might miss if their access to the Internet were cut off. Lawmakers must balance public safety with their obligation to preserve essential civil liberties. Men and women have to come to terms with what draws them to such images. And computer programmers have to come up with more enlightened ways to give users control over a network that is, by design, largely out of control."

Lucky for us, he acknowledged that "The Internet, of course, is more than a place to find pictures of people having sex with dogs. It's a vast marketplace of ideas and information of all sorts—on politics, religion, science and technology."

After telling how "ten-year-old Anders" received pornographic GIF files in unsolicited E-mail from a stranger on America Online, Elmer-Dewitt asked "When the kids are plugged in, will they be exposed to the seamiest sides of human sexuality? Will they fall prey to child molesters hanging out in electronic chat rooms?"

Elmer-Dewitt's article cited what would become the most controversial statistic from the Carnegie Mellon study: "On those Usenet newsgroups where digitized images are stored, 83.5 percent of the pictures were pornographic." The study also found that over 70% of the sexual images on the newsgroups surveyed "originate from adult-oriented computer bulletin-board systems (BBS) whose operators are trying to lure customers to their private collections of X-rated material."

Virtually all of the consumers of on-line porn were men; many of the remainder "are women paid to hang out on the 'chat' rooms and bulletin boards to make the patrons feel more comfortable." Elmer-Dewitt reported that the study illuminated an arms race among pornography suppliers on the Internet to stimulate sales by resorting to violent and kinky images. As the prime example, he zoomed in on AABBS sysop Robert Thomas. Thomas had been in a Memphis prison since February; a photograph of Thomas, gazing wistfully out the window, appeared in a sidebar to the main story. Elmer-Dewitt said of Thomas's experiments in creative copy-writing, "The words that worked were sometimes quite revealing. Straightforward oral sex, for example, generally got a lukewarm response. But when Thomas described the same images using words like choke or choking, consumer demand doubled."

Utilizing the classic "on the one hand, on the other hand" tactic of mainstream journalism, Elmer-Dewitt dutifully reported on the conflicting views of anti-porn crusader Catharine MacKinnon and ACLU president Nadine Strossen about pornography. He described both Senator Exon's assault on indecency and the civil libertarian opposition to it. He concluded with the recommendation of John Perry Barlow, the EFF co-founder: "If you don't want your children fixating on filth...better step up to the tough task of raising them to find it as distasteful as you do yourself."

> "The *Time* editors were convinced the Rimm study was their ace. Someone should have told them it was dealt from the bottom of the deck," wrote Brock Meeks in *Hotwired*. *Time* Magazine had stepped into a hole. Blinded by the subject matter and a proffered exclusive on the study, it failed to examine the underpinnings, but reported on it as if it were hard science. Most notably, it presented the Carnegie Mellon study as if it were the official work-product of the university, and described Marty Rimm only as the "principal investigator."

In fact, Rimm was a thirty-year-old college senior, and the study was a student paper prepared under the supervision of faculty advisor Marvin Sirbu. What's more, Rimm had a history of involvement in media stunts and wild self-promotions.

Rimm, a member of a wealthy, politically well-connected family, had graduated from a New Jersey high school in 1983. Now, immediately on the heels of the *Time* cover story, his hometown paper, the *Press of Atlantic City*, which has its own sophisticated site on the

World Wide Web, took an interest in him. The *Press* reported that "Fourteen years ago, when he was a sixteen year old student at Atlantic City High School, Rimm conducted a survey that purported to show that 64 percent of the students at his school had gambled in the city's casinos." The survey, which was met with skepticism by the gaming industry, prodded the state Legislature to raise the age for gambling in casinos to 21.

The *Press* reported that the sixteen-year-old Rimm "added a special flourish to the story by wrapping his head in a burnoose and infiltrating the Playboy Hotel and Casino in the guise of an Arab sheik." The *Press* later reported that Rimm had also been "suspected by state investigators of pulling two creative—and potentially expensive—pranks on the Trump Taj Mahal Casino Resort in 1990."

Rimm had self-published a book that year called *An American Playground*, a series of stories about the Atlantic City casino industry. One day, a Taj Mahal employee noticed fliers on the windshields of cars at a Northfield shopping center announcing that anyone who bought the book and presented it at the Taj Mahal would receive $25 in coins. The flier was printed on what appeared to be Taj Mahal letterhead, and falsely quoted Donald Trump hailing the publication of Rimm's book as "one of the most phenomenal literary events of the 90s."

Rimm was also suspected of involvement in a second hoax a few months later, when letters were sent on Taj Mahal letterhead to New Jersey residents informing them they had won a Rolls Royce or $10,000 in cash. The letters promised that at the awards ceremony, owner Donald Trump would give a speech entitled "Whorehouses of Emotion"—the name of one of the stories in *An American Playground*.

After the Carnegie Mellon study appeared, another of Rimm's books came to light. In March 1995, Rimm had obtained an ISBN for the self-published, 64-page *The Pornographer's Handbook: How to Exploit Women, Dupe Men & Make Lots of Money*. Rimm told the *Press of Atlantic City* that the book was a "satire on the pornography industry which was never printed, published, distributed or sold to anyone." As we will see later, this proved not to be true.

"My life," he added, "is an eclectic attempt to bridge many worlds, from the liberal arts to technology, from writing and traveling to working in the Atlantic City casinos." Marty Rimm, who in his study called Robert Thomas "the Marquis of Cyberspace," was shaping up to be the Barnum of Cyberporn.

During the June 14 debate on the Communications Decency Act (CDA), Senator Coats, its co-sponsor, had cited statistics from the Rimm study. Since the study was still under wraps for another few weeks, Coats must have received a copy—or at least some of the findings—from Rimm, one of the student editors, or one of the law professors who wrote the accompanying essays in the *Georgetown Law Journal*. As soon as the July 3 issue of Time was on the newsstands, Senators Grassley and Exon hyped the Rimm study and the *Time* story in Congress.

By its own terms, and contradicting the way it was frequently described later, Rimm's study only purported to do two things. It reviewed the descriptions of GIF files on the Thomas's Amateur Action BBS and some other private pornographic bulletin board systems; and it examined the descriptions of binary uploads of image files on selected sex-related Usenet newsgroups.

Commenting on this approach, one Georgetown law professor remarked that it was like walking into a book or video store and rating its content based solely on what is for sale in the adult section. Rimm's study was strangely ambivalent. It can be read either as a critique of the prevalence of pornography on the Internet—or as a marketing guide for pornographers wishing to improve their operations, a la the *Pornographers' Handbook*. Rimm may very well have intended it as both. He had apparently convinced the Thomases and others to cooperate with him by offering to help them increase their revenues.

Certain passages in the study sound mainly like advice to a clientele of pornographers. "Computer pornographers are also moving from a market saturation policy to a market segmentation, or even individualized, marketing phase. Until now, most have saturated customers with tens of thousands of images, reasoning that their customers would inevitably find material that they liked. However, few customers have the patience or technical resources to perform the extensive database analysis necessary to quickly download only the images they prefer. Pornographers now have sufficient information to dramatically shrink the size of their portfolios, while at the same time increasing their subscriber revenues. A few have already begun to do so."

In the weeks after the study appeared, adversaries began ripping into it, insisting that Rimm's methodology was inadequate or incompletely disclosed, and had not led to statistically valid results. The study states that the "research team" downloaded all available pornographic images from five Usenet newsgroups over a four month period. The Usenet downloads were examined with the following questions in mind: the percentage of all Usenet images that are pornographic; popularity of pornographic versus non-pornographic newsgroups; the origins of pornographic images posted to Usenet.

Next, Rimm obtained 450,620 file descriptions and corresponding download information from sixty-eight adult BBSs (the Thomases' **ALLGIF** file was one of these.) These BBSs were not connected to the Internet, and a controversial issue raised by the study's opponents was whether they were at all representative of the Net or of cyberspace in general. Although these files had been downloaded 6.4 million times, no time period is given. The text descriptions were then analyzed with the team looking at 10,000 randomly selected images to make sure they matched their descriptions. The team eliminated animations and images which lacked descriptions or which were ambiguously descibed.

Rimm spent the bulk of his study examining "(1) the availability and demand for hard-core, soft-core, paraphilic, pedophilic, and hebephilic imagery; (2) the concentration of market leaders; (3) market forces common to all 'adult' BBS; (4) 'adult' BBS demographics; and (5) the image portfolio and marketing strategies of the Amateur Action BBS as a case study."

Rimm concluded that "the new research is a gold mine for psychologists, social scientists, computer marketers and anybody with an interest in human sexual behavior." He claimed that "Every time computer users logged on to one of these bulletin boards, they left a digital trail of their transactions, allowing the pornographers to compile data bases about their buying habits and sexual tastes. The more sophisticated operators were able to adjust their inventory and their descriptions to match consumer demand."

Rimm touted the superior methodology of his study over prior studies which, he said, "depended upon the honesty of replies people give when surveyed about their sexual tastes. In contrast, this study focuses entirely upon what people actually consume, not what they say they consume; it thus provides a more accurate measure of actual consumption."

The study posited that there was a tremendous rift between the sexual acts people admitted enjoying, in their responses to conventional surveys, and their tastes as revealed by the files they chose to download from Usenet and the BBSs studied.

The Usenet study concentrated on five Usenet newsgroups: **alt.binaries.pictures.erotica,** **alt.binaries.pictures.bestiality,** **alt.sex.fetish.watersports, alt.binaries.pictures.female, and alt.binaries.pictures.tasteless**. Rimm analyzed the descriptions of 2,830 images posted in these groups. He broke the images up into two categories, those "stamped" with the name and phone number of an adult BBS, and those which were not. He reported that "seventeen of the thirty-two alt.binaries newsgroups located on the Usenet contained pornographic imagery. Among the non-pornographic newsgroups, 827 image posts were counted during the seven day period. Among the pornographic newsgroups, 4,206 image posts were counted, or 83.5% of the total posts." This passage led Elmer-Dewitt and proponents of the CDA later to claim that 83% of all images on the Internet were pornographic. But, as critics would later point out, Rimm had only counted the images in selected pornographic newsgroups.

Rimm himself, in a passage ignored by the pro-CDA forces, acknowledged that the total percentage of Internet traffic devoted to these newsgroups was very small. "The best data concerning network pornography consumption comes from the Usenet, which itself constitutes only 11.5% of Internet traffic. Of this 11.5%, approximately 3% by message count, but 22% by byte count (e.g., 2.5% of total Internet backbone traffic), is associated with Usenet newsgroups containing pornographic imagery."

Next, Rimm reported on the popularity of pornographic newsgroups at his own university, Carnegie Mellon. "Approximately 3,600 Usenet newsgroups were available to the users studied. Of these, 104, or 2.88%, were identified as pornographic. Thirteen of the forty (32.5%) most frequently accessed newsgroups were identified as pornographic." Rimm had obtained his data from publicly available files on the Carnegie Mellon server, which listed the newsgroups to which individual students subscribed. Most students were not aware these files existed and there was an outcry that Rimm had invaded the privacy of the Carnegie Mellon student body by examining them.

Rimm then looked at "world-wide" Usenet usage and reported that three of the five most popular newsgroups were pornographic and that 20% of the posts in the top forty newsgroups were pornographic. Seventy-one percent of the images posted in the top five groups originated from adult BBSs. This was a deliberate marketing strategy by sysops such as Robert Thomas. "Many of the ninety-two 'adult' BBS identified on the Usenet were unabashedly advertising their products, posting 'teaser' images on the Usenet as an essential part of their marketing strategy."

The next section of the study analyzed the 450,620 descriptions of images from the private BBSs. Rimm classified these in four categories: "paraphilia", meaning varied fetishes including bestiality, coprophilia, sado-masochism; pedo/hebephilia, meaning a preoccupation with children or young teens; hard-core (but non-paraphilic); and soft-core.

Rimm had identified approximately 1,000 adult BBSs through advertisements and lists. About half of these were no longer in business, so he decided to narrow the study to BBSs that had existed for at least 24 months, had at least four modem lines, transmitted at 14,400 baud or better, and had at least 1,000 images available for download. Rimm wrote:

"In order to collect descriptive lists of the pornographic images available on each BBS, as well as a representative sampling of the images themselves, the research team placed more than 300 hours in long distance telephone calls to the 'adult' BBS selected by the team. Every BBS asked the members of the research team to provide a real name, address, business and home phone numbers, date of birth, password, and type of computer and modem. ... Members of the research team did not, as a rule, identify themselves as researchers." Of course, university ethical standards do not usually permit research to be done "undercover"—an issue that would be raised by Rimm's critics.

Internet journalist Brock Meeks later contacted sysops of fifteen of the adult BBSs cited by Rimm, and found that none of them remembered him. Rimm wrote an E-mail message to Meeks: "Discrete [sic], ain't we?"

When Meeks asked how he was able to obtain detailed customer profiles from usually skeptical operators of adult BBSs, Rimm replied that "If you were a pornographer, and you don't have fancy computers or PhD statisticians to assist you, wouldn't you be just a wee bit curious to see how you could adjust your inventories to better serve your clientele? Wouldn't you want to know that maybe you should decrease the number of oral sex images and increase the number of bondage images? Wouldn't you want someone to analyze your log files to better serve the tastes of each of your customers?"

Unknown to Meeks, Robert and Carleen Thomas of Amateur Action BBS (AABBS) remembered Rimm well. He had been a member of AABBS, renewing once, then quitting after a feud with Robert Thomas.

Rimm relied heavily on listings like the *ALLGIF* file from AABBS, which described all of the board's image files. Additional valuable information could be garnered from the BBS software, which frequently allowed a user to see how many times a file had been downloaded and the date of the last download. Rimm used this data to compare the popularity of different types of images, thus supporting his claim that his study was the first based on objective evidence. In some cases where the bulletin board concealed download information from users, Rimm claimed that he "persuaded the sysop to provide the list privately."

Rimm next mentioned the software that he used to sort the descriptions into categories, but was somewhat mysterious about its design and function. "In order to study the vast listings of images obtained, the research team decided to construct a classification scheme that would sort the pornographic images by the different types of behavior they depicted. This proved to be no small task, given that it was impossible to sort the enormous volume of records manually. Because the descriptive listing for each pornographic image contained terms that could be mapped to specific categories defining different depictions or interests in pornography, the research team created a computerized dictionary of these terms that sorted the image descriptions into categories. Developing the dictionary required five steps. First, a classification scheme that paired terms and categories was established. Second, because of the nature of the English language, certain categories were given precedence over others. Third, certain categories were permitted to overlap with others. Fourth, images which the dictionary could not classify (e.g., none of the words used to describe the image were contained in the dictionary) were identified. Fifth, an exceptions category was created to deal with further quirks in the descriptions."

Rimm adapted his categories from an earlier published study known as "Dietz-Sears." However, he merged some Dietz-Sears categories into a single one, such as the twenty S&M-related classifications. He also added some categories which were not used in Dietz-Sears, such as "incest, hair color, obese, pedo/hebephile, 'amazing,' dogstyle, swing, muscular, sixty-nine, emotions, shower, outdoor, petting, panties, and whore." When done, Rimm had 3,823 words in sixty-three categories.

Rimm then discussed certain semantical problems. At this point, the Rimm study gets decidedly weird. "Because pornographers described images with multiple words, prioritization schemes became necessary to avoid false categorizations. For instance, if the word 'fucks' was assumed to imply the vaginal category, the computer dictionary would have classified such descriptions as 'he fucks her ass' or 'he fucks her mouth' or 'she fucks herself with a dildo' as vaginal, when clearly they were not. The research team therefore established a priority scheme that checked for the word 'fucks' appearing with the words 'ass' or 'face' or 'dildo;' otherwise the image was classified as 'vaginal.' Without such a prioritization scheme, the word 'fucks' would need to be excluded from the dictionary as too ambiguous."

Descriptions that overlapped several categories presented another inconvenient problem, which needed to be solved in the software. "A description such as 'She fists her girlfriend's pussy,' was thus classified as both a lesbian and a fisting image, while 'Three Asians going at it in bed,' was classified as both an Asian and an orgy image. Without some overlap, the classification scheme would have proven less insightful."

The Dietz-Sears study, however, had always permitted over-lap; in Rimm's opinion, this was misleading. Therefore, Rimm's remarkable software classified certain descriptions only in their "strongest" category. "A more difficult description to categorize is, 'She licks her girlfriend's asshole.' The image could be classified as oral, anal, or lesbian, but the computer classified it as lesbian, because lesbian is a more general term which may describe a variety of sexual acts, including oral, vaginal, and anal acts. Thus, general terms were given precedence over particular terms."

About 16% of the images could not be categorized, because there was no description file, or "the description contained deliberate or accidental misspellings, such as 'She socks his cock,' which the computer could not identify. ... Descriptions such as 'Blonde getting a cheeky dinner plate' were too ambiguous to assign."

Approximately 1.5% of the images were classified as "exceptions" containing double meanings or idiosyncrasies of the English language, such as "Bo Derek walks her dog on the beach," which, said Rimm, "is clearly a portrait of a movie star, not a bestiality image." The accuracy of the computer dictionary was double-checked by randomly comparing 10,000 descriptions to their classification by the dictionary.

In the acknowledgments to his study, Rimm thanked numerous people for their help, many of whom later denied being involved or distanced themselves from the results. One of these was Adam Epstein, a fellow student at Carnegie Mellon, whom Rimm had acknowledged for his assistance in creating the dictionary software. Epstein later posted the following on his personal Web page: "I've been told that I am listed as a 'contributor' to Martin Rimm's study entitled 'Marketing Pornography on the Information Superhighway'. I'd like to be able to say that this is completely untrue. Unfortunately, I did in fact write a few primitive programs which Mr. Rimm presumably used to sift through the data he collected for his study. Don't ask me what the scripts did. I couldn't tell you with any degree of certainty. I got involved because I happened to overhear my advisor say that he was looking for someone who could spend an hour or two with Mr. Rimm writing some scripts to his spec. (I figured that I could use the hours on my stipend timesheet, so I volunteered). For whatever reason, he couldn't show me his actual data. So I just worked with dummy data, which looked like 'field-1', 'field-2', etc. Beyond that, I have no knowledge of his study. I'd never met Martin Rimm before and I've had no contact with him since. I've never seen his paper. If I had been aware of its nature, I certainly wouldn't have had anything to do with it."

Thus, the dictionary software, described by Rimm almost as an artificial intelligence program able to make exceedingly fine distinctions between shades of meaning, may actually be a set of primitive scripts for the crude manipulation of text files.

To validate the descriptions against the images themselves, Rimm randomly examined 400 images, half of them from the Amateur Action BBS alone. Rimm then passes from being decidedly weird to deeply weird. "Accordingly, the judges developed several rating rules: First, a match occurred when each of the major ideas of the description corresponded to what was visible on the image. Some tolerance of wording was acceptable but nothing which contradicted the description was permitted. Second, a partial match was scored when at least one major element was described which did not appear in the image. Sources of partial disagreement typically included descriptions such as the following: ...'Brunette has big boobs! She pisses on her girlfriend's face!' (although a urophilic image, two of the judges concluded that the urine was aimed at the chest, not the face)." And he gives two other gross examples.

It is almost impossible to believe that Rimm wrote these lines with a straight face. One suspects that *Time* and Senator Exon were taken in by a farce worthy of William Burroughs. "In sum," said Rimm of his validation efforts,"validity was very high, suggesting that pornographers, as a rule, take special care to describe their images with the high degree of accuracy they consider necessary to satisfy their customers."

Rimm concluded that the "'adult' BBS market is driven largely by the demand for paraphilic and pedo/hebephilic imagery. The availability of, and demand for, vaginal sex imagery is relatively small." Rimm found that, judging from download patterns, demand far exceeded supply for "paraphilic and pedo/hebephilic images," which constituted 48.4% of all downloads. This suggested that "computer pornographers have not yet optimized their image portfolios according to consumer demand patterns." Rimm attributed the online popularity of these kinky images to the difficulty of purchasing them through "traditional outlets."

The "research team" had obtained demographics "from several leading 'adult' BBSs which indicate the age, sex, and city of origin of subscribers. These demographics were based on verified credit card information and were obtained either directly from the logfiles of 'adult' BBSs or various methodologies developed by the research team programmers...the Carnegie Mellon research team was able to identify consumers of pedophilic and paraphilic pornography via computer in more than 2,000 cities in all fifty states in the United States, most Canadian provinces, and forty countries, provinces, and territories around the world."

The next section was devoted to a case study of the "'Adult' BBS Market Leader: Amateur Action." After summarizing the facts of the Thomas case, including the convictions, Rimm noted: "116 Amateur Action BBS images were recently discovered on the Usenet. Two of these images reposted on the Usenet were among those recently found obscene by a Tennessee jury."

Rimm's "research team" analyzed the **ALLGIF** file and download information. "The computer dictionary developed for this study was able to classify 99.4% of the 22,319 AABBS images, which were downloaded 1.6 million times. The Amateur Action AABBS images were also analyzed according to a mean popularity index, which indicates the average number of times each file in each category was downloaded. This index is useful in determining whether a category is in low availability but high demand, or the reverse. The mean popularity indices show that the paraphilias were far more popular than any of the hard-core or soft-core classifications. In other words, the demand for the paraphilias exceeded the availability."

Rimm noted that "most of Thomas's files were in high demand… forcing Thomas to remove a few 'objectionable' files will have no measurable effect on his subscriber download habits or interest in his board."

According to Rimm, AABBS, now with 10,700 members as compared with the 3,500 at the time of the trial, relied on three principal tactics to market its images: "[P]ortraying a power imbalance between the sexes, including a disproportionate representation of women in acts which may be considered degrading;…deceitful marketing; and…exploitation of children." Thomas had learned, for example, that file descriptions simply referencing fellatio were not very popular; downloads for the same files vastly increased if Thomas added references to "choking." Similarly, other images described as portraying women in degrading situations were popular. Bestiality was the second most downloaded category on AABBS; some of the 852 bestiality images offered were of "exceptional" clarity.

By "deceitful marketing," Rimm meant that "Verbal descriptions enable Thomas to market his portfolio as somewhat more taboo than may be the case. Indeed, Thomas is one of the few sysops in the country to exploit fully the remarkable power of verbal descriptions to fulfill customer fantasies." A prime example were descriptions that implied acts of incest, when there was no evidence that the individuals depicted were actually related to one another.

Earlier in the study, he had lauded the "high degree of accuracy" of adult BBS descriptions and said that Robert Thomas was the most accurate of all. "None of the judges disagreed with any of the descriptions from Amateur Action BBS." There is no explanation of the contradiction.

Thomas exploited children by offering nudist material that sailed just inside the boundaries of the law. "Thomas has attempted to push the parameters and current interpretation of child pornography law. By offering more than 5000 images featuring the exhibition of genital areas of children, being careful not to depict hard-core sex acts with pre-pubescent children, and terming many of the images 'nudist' material, Thomas has attempted to skirt the attention of law enforcement. He repeatedly used marketing language in an attempt to convince his subscribers that his material depicting children was both sexually enticing and legal."

Rimm offered numerous examples of Thomas's clever copywriting. "[O]f the 22,319 image descriptions analyzed, the following generated the most downloads: 'Young amateur teen! No tits at all! She spreads her pussy!'

"An analysis of Thomas's use of five of these terms, young, amateur, teen, no tits, spreads revealed that this and similar combinations generated unusually intense download activity." Note again the ambivalence of this language: is Rimm analyzing a sociological or psychological phenomenon for the rest of us? Or advising pornographers how to write better copy? Rimm seems to be trying to do both at once, "the ultimate media hack," as Brock Meeks later said.

Rimm's conclusion, which verges on pornography itself, states that "This is as much a study of words as of images, of words that describe images, of words that are as revealing in their accuracy as in their failures to describe an image accurately. Consider the description, 'She has one fist in her girlfriend's asshole and another fist in her pussy.' Examination of the image revealed that only two fingers were in the anus; the research team interjudge reliability test did not classify this as anal fisting. However, the customer who has a fetish for anal fisting of women and who downloads an image whose description is the one described may not be upset to discover that only two fingers, and not the entire hand, are inserted in the anus. In fact, it may serve as the starting point of another fantasy; the divergence between word and image suggests a certain flux, such that two fingers are in the anus now, and the entire fist will be in the anus later. The dichotomy between now and later is an extremely clever way for the pornographer to make a still image assume a certain kind of motion. In the viewer's mind, it may even become a movie. What he actually sees, and what the words promised he would see, must converge in his mind; they must synthesize into a new form of imagery."

Bizarrely, the study ends with a tribute to Robert Thomas, entitled "The Marquis de Cyberspace"—a title borrowed by *Time* for its sidebar on Thomas. "Thomas is a brilliant marketer, presenting himself as a modern day Marquis de Sade. It is not without irony that he promotes Amateur Action BBS as 'the nastiest place on earth.'

Indeed, the parallels between the lives and 'art' of Thomas and Sade would provide fodder for a fascinating study. Both pushed 'taboos' and societal mores to the extreme; both flaunted the law and were jailed; both considered themselves renegade artists; and both revolutionized the dissemination of paraphilic pornography, Sade in print, Thomas on computer networks."

In an appendix, Rimm lists the descriptions of the most popular GIFs on AABBS. Among them is the following bizarre sidelight on the case: "Lance White NUDE! D/L this free GIF and DISTRIBUTE FREELY—Downloads: 301." Lance White, you may remember, was the undercover name of postal inspector David Dirmeyer, who busted the Thomases.

In a footnote, Rimm said "it may be difficult for researchers to repeat this study, as much valuable data is no longer publicly available." As Professor Donna Hoffman and others would later point out, he appeared to be shielding himself against the later failure of others to be able to validate or repeat his results.

In the same issue of the law review were articles by three well-known law professors with an interest in information technology, pornography, or both. Catharine MacKinnon of the University of Michigan had spoken on behalf of the anonymous Jane Doe in the Jake Baker case. Anne Branscomb was the author of a well-regarded treatise called *Who Owns Information?* Carlin Meyer had taken a libertarian stance, saying that society must come to grips with the urges that produce pornography rather than censoring it.

As Mike Godwin would point out, Marty Rimm appeared to have couched his study so that each of the three law professors would be able to find supporting data in it. MacKinnon was interested in the violence of the pornography studied by Rimm; it supported her thesis that pornography is oppression, that it creates the conditions for the rape and humiliation of women. Anne Branscomb found data to support her belief that the privacy of our personal data is in increasing danger—Rimm had sprinkled a few references throughout the text and footnotes to the idea that pornographers were relying on users' logon data and other personal information to refine their product. Civil libertarian Carlin Meyer believed that Rimm's study showed that pornography on the Net was essentially uncontrollable.

None of the law professors was a statistician; each assumed the validity of the Rimm study primarily because *Georgetown Law Journal* was publishing it. According to Godwin, Rimm asked Meyer and Branscomb to praise his efforts, and even suggested specific language to Meyer.

As soon as *Time* was on the newsstands, critics of the Rimm study began to gather on the Well on-line service and in Usenet newsgroups. Some of the early critics had known about the study for some time and had had a keen sense there was something wrong with it. Rimm had brought this on himself, by the way he had combined publicity and secrecy before publication. Rimm and others had been talking about the study since November 1994, whetting people's interest in it while consistently refusing to show any of the work product, or any early drafts, to anyone. While most scholarly works are reviewed and critiqued by experts prior to publication, Marty Rimm had "embargoed" his study, refusing to show it to people he had asked for help.

He had asked Adam Epstein to write programs without showing him the actual data. When he asked Mike Godwin, of EFF, to review the legal footnotes but wouldn't show him the main text to which the footnotes were attached, Godwin refused.

In the hours and days after the *Time* article appeared, numerous critiques of the Rimm study would be posted on Usenet and elsewhere, but the home base for such expert commentary proved to be a "Newsweeklies" forum on the Well, where journalists and those interested in their work congregated. Elmer-Dewitt was a participant here, and ended up spending many hours defending his cover story—and finally admitting his errors.

The two leaders of the onslaught against the Rimm study were Mike Godwin and Donna Hoffman, an associate professor of management at the Owen School at Vanderbilt.

Hoffman had spoken to Elmer-Dewitt while the story was in preparation. Both he and the *Georgetown Law Journal* had refused to give her a copy of the paper, citing their secrecy arrangements with Rimm. Hoffman had nevertheless been able to point out some peculiarities about the work, such as the fact that it was unusual for a sociological work to be published without peer review. Elmer-Dewitt found out, however, that law journals, which are edited and published by students, rarely have articles reviewed before publication by anyone except the student editors themselves. In discounting Hoffman's criticism, Elmer-Dewitt failed to take into account the significant distinction that Rimm's piece was not a law article, but a statistical study, very unusual subject matter for a law journal and which the student editors were not competent to evaluate without expert help.

The law journal's editors had approached David Post, a visiting professor of communications law at Georgetown, with some questions about the study's methodology. Post declined to help, however, when they refused to show him the study.

Elmer-Dewitt admitted later that he "should have had a graph" in the story that referenced Hoffman's criticism. "That was probably a screw up," he wrote on the WELL.

Donna Hoffman and her husband, Tom Novak, are professors of management at Vanderbilt University and experts on Internet traffic patterns and the use of the Web for marketing. On July 3, they posted an exhaustive critique of the Rimm study on their "Project 2000" Web pages. "We criticize the study on conceptual, logical, and process grounds, including: 1) misrepresentation, 2) manipulation, 3) lack of objectivity, and 4) methodological flaws," they said.

Their purpose was not to defend pornography. They merely wanted the national policy debate to be carried out based on accurate information. "We do not debate the existence of pornography in 'cyberspace.' ... What we dispute are the findings presented in this study concerning its extent and consumption on what Rimm calls the 'Information Superhighway.' The critically important national debate over First Amendment rights and restrictions on the Internet and other emerging media requires facts and informed opinion, not hysteria." *Time*, unfortunately, had given the study "a credibility it does not deserve."

Hoffman and Novak's first criticism was that Rimm had misrepresented the scope and import of the study. They stated that "The study is positioned as 'marketing pornography on the Information Superhighway.' Yet, it deals neither with marketing nor the Information Superhighway, and displays a considerable lack of understanding of both areas." Rimm displayed no familiarity with basic marketing literature, referencing standard sources only once in 148 footnotes.

He also had not, despite his claims, studied the "Information Superhighway"; instead, he had juxtaposed "unrelated analyses of adult BBSs and Usenet newsgroups," creating in the "casual reader's mind the impression that what is stated about adult BBSs is also true of the 'Information Highway' as a whole."

Hoffman and Novak cautioned that "this paper provides no action-able insights for policy makers about the future of Cyberspace, as the results, at the maximum, can only be generalized to all adult BBSs in the United States." Who, they asked, was the shadowy "research team" referred to continuously throughout the study? A team member making a significant contribution would typically be named as a co-author, yet Marty Rimm's was the only name on the study.

"Given established standards of authorship as ownership of intellectual property in the academic and scientific community, we can only infer from this that no one on the 'research team' felt their contributions merited the significance of shared authorship," Hoffman and Novak wrote. They also questioned Rimm's right to refer to an undergraduate paper as the Carnegie Mellon study. Was his work actually funded, or even blessed, by the university?

Next, they examined Rimm's unusual manipulation of the *Georgetown Law Journal* and of *Time*. The law journal should never have published a sociological, statistical article without insisting on peer review. "Given the vast array of conceptual, logical, and methodological flaws in this study, documented thoroughly below, *Time* magazine behaved irresponsibly in accepting the statements made by Rimm in his manuscript at face value." Instead, *Time*, blinded by its exclusive and the sexy, controversial topic, had rushed into print irresponsibly, presenting, "around lurid and sensationalis-tic art, an uncritical and unquestioning report on 'cyberporn' based on Rimm's flawed study. This has had the extremely unfortunate effect of giving the study an instant credibility that is not warranted nor deserved and fueling the growing movement toward First Amendment restrictions and censorship."

Hoffman and Novak observed that Rimm seemed more interest-ed in discussing the lurid details of the image descriptions than in revealing the methodological details of his study. "In fact, in many cases important aspects of the methodology are simply not described at all...it is impossible for other researchers to 1) determine what Rimm actually did and 2) replicate the results."

Much of the Hoffman and Novak response concentrated on Marty Rimm's magic with numbers. He spoke of files that had been "downloaded 8.5 million times," but did not specify the time period. "Was it one month? One year? Five years? Ten years?"

Whenever Rimm talks about his methodology, he stops short of telling you exactly what he did. For example, in describing the ways he validated his computer dictionary, "Rimm says that 10,000 'actual images' were 'randomly downloaded' from adult BBSs, the Usenet or CD-ROM and used to verify the accuracy of the descriptive listings. Rimm does not, however, 1) report the methodology used to randomly select the images, 2) provide frequency distributions of the images across the media they were obtained from, 3) specify the exact media used to obtain the listings (e.g. which CDROMS?), nor 4) indicate how the accuracy verification procedure was performed."

Rimm never examined the possibility of a discrepancy between what people actually download and what they view or use. Significantly, he analyzed downloading patterns only for the BBSs; on Usenet, he looked at the groups individuals subscribe to, but "no download behavior on Usenet news groups was ever examined by Rimm."

Rimm had stated that because BBS download data was "exhaustive," statistical techniques and assumptions that are commonly invoked to impute general consumer behavior "are not necessary for this dataset." Hoffman and Novak thought that "the statement that statistics are not necessary for these data is astonishing."

Rimm's statement that there was a tremendous disparity between his study and prior, conventional studies of pornography, as far as American sexual tastes are concerned, was also highly suspect. The prior study he cited was a questionnaire submitted to individuals about their sexual tastes. Rimm was comparing this with a study of download patterns on adult BBSs. "[T]he two studies examine two completely different populations. Thus, there is no basis for the conclusion that a 'tremendous rift' exists and the statement represents an 'apples and oranges' comparison."

"One of the more intriguing questions raised by this study is whether the general population will demand the same types of imagery currently in high demand among computer users."

Hoffman and Novak responded, "This statement is misleading. All computer users? Some computer users? How many are 'demanding' it now? What types? Indeed, why would the general population be expected to exhibit the same types of preferences as subscribers to adult BBSs, which is the only group of 'computer users' for which Rimm studied imagery?"

They were particularly troubled by Rimm's claims that the BBS sysops had assisted him in the study—a concern given emphasis by Brock Meeks's allegation that fifteen of the sysops did not remember having dealt with Rimm or his team. "This is a troubling statement. How was Rimm able to obtain such consent? Was it 'informed consent?' Did Rimm provide full disclosure to these operators about the nature and objectives of his study? Did Rimm 'debrief' them afterwards? Did he get the permission of the subscribers of these BBSs to examine information about their consumption habits? Did Rimm submit a proposal of his methodology for such 'persuasion' to the University Human Subjects Committee? Did they approve the research and the methodology?"

In the study's footnotes, Rimm stated, "Members of the research team did not, as a rule, identify themselves as researchers." Further disclosures, by Rimm ("discrete, ain't we?") and others made it appear that Rimm had tricked his subjects into cooperating—just one of the apparent ethical breaches that led to an internal investigation at Carnegie Mellon.

As for the Usenet section of the study, Rimm failed to explain if he was counting "images" or "posts." This is significant because images are typically uploaded in segments in multiple posts. For instance, one image uploaded to Usenet on July 1, 1995, was split into forty-one separate messages.

Use of the Carnegie Mellon log files to determine campus Usenet usage raised ethical questions similar to those involving the sysops. Rimm had seemingly used his fellow students as research subjects without their knowledge and consent.

Hoffman and Novak were extremely scornful of Rimm's claim that 83.5% of images posted to Usenet were pornographic—a statistic which by now had already been cited on the Senate floor by the pro-CDA forces. He had, without disclosing his method for doing so, arbitrarily decided that certain Usenet newsgroups were pornographic. Then, using a shifting definition of pornography, Rimm determined, based not on the images but on descriptions of them, that 83.5% of these images were pornographic. "Also, no information is provided on the degree to which these 32 groups comprise the complete universe of Usenet imagery." Rimm made no attempt to determine whether other, non-pornographic newsgroups existed in which images might be exchanged (e.g., **alt.pictures.vacation**).

Rimm's findings pertaining to the "top 40" newsgroups at Carnegie Mellon were "simply unbelievable." Hoffman and Novak wrote that "It is truly astonishing that there are no .comp or .news groups in the Top 40 Usenet news group at the university studied."

Rimm cited studies by Brian Reid of the Digital Equipment Corporation who used an "arbitron script" to measure Usenet readership. Reid, in his own writings on the subject, was careful to point out that his data shed no light on the percentage of Usenet messages actually read by those who download them. Rimm failed to repeat this caveat.

Brian Reid was also extremely distressed by Rimm's citation of his "arbitron" research regarding Usenet usage. He wrote,"Normally when I am sent a publication for review, if I find a flaw in it I can identify it and say 'here, in this paragraph, you are making some unwarranted assumptions.' In this study I have trouble finding measurement techniques that are **not** flawed. The writer appears to me not to have a glimmer of an understanding even of basic statistical measurement technique, let alone of the application of that technique to something as elusive and ill-defined as Usenet."

Even Rimm's simple statement that "71% [of the] pornographic images downloaded from the five Usenet newsgroups studied over a four month period, originated from 'adult' BBS," was unsupported. Hoffman and Novak said, "We cannot determine how Rimm arrived at this number from our reading of the manuscript. Is it an estimate? A count? How was it estimated or counted?"

Hoffman and Novak questioned the approach Rimm had used in selecting the adult BBSs. "Rimm does not indicate how many boards this represents, how they were sampled to be 'representative,' whether the list of adult BBSs Rimm sampled from was exhaustive, or whether Rimm used his 'judgment' in selecting BBSs or in generating the list of BBSs to sample from."

Similarly, his selection of the description files was infirm. They wrote, "Rimm indicated that 292,114 descriptive listings were retained for analysis. How many listings were actually collected? How many pornographic images do these listings represent? How many were movies? How many were text files? How many images were selected from the BBSs and how were they selected?"

Another major problem was the mysterious dictionary software. Rimm failed to discuss the design of the software or the algorithms it used, both mandatory topics for a serious sociological work. "In the scholarly literature it is not only customary to offer the software to those who wish to replicate your results, for some journals it is mandatory (as is making the data available). Nowhere does Rimm indicate that the data or the software that categorized the listings are 'available from the author.'"

Finally, Hoffman and Novak asked, rather mildly, "What is the point of including the Amateur Action BBS Case Study?"

Marty Rimm promised to reply to the Hoffman and Novak critique, but never did. Instead, he answered a separate commentary they wrote on the *Time* magazine article. In that piece, Hoffman and Novak pointed out the many inconsistencies between Rimm's sloppy results and the *Time* reportage.

For example, *Time* claimed that the Rimm study was "an exhaustive study of on-line porn—what's available, who is downloading it, what turns them on." Hoffman and Novak riposted that the study was "an unsophisticated analysis of descriptions of pornographic images on selected adult BBSs in the United States," masquerading as an exhaustive study of porn on the Net.

Rimm wrote, "It is not surprising that the 'critique,' which was quickly prepared (in less than five days) by two psychologists in a field (pornography on computer networks) where they have apparently done little scholarly research, falls far short of its mark."

In response to the criticism that the study was not "peer reviewed," Rimm pointed out that it was "reviewed and commented upon extensively by three outstanding scholars, each from differing perspectives." Rimm was referring to law professors MacKinnon, Branscomb and Meyer, who had accepted the statistics as gospel but presented their analyses of the legal and societal implications. Moreover, all three writers used Rimm's results to support previously-held positions about pornography or information security.

Rimm was stung by Hoffman's and Novak's accurate description of his work as an "undergraduate study." He claimed that "The Carnegie Mellon study drew on the expertise of more than two dozen researchers, many of whom hold Ph.D.s in statistics, engineering, economics, management, fine arts, psychology, history and public policy from universities such as MIT, Berkeley, Stanford and Carnegie Mellon. The formal credentials of those who assisted with, or directly participated in, this study are substantial and reflect expertise in a wide variety of disciplines."

Many of these people were already lining up, like Adam Epstein, to announce that Rimm had misled them, failed to disclose his data, or had misrepresented their role in his work. Rimm's intellectual dishonesty is exemplified by his statement that Hoffman and Novak's "claim of a 'vast array' of 'flaws' is not substantiated here or elsewhere in this 'critique.'"

Hoffman and Novak did not discuss details of these flaws in their analysis of the *Time* article; instead, they referred the reader to their essay on Rimm's study—to which Rimm never directly replied. Calling Elmer-Dewitt a "superb technology writer," Rimm attributed Hoffman, Novak and Mike Godwin's criticisms to *Time's* refusal to allow them "to censor the Carnegie Mellon research team." He claimed that Godwin had been "offered the opportunity to participate in the Carnegie Mellon research effort last year," but failed to mention that he had refused to show Godwin the study. Rimm said that none of these people were "objective experts" qualified to criticize his work.

Hoffman and Novak had questioned Rimm's method of counting images, pointing out that one image might be contained in many posts to Usenet. Rimm replied, "We were unaware of any fancy methodology necessary for counting images. We used a calculator."

He acknowledged that he had not disclosed the means by which he obtained information from BBS sysops, but claimed that his vagueness on this point was for the protection of the sysops and their users. He concluded that "It is peculiar that two business faculty from a well-known university would invest considerable effort [to] attack a study of computer pornography written by a person with a degree and an advanced background in electrical and computer engineering, published by a well respected law journal and discussed in the popular press." He called the Hoffman and Novak commentary an "overwrought critique."

Rimm would later attack Donna Hoffman personally, calling her "an instrument of the Left" on National Public Radio and hinting elsewhere about "conspiracies."

Mike Godwin of EFF, who remembered his contacts with Marty Rimm about the study's legal footnotes, joined the fray on the Well and also contributed an article to *Hotwired*.

In Fall 1994, Marty Rimm had approached Carnegie Mellon faculty to inform them that pornographic newsgroups were popular at the university. He had already studied the log files at this point. The university administration reacted—or overreacted—by cutting off all access to the *alt.sex* newsgroups and to many of the *alt.binaries* newsgroups as well. Godwin planned a visit to the school to consult privately with administrators about the First Amendment implications, and then to make a speech to a student group. Rimm E-mailed him suggesting that they meet, but failed to follow up by contacting Godwin on campus, though Godwin had E-mailed him his itinerary.

In his E-mail, Rimm told Godwin he opposed the Carnegie Mellon action based on his log files research. He tried to get Godwin involved in his study. Godwin wrote in *Hotwired* that "I can't say I thought much more about Rimm at the time. There was something that smelled a bit goofy about his research project and the weird seriousness with which he was pitching it to me. His faculty adviser, Marvin Sirbu, actually wrote me independently to suggest that EFF sponsor the Rimm project in some way. But EFF doesn't normally sponsor this sort of project, and my instincts told me we should keep our distance."

Godwin has some psychology and statistics background from college, and an early abstract of the study someone sent him from Carnegie Mellon set off many of the same alarms that would later ring for Hoffman and Novak. He also was surprised by Rimm's "evident fascination with types of porn that are, uh, not mainstream," and concluded that Rimm was an "odd duck" with "some sort of agenda."

In the months after the Carnegie Mellon flare-up, Rimm continued E-mailing Godwin, asking him to review the legal footnotes, but refusing to show him the study itself. "But even if I'd had the time to check on someone else's legal research (doing the job right would require many hours), I couldn't ethically approve of legal footnotes without seeing the text of the article they were footnotes to."

Godwin didn't worry further about the impact Rimm would have on the on-line world, however. He wrote; "I was certain the Rimm paper would never come to anything. I figured that, once the CMU censorship fracas died down, the Rimm research would sink, like most undergraduate research projects, into oblivion."

In Godwin's opinion, the publication of the Rimm study in a law review was the culmination of an extremely shrewd strategy. "If Rimm had set out to publish an article about on-line porn in a way that legitimized his article yet escaped the kind of critical review the piece would have to undergo if published in a scholarly journal of computer science, engineering, marketing, psychology, or communications, what better venue than a law journal? And a law journal article would have an added advantage—it would be read by law professors, lawyers, and legally trained policy makers and taken seriously. It would automatically be catapulted into the center of the policy debate surrounding on-line censorship and freedom of speech."

Godwin knew Elmer-Dewitt from the Well. In the days prior to the appearance of *Time*'s July 3 issue, Godwin urged him to take

Donna Hoffman's comments seriously and warned him that dignifying the Rimm study with a cover article would be a "disaster. ... It'll be used to stoke the fires of the Great Internet Sex Panic."

After the issue appeared, Godwin was invited to appear on ABC's *Nightline* to debate Ralph Reed of the Christian Coalition about the CDA. The preamble to the show would deal with the Rimm study, so Godwin tried to educate the ABC reporters about its problems. Though Godwin sensed that ABC was not greatly interested in "in hearing nerds talk about statistical inferences," ABC did schedule a conference call with Godwin, Rimm, and Elmer-Dewitt to discuss the study. Godwin had a moment of epiphany at the end of the call, when he heard the following exchange between Elmer-Dewitt and Rimm:

> "Philip: 'Marty, you there?'
>
> Rimm: 'Yes, I'm here.'
>
> Philip: [slight pause] 'Good job!'"

The beleaguered Elmer-Dewitt, on the defensive in the Well and in numerous interviews with newsmagazines tracking the "Cyberporn" controversy, regarded himself as being on the same team with Marty Rimm.

Godwin now got busy, sending copies of the Rimm study to anyone he knew who was qualified to comment on it; articles in the *New York Times* and *Washington Post* appeared as a result.

Elmer-Dewitt, formerly a friend of Godwin's from their contacts on the Well, would later call the EFF counsel a "professional lobbyist" conducting an "orchestrated campaign" to discredit him.

In the interview he granted *Hotwired* over the July 4 weekend, Elmer-Dewitt commented that the debate on the Well would itself make an interesting story for *Time*. "Frankly, I think there's a good story to be done, probably by me, in what's gone on in The Well. This might be self-serving, but it feels like poor Marty Rimm is being lynched there. He's not getting a fair trial; his study's not getting a fair trial. Mike Godwin has organized an attack, and there are precious few voices that are not already prejudiced to one side."

Interviewer Gary Brickman asked Elmer-Dewitt whether he now thought the Rimm study was "a solid piece of academic research."

"Well," answered Elmer-Dewitt, "we did have some problems with the study. I have to say I don't think it's the most mature piece of academic research I've ever seen. It's basically a descriptive study.

It's a count of how many messages of a certain type there are on adult bulletin board systems and a-less-than-satisfactory estimate of the number of those kinds of messages on the Usenet. It is sort of immature in that it doesn't have a real sharp point to be made, except here's how much stuff there is."

In July, Carnegie Mellon Provost Paul Christiano issued a press release stating that the study was the individual work of undergraduate Marty Rimm and should not be referred to—as it universally was, in *Time* and *Newsweek*, on *Nightline*, and all over the Net—as the Carnegie Mellon study. Next, following the university's internal procedure, he formed a committee of professors to determine whether a full scale investigation was necessary of the ethics of the Rimm study.

On July 11, in a typically acerb piece in his *Cyberwire Dispatch*, Brock Meeks broke the story of Rimm's *Pornographer's Handbook*. Someone named John Russel Davis had uploaded the following excerpt to Usenet: "When searching for the best anal sex images, you must take especial care to always portray the woman as smiling, as deriving pleasure from being penetrated by a fat penis into her most tender crevice. The male, before ejaculation, is remarkably attuned to the slightest discrepancy; he is as much focused on her lips as on her anus. The slightest indication of pain can make some men limp."

Many on the Well and Usenet were prepared to take this as a laughable hoax. Meeks, who had been exchanging E-mail with Rimm for some time, asked him if the *Pornographer's Handbook*— and this excerpt—were really his. Rimm replied, "The excerpts circulating around the Usenet were stolen from my marketing book, Brock. You are the only one I am telling."

Meeks says he now got Rimm to make a couple of serious admissions. Rimm had given copies of the *Pornographer's Handbook* to the adult BBS sysops, and he suspected that one of them had leaked it to Usenet. Secondly, and even more significantly, the Rimm study's claim that on-line pornographers were using "sophisticated software" to refine their marketing was a reference to Rimm's own software. Rimm, says Meeks, was working both sides of the fence, "the ultimate media hack." He complimented Rimm for the brilliance of this strategy, and Rimm replied, "If I do say so myself."

Another story that made its rounds on the Internet claims that Rimm and his faculty advisor, Marvin Sirbu, applied to the

Department of Justice for a grant supporting Rimm's work. The idea was that the Department of Justice would benefit by identifying BBSs to prosecute. This, of course violated the principal ethical rule of research that you do not harm your subjects. Illinois University professor Jim Thomas wrote, "That Rimm and Sirbu then submitted a grant to the DoJ that could be used to bust the very people who were his subjects goes beyond any breach of research ethics that I can recall, ever, in the social sciences. This is not a minor lapse of ethics or an error in judgment. It is a fundamental violation of the most basic principles of the treatment of human subjects."

On August 8, Carnegie Mellon Provost Christiano issued a memo stating that the committee had recommended a full-scale inquiry. "I expect the Committee of Investigation to examine a full range of issues relating to the article and to the research preceding it. Until the Committee of Investigation has completed its work to determine which, if any, allegations are valid, it would be inappropriate for me to comment further on this matter. Indeed, all those who believe in fairness and in due process should take special care not to prejudge the conduct of persons who have engaged in this or any other research."

Within weeks after its publication, the Rimm study had been thoroughly discredited. But the damage had already been done—Senators Grassley and Exon had waved the *Time* article around Congress; Senator Coats had quoted Rimm's phony statistics.

Rimm would later claim ingenuously that he never really meant the study to be used this way. In reply to Brian Reid's savage criticism, he said: "Frankly, my sense is that things are getting blown out of proportion because people are angry that the study will be misappropriated. Their concerns are indeed well-founded. For instance, Ralph Reed stated on *Nightline* that 'According to the Carnegie Mellon University survey, one-quarter of all the images involve the torture of women.' This is simply untrue; the Carnegie Mellon study does not report any results concerning torture. Many others on Capitol Hill have misappropriated the study as well. Whoever misappropriates the study, from whatever perspective or agenda, ought to be corrected in an open, intellectually honest manner. "

An invitation to Rimm to testify before Congress in late July was rescinded. Rumor on the Net had it that Rimm had been admitted to graduate school at MIT; however, after his last public statements in July, Rimm hired an attorney and became incommunicado.

Mike Godwin had the last word on Rimm. "The more you research Rimm, the more a portrait emerges of someone wily, subtle, glib, manipulative. Even when he tells you he's being totally honest, totally frank, you have this lurking feeling that below the surface he's calculating the precise effect his choice of words—both his admissions and his omissions—will have on you."

# Chapter

# VII

## Bomb Speech

Candyman's pages on the World Wide Web contain all kinds of useful information about hacking, drugs, phone phreaking, killing people with your bare hands, and manufacturing bombs. On his *BOOOOOOOOMMMMM!!!!!* page, Candyman proudly informs you that he was featured recently on CBS's *48 Hours,* on a segment called "Bomb Scare."

Candyman's disclaimer message is short and to the point. "The following is a collection of files related to pyrotechnics. I do not endorse, nor check for the safety, or validity of the bomb making procedures. Makers of these devices take all responsibility. Warning: All of these devices do or can pose a risk to the creators and other individuals. Please read all the safety precautions and files! ... For your safety please read the recipes carefully two and three times over before attempting. It is highly suggested that you have a background in Chemistry or get an Introductory book of Chemistry."

Candyman doesn't write very much; he compiles. Most of his information is collected from BBSs, Usenet, and suggestions received from readers. After the disclaimer, he provides a safety warning: "SAFETY TIPS—HOW NOT TO GET KILLED (Ways to avoid scoring an 'Own Goal'). An 'Own Goal' is the death of a person on your side from one of your own devices."

He gives tidbits of advice such as: don't smoke around explosives ("don't laugh—an errant cigarette wiped out the Weathermen"); grind the ingredients separately; and allow yourself extra time for your escape, in case a fuse burns more quickly than expected. The **Safety Warning** file is signed "Exodus"—like all of his files, Candyman found it somewhere else.

What interests you on Candyman's menu? There are recipes for letter bombs, toilet bombs, jug bombs, and light bulb bombs. A car bomb recipe taken from a book called *The Poor Man's James Bond*, was provided by "Lex Luthor." "The best methods of blowing up a car requires getting under the hood. Explosives are placed as near the occupants as possible. NOTE—THIS ARTICLE IS FOR THOSE OF YOU WHO ARE NOT CONTENT TO PSYCH OUT THE DRI-VER WITH SOME PRACTICAL JOKE. IF YOU HAVE HIS LAST RIDE IN MIND, THEN READ ON."

According to the author, the best way to blow up a car is with dynamite and a fuse wrapped around the exhaust pipe which will catch fire when the pipe gets hot enough. This is far superior to the usual approach of wiring the ignition, for two reasons. First, since the bomb will probably explode while the car is moving, "the wreck will do the victim in even if the blast doesn't."

Second, if your intended victim is a passenger and not the driver, an ignition bomb is less sure to injure the target because the driver may start the car before the victim has entered. "You can see how embarrassing that would be to the bomber, can't you?"

Would you like to make a bomb like the one used at the World Trade Center or in Oklahoma City? It's affectionately referred to as an ANFO, short for Ammonium Nitrate-Fuel Oil. The instructions state that "Lately there has been a lot said about various ANFO mix-ture. ... This forms a reasonably powerful commercial explosive, with its primary benefit being the fact that it is cheap. Bulk ANFO should run somewhere around 9-12 cents the pound."

The author of this file, "D.S.—Civil Engineer at Large," gives details on mixing and detonating ANFO mixtures. After telling the story of the accidental discovery of ANFO (two ships collided caus-ing a "real big bang"), he concludes by warning the readership that it should be used as soon as possible after purchase because it is dif-ficult to store and, even though anyone can purchase it, a license is required to keep it on hand.

D.S. also warns that "commercial explosives contain quantities of tracing agents, which make it real easy for the FBI to trace the explosion to the purchaser, so please, nobody blow up any banks, orphanages, or old folks homes, okay."

Candyman provides "Jolly Roger's" recipe for a letter bomb. First, make some thermite, using iron filings. Then buy a heavily padded, double layered envelope from the Post Office. Place the thermite in one layer and another explosive ingredient in the other layer. Add a "touch explosive" at the top that will ignite when the envelope is torn open, triggering the other two ingredients. "If the thermite didn't blow up, it would at least burn the fuck out of your enemy (it does wonders on human flesh!). NOW that is REVENGE!"

A fragmentation grenade may be made with dynamite and nails. This recipe was prepared by Jolly Roger and revised by Exodus, who suggests the user make certain modifications to the pipe, before it is packed with explosives. "If he was not too dumb, he would do this slowly, since the process of folding and bending metal gives off heat, which could set off the explosive."

Candyman also offers a terrorists' manual that, among other things, tells you how to steal the ingredients you need. "The best place to steal chemicals is a college. Many state schools have all of their chemicals out on the shelves in the labs, and more in their chemical stockrooms. Evening is the best time to enter lab buildings, as there are the least number of people in the buildings, and most of the labs will still be unlocked. One simply takes a book bag, wears a dress shirt and jeans, and tries to resemble a college freshman."

Like most Webmasters, Candyman invites you to send him E-mail. But he asks that you read the **FAQ** (frequently asked questions) file first, so he won't be bothered with repetitive questions that he finds boring to answer.

FAQ Question: "Why aren't you in jail? How many times have the fedz questioned you? Are the federal agents out to get you? Isn't this illegal?"

Answer: "My actions are that of a librarian or archiver of information. The action of authoring, archiving, or publishing information is protected in the United States Constitution under the 1st Amendment. [L]aw enforcement officials do not question me because providing information is not illegal in the United States of America."

Candyman is right. He not only knows how to blow people up; he knows the First Amendment. However, his original essay about censorship reveals he's not much of a writer. "I am a strong believer in a censorship-free world. I feel censorship is nothing more than government exercising mind control over the masses. Call it extreme call it what you want, but censorship bears a strong communistic resemblance. For when one allows others to control what they wish to say, speak, type, read, listen to, or watch that individual is having there education limited, their views confined, and their moral standards chosen and imposed by the censor. Who is to say what an individual in a free society is allowed to read? What makes the censor the 'god' to have his own moral standards enchained around us the individuals. Have we not our own moral standards and values that we can live our lives?"

He then quotes the late Supreme Court Justice, William O. Douglas. "Literature should not be suppressed merely because it offends the moral code of the censor."

Usenet contains an *alt.pyrotechnics* newsgroup. People who gather here like to set off explosions, but not necessarily for murderous or criminal purposes. Much of the dialog in *alt.pyrotechnics* involves people telling others how stupid or criminal they are. For example, one user described a chemical bomb that can be mixed in a two-liter bottle; "fun to put on people's door step and ring the doorbell. They get soaked!" The derisive reply: "They get soaked with NaOH! In some states, assault with a corrosive chemical is cause for Deadly Force. ... Hardly a joke." Another reader responded: "Yeah, they get soaked with chemicals that can blind them or attack their skin and you go to prison. This is a totally IDIOTIC idea."

A message asks for help designing a "vapor" bomb in a two liter bottle, "so when it is rolled over with a car it will detonate." The answer: "You want help to blow up a moving vehicle presumably with driver aboard? Not from me, pal."

After the Oklahoma City bombing in April 1995, the media went looking for bomb recipes in cyberspace—and didn't have to look very far. To the immense embarrassment of the National Rifle Association (NRA), reporters found a message from "Warmaster" on its Bullet 'N Board BBS describing how to make a bomb from shotgun shells, nails and a baby food bottle.

"These simple, powerful bombs are not very well known, even though all of the material can be easily obtained by anyone, including minors. These things are so fucking powerful, that they can destroy a car. ... Go to the Sports Authority or Herman's sports shop and buy shotgun shells. At the Sports Authority that I go to, you can actually buy shotgun shells without a parent or adult. They do not keep it behind a little glass counter or anything like that. It is $2.96

for 25 shells. ... If the explosion doesn't get them, the glass will. If the glass doesn't get them, then the nails will."

On May 5, Tanya Metaksas, the director of the NRA's Institute for Legislative Action, wrote apologetically to the NRA board of directors. "We denounce...the individual who posted the message, the message itself and attempts by others to somehow impugn NRA and me personally. This sort of one-in-a-million message denigrates the customarily high intellectual quality of the debate carried on in NRA's electronic forums day in and day out.

> "Anyone can upload anything to an open and unrestricted bulletin board system—just as anyone can mail anything to someone's mail-box at home totally outside the control of the homeowner. The bulletin board in question...purges files periodically that are distasteful and inappropriate. The file in question was uploaded onto the system, then purged at a later date. I would not be surprised to learn that the posting itself was politically motivated to embarrass me, the NRA and impugn the good will and good reputation of gun owners and NRA members who use the system."

Metaksas reminded the board how important electronic communications are to the NRA—its popular Web site has an encyclopedic collection of information on state and federal gun laws and litigation, as well as every NRA newsletter and press release. She pointed out that the NRA was not alone in struggling with the problems caused by illegal or distasteful messages, citing the problems experienced by Prodigy and America Online.

Metaksas promised that all messages would henceforth be screened before being made public. If you log on to an NRA bulletin board today, you are greeted by screen after screen of rules and disclaimers. "Member agrees to use the GUN-TALK service only for lawful purposes. Member is prohibited from posting on or transmitting through GUN-TALK ANY UNLAWFUL, HARMFUL, THREATENING, ABUSIVE, HARASSING, DEFAMATORY, VULGAR, OBSCENE, PROFANE, HATEFUL, RACIALLY, ETHNICALLY OR OTHERWISE OBJECTIONABLE MATERIAL."

Metaksas also mentioned that "when people on the system learned my gender, some few sent messages that amounted to vile, sexual advances. I didn't appreciate those messages either, and no one in their right mind would suggest that I was responsible for my own sexual harassment."

Like obscenity and most of the other "bad speech" in cyberspace, there is nothing new about bomb recipes. Books and magazines describing how to make explosive devices have always been available. The most notorious of these is a book called *The Anarchists' Cookbook* published by Barricade Books. You can find it in some bookstores or order it for $25 through an ad in *The Nation* magazine. Another well-known distributor of this kind of material is Paladin Press, co-founded by NRA board member Robert Brown, now the publisher of *Soldier of Fortune* magazine. Among Paladin's publications is *Improvised Explosives: How to Make Your Own*, described in Paladin's catalog as follows: "With ease, you can construct such devices as a package bomb, booby-trapped door, auto trap, sound-detonated bomb or pressure mine."

Some of the files on Candyland pages are taken from books such as *The Poor Man's James Bond* from Desert Press. Candyman is often asked why he does not post *The Anarchists' Cookbook*, since it is the most famous of bomb manuals. He won't, he says, because some of the recipes are inaccurate, and you may blow yourself up using them.

Law enforcement officials agree that some recipes are defective, but won't reveal where the errors lie, "preferring to pick up the pieces of wannabe bombers rather than innocent civilians," says Erik Larson, a *Wall Street Journal* reporter who has written about America's fascination with guns and bombs. Larson interviewed Billy Blann, the owner of Desert Press, who told him that anyone following the recipes in *The Poor Man's James Bond* takes a similar risk of self-immolation. Blann said that "Anybody who fools with this stuff… has got to be a fool." Blann believes most of his customers are closet commandos who just want to read about bombs, not make them.

However, bomb manuals like these are frequently found in the possession of bombing suspects. According to Larson, investigators at the site of a bombing often recognize that the device, flaws and all, came from a particular book; later they find the book in their suspect's possession when they arrest him.

As Candyman noted, people are often surprised to learn that disseminating this kind of information is protected by the First Amendment. They shouldn't be. Information, after all, is a form of speech, which is what the First Amendment protects. In order to prosecute someone for publishing information, you would have to show that his speech fits into one of the few exceptions to the First Amendment: obscenity, libel, or speech which is likely to cause immediate physical violence. Bomb recipes simply do not fit into any of these pigeonholes. Though by implication bomb recipes advocate violence, they do not cause immediate apprehension of harm in the same sense as a speaker outside a house calling for the lynching of a man inside.

In a 1969 case, *Brandenburg v. Ohio,* the Supreme Court overturned the conviction of a speaker at a Ku Klux Klan rally who said, "We're not a revengent organization, but if our President, our Congress, our Supreme Court, continues to suppress the white Caucasian race, it's possible that there might have to be some revengence taken." The Court held that the law may not forbid "advocacy of the use of force...except where such advocacy is directed to inciting or producing imminent lawless action and is likely to produce such action."

Bomb recipes in books or on the Internet do not meet this exacting standard because they are not likely to produce immediate action by readers.

"You can't say they can't print this stuff," Joe Grubisic, commander of the Chicago bomb squad, told Larson. "I don't like it, but I really don't know what the solution is. I don't want a police state."

University of Chicago law professor Cass Sunstein, a First Amendment specialist, would like to see the Supreme Court limit *Brandenburg,* to situations where there are relatively few people in the audience. Using Warmaster's baby food nail bomb as one of his examples, Sunstein argues that cyberspace and other mass media should be treated differently than more local environments where violence is advocated:

"Suppose that an incendiary speech, expressly advocating illegal violence, is not likely to produce lawlessness in any particular listener or viewer. But of the millions of listeners, one or two, or ten, may well be provoked to act, and perhaps to imminent, illegal violence. Might government ban advocacy of criminal violence in mass communications when it is reasonable to think that one person, or a few, will take action? *Brandenburg* made a great deal of sense for the somewhat vague speech in question, which was made in a setting where relatively few people were in earshot. But the case offers unclear guidance on the express advocacy of criminal violence via the airwaves or the Internet."

Sunstein suggests an alternative argument for banning bomb recipes. Information is not advocacy, and *Brandenburg* may be held to protect only advocacy. "Instructions for building bombs are not a point of view, and if government wants to stop the mass dissemination of this material, it should be allowed to do so."

Sunstein is wrong on both counts. The suggestion that an idea may be legal if told to a few people, but illegal if posted on the Internet, is shocking. No basis exists for such a double standard. National media—newspapers and magazines—existed when the Constitution was drafted. There is nothing in the First Amendment to justify the concept that ideas are protected only if they do not reach a mass audience and are in no danger of persuading anybody. This is the opposite of Justice Holmes' famous statement that "the best test of truth is the power of the thought to get itself accepted in the competition of the market." Since the First Amendment is based on the faith that good speech will always win, it is unimaginable that any speech could be ruled illegal *because* of its success in reaching a mass market.

Earlier this century, (prior to *Brandenburg*), the Supreme Court routinely upheld laws against the advocacy of crime, even when not likely to cause immediate law-breaking. The question is, where do you stop? Do you jail Gandhi or King for advocating nonviolent resistance? Do you put Thoreau in jail twice, once for refusing to pay a tax, and a second time for writing an essay about it?

Sunstein wants to have it both ways; bomb manuals are evil because they advocate violence, but may be banned because they offer only information, not advocacy. This is a false distinction. The First Amendment protects speech, not just advocacy. Information is a category of speech, whether or not it advocates anything, and is therefore protected. Again, nothing in the drafters' working papers or in case law justifies the idea that information is not speech or is of lower value than other speech.

Practically speaking, the line between information and advocacy is almost impossible to draw. Is "Fire when you see the whites of their eyes" information, or is it advocacy of resistance against the British? Almost all information implicitly advocates its own use. Birth control information, for which Margaret Sanger was prosecuted under obscenity laws, constitutes advocacy of the use of birth control. Bomb recipes advocate the use of bombs for revenge or dispute resolution. Sunstein, like so many others facing a horrible or shocking idea, is struggling for a way to say that it is not First Amendment-protected. But the First Amendment does not give this any support.

One federal law is on the books, adopted many years ago but hardly used, which makes it unlawful to "teach or demonstrate" the making of explosive materials if you know that the information will be used to break the law. This law may well be unconstitutional under *Brandenburg* because it does not require a threat of imminent violence. In a 1972 case, *United States v. Featherston*, a federal circuit court of appeals upheld the conviction of a revolutionary who conducted a class in bomb-making for his followers, based on testimony that "Mr. Featherston had taken over the class and was explaining to the group how we could use these different bombs, that everyone understood how to make them, that everyone in the organization had to learn how to make them, women and men, and 'We must keep these ingredients around the house or one or two bombs made up so we could use them on a moments notice.'"

Featherston was sentenced to four years in prison and appealed. The Court of Appeals rejected his First Amendment arguments, quoting *Dennis v. United States*, an old Supreme Court holding which relied on an earlier standard overruled by *Brandenburg*: "[T]he words cannot mean that before the Government may act, it must wait until the putsch is about to be executed, the plans have been laid and the signal is awaited. If Government is aware that a group aiming at its overthrow is attempting to indoctrinate its members and to commit them to a course whereby they will strike when the leaders feel the circumstances permit, action by the government is required." The Court of Appeals failed to discuss the *Brandenburg* ruling of three years earlier.

Whether or not *Featherston* was unconstitutional—it never reached the Supreme Court—the behavior involved was very different from that of Candyman or Warmaster, or, for that matter, of Paladin Press or Desert Press. Featherston got a group of people together in a room and taught them how to make bombs, with the intention that they would go out and commit particular crimes. His case, though brought under the federal "bomb training" law, was similar to a traditional conspiracy case where people act together to plan a crime. As Columbia law professor Kent Greenawalt notes, there is a point at which speech becomes "situation-altering...much more 'action' than 'expression'." Publishers of bomb information, whether in paper or on the Internet, don't cross this line because they don't typically meet their readers or know which of them will use the information to commit a crime.

Nevertheless, at least one BBS sysop has been charged with maintaining bomb files: 21-year-old Michael Elansky was arrested in Connecticut in August, 1993 after a fourteen-year-old complained about a file called ANARC2. Elansky had not written ANARC2; it had been uploaded by a user. Elansky was charged under two state laws that have nothing to do with either cyberspace or bombs: inciting injury to persons and property and endangering a minor (the 14-year-old user who downloaded ANARC2).

Elansky's arrest in August, 1993 brought significant comment from on-line civil libertarians. "It appears," said David Banisar of Computer Professionals for Social Responsibility, "that the prosecutor doesn't realize that electronic publications have the same protections as printed publications." Mike Godwin of EFF added that "the prosecutor in this case has shown monstrous disregard for the Constitution that he has sworn to uphold."

The author of ANARC2 was 19-year-old Lucas Benfry of Tewksbury, Massachusetts, aka Deth Vegetable, who had written the file four years before. "I kind of thought of it all as a big joke," he said. Benfry was never charged with any crime, although later that year three teenagers in Laval, Canada were seriously injured when they built a pipe bomb following one of his recipes. One boy lost two fingers when the pipe bomb exploded.

After spending more than three months in prison awaiting trial, Elansky pled guilty to violation of his probation on a prior conviction for the possession of two pipe bombs. His attorney, Richard Brown, claimed that while in prison, Elansky had been assaulted twice, had witnessed a hanging, and had to bribe other inmates daily to assure his own safety. Judge Thomas Miano sentenced him to 28 months imprisonment, and five years probation. The conditions of probation were unusual—Judge Miano prohibited Elansky from allowing anyone under eighteen years old on his BBS, or posting any pyrotechnic or other harmful information. In addition, a probation officer would have the right to search the BBS at any time to make sure Elansky was complying. "It's not going to make him a better person by keeping him in jail," said Elansky's stunned father, who had expected his son to walk out of court free that day.

Senator Diane Feinstein of California believes bomb recipes should be illegal, and has introduced a bill that would ban them.

Feinstein's bill, S. 735, presented in 1995 as a part of President Bill Clinton's Counterterrorism Act, would amend the "bomb training" law, making it illegal to distribute bomb information "by any means" if the distributor "intends or knows" that the information will be used to commit a crime. The penalty: up to 20 years in prison and a fine of $250,000.

Though propelled by concern about bomb recipes on the Internet, S. 735 was not restricted to cyberspace. The words "by any means" mean that if S. 735 becomes a law, Billy Blann of Desert Press is in as much trouble as Candyman.

Feinstein, elected to the Senate in 1992, is a moderate Democrat who was the mayor of San Francisco for ten years. She has a background in criminology and is on the Senate Judiciary Committee. Feinstein was the target of an attempted bombing that failed because unseasonably cold weather froze the fuse. Later in 1995, she would vote in favor of a constitutional amendment banning flag burning—further calling into question her commitment to freedom of speech.

On May 11, the Senate Judiciary Subcommittee on Terrorism, Technology and Government Information held a hearing on Feinstein's bill. "This hearing," said chairman Arlen Specter, "focuses on the use of the Internet by a variety of groups and individuals to propagate 'mayhem manuals,' which, as their name suggests, are guides to assist people in committing acts of violence."

Referring to the Internet as the "most democratic means of communication today," he went on to warn of its dangers: "Among those who communicate on the Internet are purveyors of hate and violence. Among the full text offerings on the Internet are detailed instruction books describing how to manufacture a bomb. I am troubled that we may one day fondly recall the days of prank phone calls once these mayhem manuals permeate our schools. Already, one inquiry on how to construct a bomb reportedly was made by a 13-year-old. I doubt that this inquiry was the result of a school project."

Another horrifying example, he said, was "this anonymous message posted on an Internet electronic bulletin board shortly after the Oklahoma City bombing: 'Are you interested in receiving information detailing the components and materials needed to construct a bomb identical to the one used in Oklahoma.' The information specifically details the construction, deployment, and detonation of high powered explosives. It also includes complete details of the bomb used in Oklahoma City, and how it was used and how it could have been better."

Senator Specter did not take a stand on the legislation before the committee, in fact, he intimated that he knew it was unconstitutional. "Even if the technological issues can be resolved, there remain significant First Amendment concerns," he said. He summarized *Brandenburg*, then concluded, "Cases upholding restrictions on speech are extremely rare." He noted that certain scholars, such as one-time Supreme Court nominee Robert Bork, believed that the First Amendment protects only political speech. "While that may be too narrow a reading of the First Amendment, we should not forget the warning of Justice Robert Jackson that the Bill of Rights must never be converted into 'a suicide pact.'"

Deputy Assistant Attorney General Robert S. Litt was the first to testify in front of the subcommittee. Like everyone else that day, he started off with a couple of bomb stories. Then, commendably, he told the Senators that the bill was unconstitutional.

> "When we address not conduct but possibly protected speech, the power of law enforcement is restricted by the First Amendment. As the Committee well knows, we must guard the public's right to free speech even while protecting the public from criminal activity. The Constitution imposes stringent limits on our ability to punish the mere advocacy of principles or the mere dissemination of information, without more, even if the communications in question are utterly repugnant."

Litt reminded the subcommittee that the "bomb teaching" laws permitted the prosecution of those who taught bomb-making classes like Featherston. But, he added, bomb recipes on the Internet probably did not meet the *Brandenburg* requirements, because they did not incite imminent lawless action.

> "In sum, it is generally not possible to penalize speech unless the speech crosses the line from providing information or mere advocacy to inciting imminent lawlessness or participation by the speaker in illegality. This protection applies to speech on the Internet as well as on the street corners; to bomb manuals posted on electronic bulletin boards as well as bomb manuals for sale in corner bookstores."

Litt undercut his admirable disquisition on Constitutional law at the very end, by making a plea for support of funding for the Digital Telephony Act, and against encryption and anonymity on the Net.

> "Privacy rights should generally be protected, but society should continue to have, under appropriate safeguards and when necessary for law enforcement, the ability to identify people and hold them accountable for their conduct. In the case of encryption, the appropriate balance can be achieved by the widespread use of reliable, strong cryptography that allows for government access, with appropriate restrictions, in criminal investigations and for national security purposes."

Rabbi Marvin Hier of the Simon Wiesenthal Center in Los Angeles, which tracks hate groups, acknowledged that the First Amendment applied to cyberspace, and called for action against bomb components, not bomb manuals.

> "The Wiesenthal Center has located, both prior to and since the Oklahoma massacre, numerous 'recipes' for building bombs. Information once only available behind the counter of a few counterculture bookstores is now being promoted into millions of homes in America on a daily basis. Under our system of laws and freedoms, we are unable to stop the flow of such dangerous information to people bent on destruction. But America can, and must, prohibit the over-the-counter sale of large quantities of chemicals like ammonium nitrate and other explosives or toxic substances to people who have no legitimate use for them."

The Internet's great danger lay in the pervasiveness of information. "Cyberspace offers direct instantaneous, cheap, mainstream communications in the marketplace of ideas. Further, young people—a target group for racists— are especially drawn to this cutting edge of technology."

Rabbi Hier called for better monitoring capabilities for law enforcement, and for on-line services to exercise some censorship of their own, by denying hate groups a forum. He also recommended limitations on anonymity on the Net. "We need to keep in mind that the obscene or threatening phone caller has neither his privacy nor his speech protected when he threatens a member of the community via the phone - why are those protections afforded if he launches the same attack via the Internet?"

The next witness was Jerry Berman of the Center for Democracy and Technology, who said, "Yes, there is information on the Internet about how to build bombs, reasons to overthrow the United States Government, and how to organize violent militia groups. The question facing us, as an open society, is how to respond to the most controversial and extreme uses of this new technology, this electronic, global Gutenberg printing press that turns all citizens into publishers who can reach thousands and even millions of people around the country and the world.

> "As an open society, governed by the democratic principles of the First and Fourth Amendments, we tolerate and even encourage robust debate, advocacy and exchange of information on all subjects and in all media of expression, without exception. Prior restraint or any government action, which might chill speech have long been labeled intolerable, except in the few circumstances in which that speech advocates imminent violence and is likely to produce such violence. Even in these cases, Constitutional law and long-standing law enforcement policy have dictated great restraint in order to avoid chilling legitimate speech activity."

Berman cited a frequently used example of speech that is not protected by the First Amendment: shouting fire in a crowded theater, which triggers panic and injury. But, he asked, how exactly do you shout "Fire!" in cyberspace?

> "We believe that shouting fire in cyberspace is actually *far less threatening*, and thus less deserving of censure, than the equivalent act in the physical world. Though one can shout fire in an E-mail message or on an Internet newsgroup, the likelihood that it will incite readers to imminent, criminal action is much reduced because the readers are dispersed around the country, and even around the world."

Berman only meant that the immediacy required by *Brandenburg* would be hard to accomplish in cyberspace. But he sounded like he was arguing for a double standard—that information on the Net is less dangerous than the same information offline. These days, all sorts of crimes—conspiracies, frauds, thefts—take place over the wires and involve people who are physically remote from one another. The challenge is to persuade judges and legislators that the Net should be treated *the same as,* not *worse than,* print media. Arguing that it should be treated *better* is risky because it may backfire.

Berman climbed onto more solid ground by arguing that the open, free debate on the Internet bolsters democracy.

"Given the political character of communication in online environments, it is especially important that First Amendment activity and privacy rights be protected.

"Indeed, in the face of terrorist threats, it is particularly important to maintain an open society in order to minimize public paranoia about the government and to discredit the arguments of those who advocate the destruction of our government. The openness of the Internet and other interactive media should be seen as a great boon to our democracy, not as a threat to order."

Berman concluded: "As passionate and vehement as speech on the Internet may be, it remains only speech, with no immediate nexus to violence in most situations."

Law professor Frank Tuerkheimer came next. Like all the other witnesses, he warned the subcommittee that S.735 was unconstitutional. Bomb information is widely available—in the *Encyclopedia Brittanica*, and in the *Blaster's Manual* published by the U.S. Department of Agriculture (both containing recipes for an ANFO bomb like the one in Oklahoma City)—and the First Amendment does not permit us to outlaw it. Responding to the subcommittee's concern about children building bombs, he said drily, "If parents are concerned their children will obtain information they can use for the wrong purposes, they can take steps to ensure that their children do not do so. Despite the distressing number of accidents involving children and firearms, in all the discussion on regulation of firearms, no one has yet proposed that people with children in the house be prohibited from owning guns."

Tuerkheimer argued that the Internet does not require laws different from those governing any other forms of communication, because it is essentially similar to them. "The Internet is a method of communicating information, quickly, to many people, and for great distances. ... In the end, however, it is just another method of communicating, and when the issue of regulating it arises, this cannot be overlooked."

Tuerkheimer, as a young Wisconsin prosecutor, had worked on the *Progressive* case, in which a court issued an extremely rare preliminary injunction under a nuclear secrets law, banning the distribution of a magazine containing an article on how to build an atomic bomb. He had been skeptical then and is even more so now. (The case became moot when another magazine ran the article.) "Even my limited enthusiasm waned considerably once the case took the turn of attempting to enjoin the publication of information gathered from the public domain," he said.

Remarkably, given that every one of the witnesses said that S.735 was unconstitutional, the Senators voted to report Senator Feinstein's bill for consideration by the full Senate.

On June 5, the Senate debated the Counterterrorism Act. (Civil libertarians opposed the Act for reasons other than S. 735: it would generally increase police surveillance and wiretapping ability while cutting back the procedural rights of suspects.) Senator Feinstein told the story of the attempted bombing of her house, then described a cartoon from *USA Today* that shows "a youngster sitting in front of his computer learning how to put together a bomb. Here is the mother on the phone saying, 'History, astronomy, science, Bobby is learning so much on the Internet.'"

With the same showmanship that Senator Exon would exhibit nine days later during the Internet indecency debate, Senator Feinstein showed the Senate an enlargement of a screen captured from the Net advertising the *Terrorist Handbook*. "Whether you are planning to blow up the World Trade Center, or merely explode a few small devices on the White House lawn, the Terrorist Handbook is an invaluable guide to having a good time. Where else can you get such wonderful ideas about how to use up all that extra ammonium triiodide left over from last year's revolution?"

Senator Feinstein responded to Tuerkheimer's point that explosives-related information can be found in many innocuous places, such as federal agricultural manuals and the *Encyclopedia Brittanica*. "Now, I have heard people say, oh, but the *Encyclopedia Britannica* has eight pages on explosives, and nobody criticizes that. Well, I have read the eight pages on explosives, and it does not say how to make a toilet paper roll booby trap. What legitimate purpose is there for a toilet paper roll booby trap other than to kill somebody? You do not blast out the stump of a tree. You do not need it for mining. You need it for no civilian or military purpose other than to kill."

Senator Feinstein also quoted a Usenet message sent on April 25, after the Oklahoma City blast: "I want to make bombs and kill evil Zionist people in the Government. Teach me, give me test files. Feed my wisdom, O Great One."

Feinstein listed a few bomb-making books of the *Anarchists'* *Cookbook* genre, quoting from recipes for booby traps and murder devices of various kinds. "Well, there are those who would say this is just a simple first amendment exploration. Do not worry about it. People are just curious. Well, let me tell you that on Friday, Orange County bomb squad Sgt. Charlie Stump told me that a 14-year-old was in his garage making a pipe bomb with an 11- and 12-year-old watching him do it. The information to make this pipe bomb came from the *Improvised Munitions Black Book*, which can be obtained in any gunshop through the Paladin Press mail order outlets. So this youngster blew himself up, and right next to him was the handbook that he used. Another example. In Mission Viejo, a 20-year-old junior college student went into the so-called survivalist movement and accidentally set off his own bomb and killed himself. Again, the manual was sitting right next to him."

A rule of political sophistry: when urging censorship of abhorrent speech, say that you can't believe that the First Amendment was written in order to protect such horror or filth. (Senator Exon would say a few weeks later that Jefferson, Madison and Co. did not stay up all night to find a way to protect pornographers.) Senator Feinstein used this tactic to sidestep the First Amendment issue:

"Enough is enough. Common sense should tell us that the First Amendment does not give someone the right to teach others how to kill people. The right to free speech in the First Amendment is not absolute, and there are several well-known exceptions to the First Amendment which limit free speech. These include obscenity; child pornography; clear and present dangers; commercial speech; defamation; speech harmful to children; time, place, and manner restrictions; incidental restrictions; and radio and television broadcasting. I do not for one minute believe that anyone writing the Constitution of the United States some 200 years ago wanted to see the First Amendment used to directly aid one in how to learn to injure and kill others."

Senator Feinstein was wrong. The Founders correctly did not have to foresee the particular types of speech the First Amendment would one day protect—they made it virtually absolute so that it could be used to shelter any type of speech. The moral force of the First Amendment is in the fact that it does not just protect the speech of which we approve.

Senator Feinstein did not claim that bomb information fell into any of the categories that she listed. Therefore, at the same time that she claimed that S. 735 would not trample on the First Amendment, she tacitly acknowledged that she was creating a brand new category of prohibited speech.

The proof that this is true is in the image not of Candyman, but rather that of Billy Blann being led away in handcuffs. It has been more than thirty years since a book publisher was jailed for his publishing activities. Since text is never held obscene anymore, there is virtually nothing you can say in a book that can get you arrested. And, since Candyman is in effect a publisher like Billy Blann, there is no legal justification for treating him any differently. Senator Feinstein wants to roll back the clock to the days when words, not coupled to acts, could be regarded as dangerous.

She called for the Supreme Court to reconsider *Brandenburg* if necessary, echoing Cass Sunstein's argument that speech is more dangerous when heard by millions:

> "The last time the Supreme Court directly dealt with the issue of freedom of speech restrictions was [in *Brandenburg*]...I think it may be time, especially in light of Oklahoma City and the World Trade Center bombings, for the Supreme Court to deal with this issue again. In today's day and age, when violent crimes, bombings, and terrorist attacks are becoming too frequent—2,900 bombings a year, 541 in California alone in the year 1993—and when technology allows for the distribution of bombmaking material over computers to millions of people across the country in a matter of seconds, I believe that some restrictions on speech are appropriate."

Senator Feinstein finished her speech by quoting the judge in the *Progressive* case:

> "'While it may be true in the long run, as Patrick Henry instructs us, that one would prefer death to life without liberty, nonetheless, in the short run, one cannot enjoy the freedom of speech or the freedom of the press unless one first enjoys the freedom to live.' I could not agree more with Judge Warren. Enough is enough. I do not believe the first amendment gives anyone the right to teach someone how to kill other people. ... Even our most precious rights must pass the test of common sense."

Nine days later, Senator Exon's "decency" bill would have a formidable opponent in Senator Leahy, but at this hearing no one thought it would be politically profitable to defend bomb manuals, or the First Amendment, against Senator Feinstein. S. 735 went almost unopposed. Only Senator Orrin Hatch rose to request any changes to it. The conservative Republican Senator from Utah, elected in 1976, is no friend of civil liberties. Senator Hatch was concerned by the language "knows or intends" and wanted to delete "knows". Hatch was concerned that the publisher of a bomb recipe might be a criminal if he merely *knew* that his work might be used for criminal purposes, even though he didn't *intend* that it be used this way. That day, Hatch would also oppose another provision of the Counterterrorism Act calling for the introduction of chemical taggants into explosives to make them traceable. In both cases, Hatch explained that he was concerned for the mining companies in his state, who use explosives.

Feinstein replied that she saw the change as a way to let bomb manual publishers off the hook: "What concerns me is somebody writes a terrorist handbook. We have that case. And they tell somebody how to steal; how, in detail, to put together, let us say, a light bulb bomb. You come to them and say, 'You violated a criminal law.' They say, 'I did not intend this to be used for crime.' Then the comeback is, 'You should know it is going to be used for crime because that is the only purpose for a light bulb bomb. It is the only purpose for a toilet paper bomb, for a candy box bomb.'"

Senator Joseph Biden agreed. He pointed out that, along with Senator Leahy, the ACLU always rated him highly as a defender of the First Amendment. Nevertheless, he believed S. 735 was constitutional and necessary, and opposed Senator Hatch's proposed change. "If I walk in to you and you are selling the handbook, you have the handbook and I say, 'Ma'am, I would like to buy a handbook that would teach me how to—do you see the cop down there in the corner? I want to put a pipe bomb in that trash can where he stands every morning from 8:30 to 9. I want to blow that SOB up,' and you say, 'I have just the thing for you,' and you walk over and you hand him the handbook, it seems to me you knew the information that is available to you to do something terrible, kill that policeman standing at the corner. It would be awfully hard to prove, though, that, if you sold that handbook to me, you intended for me to kill that policeman. ... So my concern is, if it gets even narrowed further to say only 'intends the information to be used in a criminal enterprise or criminal act,' then it is so narrow that you are not going to catch in that net people who I think we should catch." Hatch agreed to drop his request.

The Senate adopted S. 735, then the Counterterrorism Act of which it was a part. The Act, however, bogged down in the more conservative House. Involved in hearings about FBI and Bureau of Alcohol, Tobacco and Firearms overreaching at Waco and Ruby Ridge, the Republican majority didn't want to pass legislation which would increase the police powers of the Clinton administration.

The freedom of speech is the shield that protects all our other freedoms. Walt Kelly's famous dictum in the *Pogo* comic strip was, "We have met the enemy—and he is us." If we must—as Senator Feinstein argues—strip away the Constitution to fight terror and anarchy, all we will have left at the end of the day are anarchy and terror. We will have destroyed everything we were fighting to save. Freedom of speech means we must tolerate Candyman.

# CHAPTER

# VIII

## THE NEW COMSTOCK

The new Anthony Comstock stood up in front of the United States Senate on June 9, 1995, and waved his blue book of pornography from the Internet. He is Senator James Exon, a Democrat from Nebraska. He told his fellow members of the most exclusive club in the world: "This is a sample of what is available today free of charge: Click, click, click on the computer, on the information superhighway. To give an idea, let me read through some of the listings that appear on the bulletin boards....

> Multimedia erotica; erotica fetish; nude celebrities; pictures black, erotic females; pictures boys; pictures celebrities; pictures children; pictures erotic children; pictures erotica; pictures erotica amateur; pictures erotica amateur females; pictures erotica amateur males; erotica animal; erotica auto; erotica bestiality; erotica bestiality, hamster, duct tape; bestiality, hamster, duct tape; [two of those] erotica black females; erotica black males; erotica blondes; erotica bondage; erotica breasts. Here is a good one: Erotica cartoons; erotica children; erotica female; erotica female, anal; erotica fetish; erotica fury; erotica gay men; erotica male; erotica male, anal; erotica Oriental; erotica porn star.

"This goes on and on and on—so much repetition. But it is startling, page after page after page, on screen after screen after screen—free, free of charge, with a click, click, click." The cadence is hypnotic, reminiscent of James Joyce's "ever, never."

Bad, frightening speech exists on the Internet, and the Senator has made that his issue, much as Senator McCarthy had enlivened a dull career by complaining about Communists in the State Department. Senator Exon has served since 1978; before that, he served two terms as governor of Nebraska. He is a graduate of the University of Omaha, served in World War II, and is Episcopalian. The ACLU, which rates Congresspeople for their dedication to civil liberties, gave him a rating of 45 in 1992, placing him squarely in the center of his peers. (Senator Kennedy received a 95 and Senator Helms a 5 the same year.) The ACLU will certainly give him a lower rating next time because of his sponsorship of the Communications Decency Act (CDA).

During 1994, Senator Exon first introduced the CDA as a rider to the Telecommunications Reform Act but Congress adjourned for the year without voting on it. With a conservative majority in Congress as a result of the 1994 elections, and a lot more interest in the lamentable state of speech on the Net, the CDA had another chance.

The CDA, innocuous or even incomprehensible on a first reading, was a radical attack on the First Amendment protection of free speech and the Supreme Court's settled and rather simple rules interpreting the First Amendment.

First, the Court had established that the only category of sex-related speech that was not protected by the First Amendment is obscenity, defined as prurient, patently offensive speech lacking in scientific, literary, artistic, or political value. Second, the case law of recent decades strongly indicates that the printed word, which includes words on a computer screen, can never be obscene—no matter how raunchy or shocking. Only pictures and films have been the subject of prosecution in recent years. Third, the Supreme Court made clear that indecent (as opposed to obscene) communications could be regulated to protect minors, but could not be banned.

Senator Exon proposed to return to the days of Anthony Comstock by restoring a long-discredited indecency standard, which the CDA made no attempt to define. Laws barring indecency have a long, disreputable history in the United States. Even more so than obscenity laws, they have been used to censor and criminalize political or sexual speech. The original Comstock law targeted indecent material. Indecency laws have reached the Supreme Court in several contexts since then. In 1971, the Supreme Court overturned the conviction of an anti-war protester arrested in Los Angeles for wearing a jacket emblazoned with the words "Fuck the Draft." The Court said that a state "has no right to cleanse public debate to the point where it is grammatically palatable to the most squeamish among us...[it is] often true that one man's vulgarity is another's lyric." The following year, the Court vacated the convictions of three individuals who had used vulgar language at school board meetings or in confrontations with policemen.

The Court and the Congress have established one zone in which indecency laws have sharper teeth, communications media regulated by the FCC. In 1978, the Court upheld the right of the FCC to penalize a radio station that broadcast, in midafternoon, comedian George Carlin's routine about the seven dirty words the FCC won't let you say on the air. While a late-night broadcast would have been permissible, it was aired at a time when children were listening.

The FCC's ability to apply greater restrictions to radio and television than are permissible for other forms of speech is derived from the scarcity of bandwidth. Because there are a limited number of radio and television channels available, the government, which assigns them to broadcasters, is thought to have the right to monitor content for indecency. This is, of course, the wrong analogy for the Internet. Bandwidth on the Net is unlimited, and the government's permission is not required to attach a server to it. Content providers on the Internet are publishers, not broadcasters.

The concept of decency has been injected into another area of public regulation in recent years, the phone companies. An explosion of 900-line services in which callers, including minors, could hear explicit sexual messages, led Congress to ban telephone indecency. In 1989, the Supreme Court threw out this law as overly broad, reminding the lawmakers that they can only regulate indecent expressions, not ban them. After a series of attempts to tailor the law, Congress finally settled on language requiring the 900-line services to take steps to ensure that minors do not hear explicit messages. Senator Exon's rationale for the CDA was that logging on to the Internet also involves a telephone communication, and that any regulation that was valid for the 900-line services should be valid for electronic information providers. However, because of the vagueness of its drafting, the CDA would actually go far beyond that. Its ban on on-line indecency, for example, would mean that the words "Fuck the CDA," legal on a jacket, might be illegal on your Web pages.

The CDA proposed several new categories of felony crimes, punishable by up to two years in prison or a $100,000 fine. The first new category involved initiating "the transmission of any comment, request, suggestion, proposal, image, or other communication which is obscene, lewd, lascivious, filthy, or indecent, with intent to annoy, abuse, threaten, or harass another person." Senator Exon had borrowed the language from the Communications Act of 1934, which regulated telephone and radio communications.

Another new crime involved knowingly making, or making available, "any obscene communication in any form including any comment, request, suggestion, proposal, or image regardless of whether the maker of such communication placed the call or initiated the communications." This section specifically included communications originating outside the United States, laying the groundwork (shades of Iran and Salman Rushdie) for American prosecutors to attempt to indict porn sysops operating Internet-linked services in other countries.

Another significant provision barred anyone from knowingly sending indecent communications to a minor. Both the obscenity and indecency provisions also specified that it was a crime to permit a telecommunications facility, such as a BBS or Internet server, to be used for such obscene or indecent purposes. The CDA included several exceptions that information providers could rely on as defenses to a charge of obscenity or indecency. These exceptions had mostly been added since the 1994 version of the bill was dropped and lobbyists for the large on-line services began whispering in Exon's ear.

The first of these exceptions provided that no one would be held responsible "solely for providing access or connection to or from a facility, system, or network over which that person has no control." In other words, Netcom couldn't be liable for dealing in smut just because it provides Internet connectivity. In order to be convicted of a crime, a party would have to have a closer relationship to the smut. In the CDA debate, Senator Exon said that a page of World Wide Web links to indecent or obscene pages would be enough to deprive a defendant of this defense.

Second, an employer wouldn't be held responsible for an employee's actions unless the employer authorized the behavior.

Third, the CDA created an affirmative defense of "reasonable, effective and appropriate actions in good faith" to restrict or prevent indecent communications. A defendant could use this defense if he could show that he had implemented reasonable means of avoiding the illicit communications. The CDA also provided immunity from lawsuits to service providers who took such actions in good faith.

This last exception appears to be intended to reverse the result in the *Prodigy* case. Though vaguely drafted, these defenses shield on-line services against liability based on unsuccessful attempts to avoid illegal communications.

The opening salvo in the Senate's CDA debate was fired by Dr. Lloyd John Ogilvie, the chaplain who offered the Senate's daily prayer on June 12, 1995. Dr. Ogilvie said, "Almighty God, Lord of all life, we praise You for the advancements in computerized communications that we enjoy in our time. Sadly, however, there are those who are littering this information superhighway with obscene, indecent, and destructive pornography. Virtual but virtueless reality is projected in the most twisted, sick misuse of sexuality. Violent people with sexual pathology are able to stalk and harass the innocent. Cyber solicitation of teenagers reveals the dark side of on-line victimization.

"Lord, we are profoundly concerned about the impact of this on our children. We have learned from careful study how children can become addicted to pornography at an early age. Their understanding and appreciation of Your gift of sexuality can be denigrated and eventually debilitated. Pornography disallowed in print and the mail is now readily available to young children who learn how to use the computer.

"Oh God, help us care for our children. Give us wisdom to create regulations that will protect the innocent. In times past, You have used the Senate to deal with problems of air and water pollution, and the misuse of our natural resources. Lord, give us courage to balance our reverence for freedom of speech with responsibility for what is said and depicted.

"Now, guide the Senators as they consider ways of controlling the pollution of computer communications and how to preserve one of our greatest resources: the minds of our children and the future moral strength of our nation. Amen."

On June 14, debate on the CDA commenced by way of an arcane gambit. Senator Patrick Leahy of Vermont, champion of the anti-CDA forces, attempted a preemptive strike by offering his own bill as an amendment to the Telecommunications Reform Act. Senator Exon then proposed an amendment to Senator Leahy's amendment: his proposal, of course, was to delete the entire text of the Leahy amendment and substitute the CDA. The debate then centered on whether the Senate would adopt the Leahy amendment or Senator Exon's amendment to the Leahy amendment, the CDA.

Senator Leahy, like Senator Exon a Democrat, was elected to the Senate in 1974. He has an ACLU rating of 95, more than twice Senator Exon's. He sits on the Agriculture Committee and has been interested in technology and the Internet for years.

Senator Leahy's amendment, which was strongly supported by on-line civil liberties groups such as the EFF, was both cautious and politically shrewd. He proposed that the Senate table the CDA, take no immediate action, and commence a study of the best way to regulate the Internet. The study would be the responsibility of Attorney General Janet Reno and must be completed within 150 days. It would concentrate on three areas: determining whether existing obscenity and child pornography laws are adequate to prosecute computer-transmitted pornography; assessing whether adequate law enforcement resources are devoted to combating pornography at the federal, state, and local levels; and evaluating the technical mechanisms available "to enable parents to exercise control over the information that their children receive by interactive telecommunications systems so that children may avoid violent, sexually explicit, harassing, offensive, and other unwanted material on such systems." The amendment ended with a sober directive "to promote the free flow of information, consistent with the values expressed in the Constitution, in interactive media."

On the one hand, the Leahy amendment was practical, because it advised the Senate not to rush in without studying the terrain. On the other hand, it was passive enough to expose itself to the criticism that, when you wish to do nothing, you call for a study. Senator Exon repeatedly said that afternoon that America couldn't wait 150 days to protect its children from computer indecency.

The first order of business was the meta-debate, a discussion of how best to debate the CDA. It was decided that two hours would be evenly divided between the Leahy and Exon forces to consider the CDA, with another twenty minutes evenly divided on the Leahy amendment.

Senator Pressler, who was presiding over the Senate that day, said, "I wonder if I should not try to reserve 10 minutes of time within that in case some Senator, from whom we have not heard, feels an irrepressible urge to make a speech." To which Senator Leahy replied, "That sometimes happens, Mr. President, in this body. It is rare, but it sometimes happens."

Senator Exon, in charge of the pro-CDA hour, yielded himself ten minutes and reread the prayer by Chaplain Ogilvie with its condemnation of "virtual but virtueless reality." He said, "If in any American neighborhood an individual were distributing pornographic photos, cartoons, videos, and stories to children, or if someone were posting lewd photographs on lampposts and telephone poles for all to see, or if children were welcome to enter and browse adult bookstores and triple-X-rated video arcades, there would be a public outrage. I suspect and I hope that most people, under those circumstances, would immediately call the police to arrest and charge any person responsible for such offenses. I regret to report that these very offenses are occurring everyday in America's electronic neighborhood." Senator Exon warned that "if nothing is done now, the pornographers may become the primary beneficiary of the information revolution."

It was now Leahy's turn, and he yielded himself "whatever time I may consume." He said, "I also use the Internet. I do town meetings on the Internet. I correspond with people around the world with the Internet. I call up information I need and plan trips to other countries. I call up information and maps, and so on. I find it is a most marvelous tool." He had been appalled by what he saw in Senator Exon's blue book, but he had been unable to find that kind of thing himself on the Internet.

"I do worry about the universal revulsion for that kind of pornography—I assume it is universal in this body—and that we do not unnecessarily destroy in reaction what has been one of the most remarkable technological advances, certainly in my lifetime—the Internet. It has grown as well as it has, as remarkably as it has, primarily because it has not had a whole lot of people restricting it, regulating it, and touching it and saying, do not do that or do this or the other thing. Can you imagine if it had been set up as a government entity and we all voted on these regulations for it? We would probably be able to correspond electrically with our next-door neighbor, if we ran a wire back and forth, and that would be it."

Senator Leahy had started his speech with a reminiscence—his parents owned a publishing company and a weekly newspaper, and they had encouraged him to read, which had stood him in good stead the rest of his life. Now he said simply, "Maybe we can do it the same way my parents did. They guided me when we read." Rather than Congress telling people what they can write on the Internet, parents should judge what their children should read on the Internet.

Senator Leahy also had a comment, in passing, for Chaplain Ogilvie: "I suggest to the Chaplain—who may be a very fine man, for all I know—that perhaps he should allow us to debate these issues and determine how they come out and maybe pray for our guidance, but allow us to debate them. He may find that he has enough other duties, such as composing a prayer each morning for us, to keep him busy."

In examining the consequences of passing the CDA, Leahy said, "I do not think under this amendment a computer user would be able to send a private or public E-mail message with the so-called seven dirty words. Who knows when a recipient would feel annoyed by seeing a four-letter word on-line?"

Two organizations had set up electronic petitions against the CDA that could be signed via E-mail or on the World Wide Web. Senator Leahy had been sent the signatures, as a sympathetic figure likely to show them off on the floor of the Senate. He did so, waving a pile of printouts. The reply to Senator Exon's blue book was Senator Leahy's 35,000 electronic mail messages. Leahy continued, "When it came out that I was looking for an alternative approach, one that would allow the Justice Department to find a way to go after pornographers but to protect the free use of the Internet, I received these petitions almost immediately. Every page of this stack of documents that I am holding has dozens and dozens of names from across the Internet. These are people saying yes, that is the way to do it. Find out how to go after the pornographers, but keep our Internet working. There were 35,000 petitions, in a matter of days."

Senator Leahy yielded and Senator Exon called on his cosponsor, Republican Senator Daniel R. Coats of Indiana. Coats gave a few dubious statistics about the Internet from the as-yet-unreleased Marty Rimm study. Senator Coats said 450,000 pornographic images and text files were on the Net, which had been accessed 6.4 million times in the last year. He further claimed that "by one estimate, about a quarter of the images available involve the torture of women. We are dealing in many, many cases with perversion and brutality beyond normal imagination and beyond the boundaries of a civil society."

To Coats, the reason why the Internet is dangerous is that "[T]he Internet is the one area of communication technology that has no protection at all for children." He bragged that he didn't even know how to use his VCR. "I have a blinking 12:00 I do not know how to get rid of." Children, however—the group most at risk from the evil speech on the Internet—are also the most technologically astute, and therefore the most capable of accessing the evil speech.

More of Coats's statistics; of the 6.8 million families on-line, 35% had children under the age of eighteen. Senator Coats stated that "the only barriers between those children and the material—the obscene and indecent material on the Internet—are perfunctory on-screen warnings that inform minors they are on their honor not to look at this. The Internet is like taking a porn shop and putting it in the bedroom of your children and then saying `Do not look.'" Quite a statement from a man doomed to live eternally with a blinking 12:00 on his VCR—the Internet is not a bookstore. It is not a community; it is a porn shop in a child's bedroom.

Professor Catharine MacKinnon then had her moment in the sun. Senator Coats did not mention her by name, but she was there in spirit in Coats's assertion that "A vote for the Exon-Coats amendment is a way to side with women endangered by rape and violence" caused by on-line pornography. The Internet, Coats said, "destroys...innocence." He told his fellow senators that the CDA would simply apply some existing standards for voice communications to modem communications: "It is just simply a different means of bringing a communication into a home—through the computer rather than through the phone."

The regulations on indecent, adult phone services did not eliminate the services. Instead, new rules simply forced the operators to be more careful about the age of their users. While the CDA would confirm the existing ban on obscenity, it would also force purveyors of indecent communications to make sure that children could not access it.

Senator Feingold of Wisconsin, a cosponsor of the Leahy amendment, pointed out the impact of creating a new indecency rule for cyberspace: "[I]f this legislation became law, an adult participant on a bulletin board who posted a profane message using some of the `seven dirty words' on any subject could be subject to criminal penalties of up to two years in prison or a $100,000 fine, if a minor might read the message posted on that bulletin board. ... Communication between adults through the Internet would likely be reduced to the lowest common denominator—that which is appropriate for children. Mr. President, that is not free speech."

Feingold did not cite *Butler v. Michigan*, but his words evoked that 1957 Supreme Court decision, which held that the First Amendment did not permit a state to limit adult speech to the level acceptable for children. He pointed out another danger; the most relevant regulations, those of the FCC pertaining to broadcast media, applied the community standard test to indecency. But, Feingold asked, whose community standards applied?

Referring to *Amateur Action*, Feingold asked, "Will all free speech on the Internet be diminished to what might be considered decent in the most conservative community in the United States?" He wondered what would become of medical sources on the Internet, or those discussing sexual abuse, or the prevention of AIDS. All might be considered indecent, if a minor got access.

"Adults will be forced to self-censor their words, even if they did not intend those words for children and even if they are protected by the First Amendment." Senator Feingold decried the CDA's double standard; the indecent speech it condemned on computer networks "would be perfectly legal, and fully protected under the Constitution, in a bookstore or a library."

The Internet is unique, he said, and cannot really be compared to broadcast or print media because "an individual on the Internet can be both a communications recipient and originator simultaneously. Congress needs to understand these differences before we can determine how best to protect children and the constitutional rights of Americans."

In response to the fears of Senators Exon and Coats that children would stumble across obscenity, Feingold said, "Users of the Internet and other on-line functions typically do not stumble across information, but go out surfing for materials on a particular subject." It would be unlikely that a child would find a pornographic site by accident, because most are named to identify them clearly. He observed that Internet access providers like America Online had the capability of blocking access to the raunchiest Usenet newsgroups. If access providers took censorship into their own hands, Feingold implied, Congress wouldn't have to pass laws like the CDA, and the First Amendment would not be violated. He pointed out that parents, using products like Surfwatch, could block out pornographic, indecent, or violent sites.

Existing laws might be sufficient to combat on-line obscenity. Feingold said that "The truth is we just do not know at this point. We need more information. However, it is entirely clear to me that Congress certainly should not abridge constitutionally protected speech if there are less restrictive means of serving the compelling government interest."

Senator Exon rose again and read a series of letters into the record in support of the CDA from organizations such as the Christian Coalition and the National Law Center for Children and Families. He went on the counterattack against Senator Leahy and his supporters: "What they propose to do with the underlying amendment is to punt." He derided Senator Leahy's 35,000 E-mail messages, by reading a copy of an article by Brock Meeks in the June 1995 issue of *Wired*, widely distributed on the Internet, called "The Obscenity of Decency"—an article he blamed for generating many of the petition signatures. Meeks' article was subtitled: "With the introduction of Senator J.J. Exon's Communications Decency Act, the barbarians are really at the gate." Exon said, "I have been called many things in my life, but never before have I been called a barbarian. I would hope that the Senator from Vermont would advise the people that he is using here as support for his position that his mutual friend, Jim Exon, is not a barbarian under any normally accepted definition of the term."

Brock Meeks is the Washington columnist for *Interactive Week* and a regular contributor to *Wired*. He has been covering the computer industry since the early 1980s. In addition to his paid journalism, he publishes a World Wide Web newsletter as a labor of love, covering Internet developments such as the CDA. Meeks is a truly original voice, impassioned, in love with the Net, sarcastic almost to the point of an angry howl when it comes to attacks on the freedom of the Internet. He believes that passage of indecency language would force him to censor his reportage, or risk running afoul of the law. However, Meeks says, he cannot take credit for the phrase "Barbarians at the Gate," which appeared as a subtitle to his article. Meeks explained that "an editor at *Wired*...actually created and placed that subtitle on the article. So the *real* story is that some 'faceless' WiredScribe got his digs in but good."

Senator Exon then cited another statistic worthy of Senator McCarthy and his obscure, shifting counts of Communists. "I do not know the authenticity of the statement that I am about to make. But I have read that it has been estimated that up to 75%, Mr. President, of present computer owners have refused to join the Internet system with their home computer, precisely because they know and they fear—and evidently they have seen or been advised—as to what I have here in the blue book."

This, of course, is nonsense. People are getting on the Net in droves, and the Net itself is growing at a rate that baffles measurement. There probably are a few Americans who have refused to join it because of indecency, which is their right.

Senator Exon continued, "And to the 25,000 [sic] people who want to call this Senator a barbarian, I simply say that, evidently, they are so selfish—at least their actions are so selfish—that they simply say: We do not want to give up anything. We want to be able to see what we want to see, where we want to see it, any time we want to see it."

In other words, it is selfish of us to want to exercise our First Amendment rights without being chilled.

Exon went on to say that pornography is pervasive on the Net. "I think too many people believe that because the pornography bulletin board is sitting out here to the side that you have to work to get to the pornography bulletin board. The pornographers have invaded the Internet down here, so that it is freely available, without cost— all of the outlandish, disgusting, pornographic pictures of the worst type, that some of my colleagues think we can handle by punting. This is not a time to punt; this is the time to act."

His point was that, like the Amateur Action sysops, many pornographers who run private commercial bulletin boards advertise their wares on Usenet, where a large percentage of the pictures distributed in alt.sex newsgroups bear the name and modem number of a porno BBS. "If you like this picture, come into our porno shop over here. For a small fee, we will show you the real thing."

It was Senator Leahy's turn to respond. He gave examples of some of the hypothetical horrors that could arise under the CDA. "This also means that if you are part of an on-line discussion group on rape victims, your computer is programmed to automatically download messages sent into the discussion group. If a participant sends into the group a graphic story about a rape, which could be deemed obscene, this story will automatically be downloaded onto your computer, and you would be criminally liable under this amendment, even before you read the story."

Since minors participate in virtually all Internet newsgroups on any topic, Senator Leahy pointed out that no areas of truly free-ranging discourse would remain, because the entire Net would have to make itself decent: "Under this provision, no indecent speech could be used on electronic bulletin boards dedicated to political debates, since kids under eighteen may access these boards. This will certainly ensure that civility is reintroduced into our political discourse when we are on-line. But this also means that works of fiction, ranging from *Lady Chatterley's Lover* to Newt Gingrich's science fiction novel *1945*, which contains some steamy scenes, could not be put out on the Internet because of the risk that a minor might download it." Internet users "would have to speak as if we were in Sunday School every time we went on-line." Senator Leahy then apologized to Senator Exon for the subtitle on Meeks's article: "I tell my good friend from Nebraska, I hope he realizes I would never call him a barbarian. We know each other too well and we are too good of friends for that."

But Senator Leahy took exception to Senator Exon's comment that the Leahy amendment "punts". "I believe the Exon-Coats amendment punts, because it punts to the FCC the task of finding ways to restrict minors' access to indecent communications so users can implement them and have a defense to criminal prosecution," Leahy said. He read into the record a letter from Assistant Attorney General Kent Markus, who stated that the CDA as drafted was confusing and unenforceable. The indecency sections suffered from the same infirmity as the child pornography statute; there was no clear requirement of knowledge that the individual to whom indecent communications were sent was a minor. The section as written could forbid explicit communications between consenting adults, a clear First Amendment violation.

However, the Justice Department also felt that, in one respect, the CDA tipped the balance in favor of pornographers. The affirmative defenses Senator Exon had added to the draft bill might make it difficult for the government to prosecute an on-line service or Internet access provider.

Senator Leahy concluded that "no member disagrees that we want to keep smut out of the hands of our children. I would remind everybody that the Internet has become the tremendous success it is because it did not have Big Brother, the federal government, trying to micromanage what it does and trying to tell users what it could do."

Senator Leahy yielded back the last twenty minutes of his time, and Senator Exon rose to deliver one last sound bite. He stated that "Every day the Congress delays in dealing with this problem, the pornographers, pedophiles, and predators secure a much stronger foothold in what will be a universal service network."

Senator Exon discussed the movement to make parents responsible and the growing field of products like Surfwatch to accomplish this, then took a side swipe at the EFF. He said, "For all the talk about 'technological fixes,' it is ironic that one group, the Electronic Frontier Foundation, who opposes this measure in favor of more of the so-called parental control, posts on the Internet instructions on 'How to Access Blocked Groups.' The fact of the matter is that kids, not their parents, know how to access everything. ... We should not throw our hands up and allow every child's computer to become a branch office of Pornography Incorporated."

Senator Exon never acknowledged, and possibly doesn't understand, that a child cannot simply connect a computer to the Internet without going through an access provider and giving a credit card number. If the child is using a parent's existing account, then a parental choice has already been made. The parent could have chosen not to give the child the password, or, conversely, to obtain access through a "child-safe" service like Prodigy.

The official debate concluded and the floor was open for a few last questions and comments. Senator Coats talked about the Prodigy case because he wanted to make sure that the Senators understood that the CDA would overrule the *Prodigy* decision and would encourage on-line services to take action against indecency without exposing them to liability as a publisher if they did so.

Senator Biden of Delaware had the last word. "If the Exon-Coats provision passes, we will have mountains of litigation over its constitutionality, dragging on for years and years—and all the while, our kids will be doing what they do best: finding new and better ways to satisfy their curiosity."

The CDA—or, technically speaking, Senator Exon's amendment to Senator Leahy's amendment to the telecommunications bill—was finally put to a vote. Every Senator was present. Eighty-four voted in favor of the CDA and sixteen against it.

Following Senate procedure, a second vote had to be taken to determine whether the CDA would actually be added to the telecommunications bill. As a formality, this was done by voice vote and the CDA became part of the Telecommunications Reform Act, which itself was adopted later in the day. The Senate had concluded a satisfying day's work and it was up to the House of Representatives to determine whether the CDA would become law or would stall in its tracks.

The fate of the CDA in the House was in the hands of Speaker Newt Gingrich. Not only does Mr. Gingrich run the House very tightly, but he has also positioned himself as a defender of the Internet.

Mr. Gingrich sometimes seems like a traditional, old-fashioned conservative, whose rhetoric would not have sounded out of place in the 19th century. But Mr. Gingrich also presents himself as a lover of technology, of communications, of the Net's impact on democracy. In his book *To Renew America*, he describes the "Third Wave Information Age" as offering "potential for enormous improvement in the lifestyle choices of most Americans," including the opportunity for "continuous, lifelong learning." In an interview with Esther Dyson in *Wired* magazine, Mr. Gingrich had spoken at length about the profound importance of the Net, but declined to take a position on the CDA, merely saying he was studying it.

However, Mr. Gingrich did state, "To be honest, I don't understand all the details of that. I didn't do adequate research. My bias is against trying to censor the Net and in favor of going after people who, for example, try to entice minors. In the long run, the Net as a community may have to develop a further sense of its own identity rather than having it done by Congress."

A few weeks prior to the Senate's debate on the CDA, Mr. Gingrich took a stand when, in a PBS interview, David Frost asked him about the CDA. Mr. Gingrich surmised that "It's probably illegal under our Constitution is my guess."

The week after the Senate adopted the CDA, Mr. Gingrich elaborated his position in an interview on a conservative cable channel. "I think that the amendment you referred to by Senator Exon in the Senate will have no real meaning and have no real impact and in fact I don't think will survive. It is clearly a violation of free speech and it's a violation of the right of adults to communicate with each other. I don't agree with it and I don't think it is a serious way to discuss a serious issue, which is, how do you maintain the right of free speech for adults while also protecting children in a medium which is available to both? That's also frankly a problem with television and radio, and it's something that we have to wrestle with in a calm and mature way as a society. I think by offering a very badly thought out and not very productive amendment, if anything, that put the debate back a step." Given the Speaker's power, this was tantamount to a declaration that the CDA would not pass the House.

That week, Senator Exon appeared on PBS to debate Jerry Berman, a civil libertarian lawyer who is executive director of the Center for Democracy and Technology (CDT). CDT had organized one of the petitions Senator Leahy had displayed on the Senate floor.

Senator Exon, possibly nettled because the show began with clips of Speaker Gingrich trashing the CDA, lashed out at Berman with the hackneyed claim that the founders never intended to protect disfavored speech: "One of the problems that we have today is we tried to work with Jerry, but we found out that basically Jerry goes back to the old idea that I think is kind of foreign that Thomas Jefferson and all of the good people who wrote the Constitution worked overnight and planned and plotted to make sure that the Constitution protected the most gross pornographers, pedophiles, those who are trying to lure children today."

This time, Exon really had behaved like a barbarian. Perhaps the drawn-out saga of the CDA had overwhelmed the Senator; it had died in 1994, triumphed in 1995, and now seemed to be cruising at 65 miles per hour toward a brick wall erected by the Speaker of the House. But Senator Exon himself, the new Comstock, the purveyor of decency, had finally become indecent.

Berman's response was proud though mild-mannered. He said, "If I am associated with the gang that goes back to Thomas Jefferson, I'm quite proud of that association."

During the last week of June 1995, *Time* Magazine presented the Marty Rimm "Cyberporn" study to the nation and Senator Grassley of Iowa inserted the *Time* article into the Congressional Record. Senator Exon stood up and thanked him and stated, "I would reference the graphic picture on the front of *Time* Magazine today, which I think puts into focus very distinctly and directly what my friend from Iowa and this Senator have been talking about for a long, long time."

Senator Exon introduced into the record a parallel article from *Newsweek*, which said that the CDA was in terrible trouble in the House. He then adopted what sounds almost like an elegiac tone in reminiscing about his own role in introducing the CDA: "Once again, I emphasize this Senator has followed with keen interest the development of the Internet. It so happens this Senator probably is one of the few members of this body who was on the original Internet. The original Internet, the only thing like it, was the amateur radio network that I became involved as a very young lad, sixteen or seventeen years old, growing up in Lake Andes, South Dakota, and I communicated, dit-dit da-dit, with people all over the United States. Of course you had to have a license to be an amateur radio operator; you had to pass certain tests. I guess no one ever thought about that first Internet being used for the purposes that this Internet is being used."

In an apparent appeal to the House, Senator Exon added, "[T]his Senator simply says I am willing to listen to any improvements or changes that should be made in this bill. But I certainly am not going to stand by and see it watered down to the place where it is totally meaningless." He asked Congress and everyone else involved in the debate not to listen to the voices who say, "I want what I want when I want it on the Internet and I don't care what ill effect that might have on kids."

On August 4, 1995, the House passed its answer to the CDA, the Cox-Wyden bill. There was no debate in the House pertaining to the CDA, pornography, or cyberspace. Cox-Wyden provided that "FCC regulation of the Internet and other interactive computer services is prohibited—nothing in this act shall be construed to grant any jurisdiction or authority to the Commission with respect to economic or content regulation of the Internet or other interactive computer services."

The Cox-Wyden bill also addressed the *Prodigy* case. "No provider or user of interactive computer services shall be treated as the publisher or speaker of any information provided by an information content provider. No provider or user of interactive computer services shall be held liable on account of:

"(1)   any action voluntarily taken in good faith to restrict access to material that the provider or user considers to be obscene, lewd, lascivious, filthy, excessively violent, harassing, or otherwise objectionable, whether or not such material is constitutionally protected; or

"(2)   any action taken to make available to information content providers or others the technical means to restrict access to material described in paragraph (1)."

In other words, the good news from the Cox-Wyden bill was that on-line services such as Prodigy were not publishers but distributors of information. They did not become publishers, with the corresponding higher liability, simply because they took measures to screen out obscene material.

The bill also included a series of Congressional findings about the Internet, such as: "The Internet and other interactive computer services offer a forum for a true diversity of political discourse, unique opportunities for cultural development, and myriad avenues for intellectual activity." A far cry from the many-headed hydra corrupting America's children as perceived by Senator Coats.

However, in a "manager's mark-up" of the telecommunications bill, two amendments were introduced which effectively resuscitated the CDA, though in different words. Most of the house members who voted in favor of the telcom bill were unaware that this language had been added. One provision amended the postal obscenity law to specify that computer communications were covered. This was the law that had been used to prosecute Robert and Carleen Thomas. On appeal, their attorneys had argued that this law covered only tangible materials, such as magazines or photographs and could not be applied to GIF files transmitted by modem.

Another provision was directed to the protection of minors and provided that anyone transmitting via computer "patently offensive" material depicting or describing "sexual or excretory activities or organs" could be imprisoned for five years. This provision, introduced by conservative Republican Henry Hyde, was copied from regulations formulated by the FCC some years before to govern indecent speech on radio and television.

Like the CDA, the Hyde amendment represented the worst nightmare of those committed to free speech on the Net. It implemented a broadcast-style indecency standard, with no exceptions for material with scientific, literary, artistic, or political value. Therefore, it would ban serious discussion of rape, safe sex, or breast cancer on the Net. And it reaffirmed, with a vengeance, the applicability of geographic community standards.

Jerry Berman's CDT issued a press release commenting that "CDT believes that these amendments are unconstitutional and overly broad. They would criminalize constitutionally protected speech and would make service providers liable merely for providing access to the Internet to a minor. CDT will work vigorously to ensure that these provisions are removed from the final telecommunications reform bill."

The House and Senate versions of the telcom bill now went to a House-Senate conference committee. Representative Rick White, a Cox-Wyden cosponsor, made an attempt to replace the Hyde amendment and the CDA with language of his own that reaffirmed the *Miller* standard for cyberspace, but substituted a national standard for *Miller's* local communities. To no avail; the House conferees voted to keep the Hyde amendment. Speaker Gingrich, reputed to be working behind the scenes to moderate the discussions , made no public statement.

The CDT and another organization, Voter's Telecommunications Watch, put out an appeal to netizens to contact the Senators on the Conference Committee. Shortly after the Hyde language merged with language from Senator Exon's CDA, it passed into law. That same day, the ACLU and a coalition of other organizations and individuals (including one of the authors of this book) filed suit in federal court to overturn the CDA. On December 12, the Senate switchboard lit up with an estimated 50,000 telephone calls—proof of the nascent political power of the Internet and the commitment of its users to the freedom of speech.

# CHAPTER

# IX

# A COMPASS FOR CYBERSPACE

In this chapter, we make some substantive recommendations for laws and policies concerning cyberspace. We also describe a way of thinking, a moral, political, and legal framework for the decisions that must now be made by Congress and the courts. In other words, we attempt to provide a compass for cyberspace.

A brilliant judge once admitted, in a series of lectures on the judicial process, that a judge does not find a human law the same way that a scientist discovers a natural law. Instead, Benjamin Cardozo said, the judge "makes" the law, almost as a legislator does, based on such factors as analogy and history.

Cardozo said, "I do not mean that the directive force of history, even when its claims are most assertive, confines the law of the future to uninspired repetition of the law of the present and the past. I mean simply that history, in illuminating the past, illuminates the present, and in illuminating the present, illuminates the future." He quoted an earlier legal commentator, "Today we study the day before yesterday, in order that yesterday may not paralyze today, and today may not paralyze tomorrow." Courts and legislators facing the issues raised by new technologies must proceed as Cardozo recommended, searching history for the right analogy.

Ithiel de Sola Pool's 1983 book, *Technologies of Freedom*, clearly states the danger of applying old laws carelessly to new technologies. "Each new advance in the technology of communication disturbs a status quo. It meets resistance from those whose domain it threatens, but if useful, it begins to be adopted. Initially, because it is new and a full scientific mastery of the options is not yet at hand, the invention comes into use in a rather clumsy form. Technical laymen, such as judges, perceive the new technology in that early, clumsy form, which then becomes their image of its nature, possibilities and use."

As soon as the possibilities of a new technology are dimly understood, Pool said, entrepreneurs, interest groups, and political organizations begin fighting to control it, and courts and government agencies then act as arbiters. Pool wrote, "The arbiters, applying familiar analogies from the past to their lay image of the new technologies, create a partly old, partly new structure of rights and obligations. The telegraph was analogized to railroads, the telephone to the telegraph, and cable television to broadcasting." While sometimes the resulting legal rules are "a tour de force of political creativity," more often they are simply inappropriate to "more habile forms of the technology which gradually emerge."

Twelve years ago, Pool ably forecast the current battle in which Senator Exon, Mike Godwin, and other figures in this book are soldiers. "The onus is on us to determine whether free societies in the twenty-first century will conduct electronic communications under the conditions of freedom established for the domain of print through centuries of struggle, or whether that great achievement will become lost in a confusion about new technologies."

We believe that the following review of history establishes that only one correct analogy exists for the Internet: *it is a constellation of printing presses and bookstores,* and thereby entitled to the full protection of the First Amendment.

Throughout history, each major innovation in communications technology has caused distress and confusion similar to what society is experiencing today about the Internet. The introduction of writing, the printing press, the telegraph, the telephone, the radio, and the television all raised similar issues. Key decisions determining the future of the Net cannot be made without knowledge of the past.

This is not to say that the advocates of Net censorship lack *all* knowledge of the past, or are unable to proceed by analogy. Instead, they are relying on partial knowledge to apply the wrong analogy. Both the CDA and the Hyde amendment attempt to apply language written for broadcast media to the very different world of cyberspace. Public figures like Senator Exon, who may feel pride in what they regard as a battle against forces of darkness, should, however, recognize the similarity of their rhetoric to the critics who saw each of the major waves in communications technology as heralding the end of civilization.

The following examines the lessons to be learned from earlier communications revolutions.

The first revolution was writing. Plato, whose life spanned the fifth and fourth centuries B.C., tells a story in his dialogue *Phaedrus* about a conversation between two Egyptian gods, Theuth, the inventor, and Thamus, ruler of Egypt. Theuth was demonstrating a variety of his inventions to Thamus, in the hope that Thamus would permit their use by the Egyptians. One of Theuth's innovations was writing, which he said would "make the Egyptians wiser and give them better memories."

Thamus replied, "[T]his discovery of yours will create forgetfulness in the learners' souls, because they will not use their memories; they will trust to the external written characters and not remember of themselves. The specific which you have discovered is an aid not to memory, but to reminiscence, and you give your disciples not truth, but only the semblance of truth; they will be hearers of many things and will have learned nothing; they will appear to be omniscient and will generally know nothing; they will be tiresome company, having the show of wisdom without the reality."

Social critic Neil Postman, the gloomiest of commentators on the effects and prospects of new communications technologies, comments that Thamus was correct about writing's damage to memory and the creation of false wisdom. "Thamus's error is in his believing that writing will be a burden to society and nothing but a burden. For all his wisdom, he fails to imagine what writing's benefits might be, which, as we know, have been considerable. We may learn from this that it is a mistake to suppose that any technological innovation has a one-sided effect. Every technology is both a burden and a blessing..."

Despite lip service to the Internet's benefits, Senators who use rhetoric like "a porn shop in a child's bedroom" and who propose laws which would severely restrict on-line discussion, place themselves squarely in Thamus's camp.

The second communication revolution came with the invention of printing. In the fifteenth century, Johannes Gutenberg introduced the printing press to Europe. Printing had already been in use in Asia for some time, in a somewhat different form. An apocryphal story relates that Gutenberg's partner was almost lynched by the copyists of Paris when he attempted to sell printed Bibles there, because "such a store of valuable books could [only] be in one man's possession through the help of the devil himself."

At first, however, the church welcomed printing—as everyone knows, the first book published by Gutenberg was the Bible. Elizabeth Eisenstein, foremost scholar of the printing press's social effects, says, "There is considerable irony about the enthusiastic reception accorded to printing by the church. Heralded on all sides as a 'peaceful art', Gutenberg's invention probably contributed more to destroying Christian concord and inflaming religious warfare than any of the so-called arts of war ever did." In *Notre Dame de Paris*, Victor Hugo describes a scholar examining his first printed book in the shadow of the cathedral and proclaiming, "ceci tuera cela" (this will kill that).

Within a few years, the Catholic church recognized its error. In 1475, the Vatican first asked the University of Cologne to intervene against the printers, publishers, authors, and even the readers of "pernicious" books. In 1486, acting pursuant to a Bull of Pope Innocent VIII, Archbishop Berthold of Mainz appointed two priests and two "learned doctors" to examine all books in the vicinity. In 1496, the Archbishop went one step further; he forbade the publication of any book he had not approved, under penalty of excommunication.

In 1501, Pope Alexander VI issued his Bull Inter Multiplices, establishing preventive censorship throughout Germany. No book could be printed without ecclesiastical authorization. Pope Leo X established a central system of censorship; in Rome, all books had to be approved before publication by the papal vicar or the head of the Holy Office; elsewhere, the task of censorship was carried out by the local bishop or an Inquisitor General. So many confusing edicts were issued against particular books that the Church saw fit to establish the Index Librorum Prohibitorum, a central listing of banned books. Eisenstein says, "Given the existence of profit-seeking printers outside the reach of Rome, Catholic censorship boomeranged in ways that could not be foreseen. The *Index* provided free publicity for the titles listed thereon."

The triumph of Lutheranism as an alternative to Catholic Christianity owed much to the printing press, which was used to produce posters, versions of the Bible, works of proselytism, and even children's books with a Lutheran angle. "Lutheranism was from the beginning the child of the printed book." The Catholic battle against printing took on new vigor as a way of combating the principles of Martin Luther; the French, enthusiastically led by their King, became the foremost enemies of books. In 1531, the High Court of Parliament sent out two members to inspect all books on sale and seize any containing "false doctrine." Matters came to a head in 1534 and 1535 with the "affaire des placards" (Lutheran posters anonymously placed around town). French authorities burned print- ers and booksellers at the stake, throwing their books into the flames for good measure. In January 1535, Francois I forbade any new books to be published in France, upon pain of hanging—an edict he was soon persuaded to revoke.

Of course, censorship—even killing—was completely ineffective in staunching the distribution of books, which were printed out of the country, then smuggled in as avidly as drugs are today. Historians Lucien Febvre and Henri Jean Martin say that even at its height, the campaign against "false doctrine" was conducted hypocritically. They said, "Among the real victims of the repression there cannot be found a single name belonging to one of the great printing dynasties that dominated the trade...above all, the big publishers had too many connections and more than enough sources of protection."

In the 1540s, Rabelais's *Gargantua* and *Pantagruel* were on the list of banned books, and at one point, Rabelais had to flee to Metz to avoid prosecution. Domestic publishers of authors such as Rabelais took to publishing anonymously, without the publisher's name and address on the title page. "Nothing," say Febvre and Martin, "could impede the invasion of France by forbidden literature."

In 1563, Charles IX required all books to be licensed in advance of publication and appointed Sorbonne theologians as his censors. "The number of books liable to incur official displeasure was so great that even the most law-abiding booksellers could always expect to be prosecuted." Attempts were made to limit the number of publishers and to concentrate them all in Paris, where they could be more close- ly watched. By the following century, these measures succeeded in creating a thriving underground book publishing business outside of France's borders, which smuggled its products, a few copies at a time, to an avid readership. "It is evident that official censorship as it was then understood had proved to be ineffectual."

Other countries, with other forms of government, also recognized the dangers of printing. In England in 1643, Parliament issued an order requiring the licensing of printing presses and of all books before publication, which provided that the Stationers' Company (a government monopoly) was "authorized to search for unlicensed presses, and to break them up; to search for unlicensed books, etc., and confiscate them; and to 'apprehend all authors, printers and others' concerned in publishing unlicensed books." John Milton issued his famous address to Parliament, *The Aeropagitica*, in which he said that "this Order avails nothing to the suppressing of scandalous, seditious, and libelous books, which were mainly intended to be suppressed...it will be primely to the discouragement of all learning, and the stop of truth, not only by disexercising and blunting our abilities in what we know already, but by hindering and cropping the discovery that might be yet further made both in religious and civil wisdom."

In Milton's estimation, it was as evil to kill a book as a man. Milton said, "Who kills a man kills a reasonable creature, God's image; but he who destroys a good book, kills reason itself, kills the image of God, as it were in the eye. Many a man lives a burden to the earth; but a good book is the precious life-blood of a master spirit, embalmed and treasured up on purpose to a life beyond life. 'Tis true, no age can restore a life, whereof perhaps there is no great loss; and revolutions of ages do not oft recover the loss of a rejected truth, for the want of which whole nations fare the worse."

Rather than censoring works of bad doctrine, he said, "Read any books whatever come to thy hands, for thou art sufficient both to judge aright, and to examine each matter. ... Prove all things, hold fast that which is good. ... Bad meats will scarce breed good nourishment in the healthiest concoction; but herein the difference is of bad books, that they to a discreet and judicious reader serve in many respects to discover, to confute, to forewarn, and to illustrate."

Scholars of the social effects of the printing press are careful to acknowledge that some of its effects were negative—just as some effects of the Internet are. Print could be used as a way to avoid dialog and interaction. Cardinal Richelieu substituted a government-controlled gazette for a volatile assembly as a medium for announcing policy. More seriously still, print was a way of flooding the world with more bad ideas faster—the precursor of the criticism leveled at the Net by Senators Exon, Feinstein, et al. "Thus, when 'technology went to press', so too did a vast backlog of occult practices and formulas, and few readers were able to discriminate between the two. ... What later came to be described as a 'natural history of nonsense' was greatly enriched." And, of course, a marketplace for bawdy, lascivious literature—what we call pornography today—was created by the printing press.

In the American colonies, the printing press was a potent tool of revolution. *Common Sense*, a polemic published anonymously by the then-unknown Thomas Paine, captured the public imagination with its succinct statement that the colonists could only pursue their own destiny by separating from England—and sold half a million copies in its first year as a result. Historian Daniel J. Boorstin has pointed out that the United States Constitution is "probably the first printed constitution and surely the oldest printed constitution by which a nation still lives." The Constitutional Convention disseminated a printed draft throughout the Colonies so that the people could review it and comment; within a month, 75 of the existing 80 newspapers in America had reprinted the Constitution for their readership. "The multiplying copies of the printed proposed Constitution were symbols of an opening society in which eventually all would have the right to know and judge the public business."

The Founders drafted the First Amendment with the printing press in mind; its dictates, as interpreted by the Supreme Court, against taxation and licensing of presses, prior restraints on publication, and other forms of censorship, represent the American commitment not to repeat the errors of the Vatican, France, and England. Ithiel de Sola Pool lamented that the Supreme Court, which excels at recognizing First Amendment protection of the media "used for discussion of public affairs in the seventeenth and eighteenth centuries", has a far more ambiguous record of vigilance when it comes to other forms of communication. First Amendment scholar Zachariah Chafee, writing in 1942, commented that "Newspapers, books, pamphlets and large meetings were for many centuries the only means of public discourse, so that the need for their protection has long been generally realized; on the other hand, when additional methods for spreading facts and ideas were introduced or greatly improved by modern invention, writers and judges had not got into the habit of being solicitous about guarding their freedom. And so we have tolerated censorship of the mails, the importation of foreign books, the stage, the motion picture, and the radio."

Writing 182 years later in *Tornillo v. Miami Herald*, the Supreme Court described the social climate in 1791, when the First Amendment was ratified. "The press was broadly representative of the people it was serving...[it] collectively presented a broad range of opinions to readers. Entry into publishing was inexpensive; pamphlets and books provided meaningful alternatives to the organized press for the expression of unpopular ideas and often treated events and expressed views not covered by conventional newspapers. A true marketplace of ideas existed in which there was relatively easy access to the channels of communication." Thomas Jefferson commented, "The basis of our government being the opinion of the people, the very first object should be to keep that right; and were it left to me to decide whether we should have a government without newspapers, or newspapers without government, I should not hesitate a moment to prefer the latter."

In 1831, Alexis de Tocqueville made his visit to the United States. Immediately upon arriving, he saw a newspaper which called President Jackson a "heartless despot." In *Democracy in America*, he commented, "The sovereignty of the people and the freedom of the press entirely support each other: by contrast, censorship and universal suffrage contradict each other and cannot co-exist for very long in the political institutions of a nation." Complaining of its violent rhetoric and gutter instincts, he commented that the American press, like that of France, was "a strange combination of good and evil; without the press, liberty could not exist; with the press, order can hardly be maintained." He concluded that "the best way to counteract the influence of newspapers, is to have as many as possible." In his recent book *To Renew America*, Newt Gingrich commented that "While the Industrial Revolution herded people into gigantic social institutions—big corporations, big unions, big government—the Information Revolution is breaking up these giants and leading us back to something that is—strangely enough—much more like de Tocqueville's 1830s America."

A Senate report of 1832 said, "A concentration of political power in the hands of a few individuals is, of all things, most to be dreaded in a republic...nothing will tend so effectually to prevent it as the sustaining of the newspaper establishments in the different towns and villages throughout the country." The perceived villain was not government, but the powerful, anti-democratic big-city press. In the 1850s, Congress intervened to protect rural newspapers from competition from their big city brethren, by granting the former inexpensive or even free postage. "The poisoned sentiments of the city, concentrated in their papers, with all the aggravation of a moral and political cesspool, will invade the simple, pure, conservative atmosphere of the country," said a Southern congressman in 1850, expressing fear that the city press would ultimately destroy "that purity of sentiment and of purpose, which is the only true conservatism." His concerns were echoed later both in the Supreme Court's creation of the "community standards" rule in *Miller v. California* and in present day hysteria about bad speech on the Net.

In 1859, philosopher John Stuart Mill published *On Liberty*, in which he argued that "the only purpose for which power can be rightfully exercised over any member of a civilized community, against his will, is to prevent harm to others. His own good, either physical or moral, is not a sufficient warrant." In the chapter, *Of the Liberty of Thought and Discussion*, he wrote, "The time, it is to be hoped, is gone by, when any defense would be necessary of the 'liberty of the press' as one of the securities against corrupt or tyrannical government. ... The power [to censor] is illegitimate. The best government has no more title to it than the worst. It is as noxious, or more noxious, when exerted in accordance with public opinion, than when in opposition to it. If all mankind minus one were of one opinion, and only one person were of the contrary opinion, mankind would be no more justified in silencing that one person, than he, if he had the power, would be justified in silencing mankind. ... [T]he peculiar evil of silencing the expression of an opinion is, that it is robbing the human race; posterity as well as the existing generation; those who dissent from the opinion, still more than those who hold it. If the opinion is right, they are deprived of the opportunity of exchanging error for truth: if wrong, they lose, what is almost as great a benefit, the clearer perception and livelier impression of truth, produced by its collision with error."

This is a truth that every generation must learn anew, and of course, there are some who will never learn it. The attempt to ban books because of the ideas they express, which began in this country with Anthony Comstock and the New York Society for the Suppression of Vice in the 1870s, continued well into this century and has not entirely ceased today. Comstock succeeded in banning works of Balzac and Tolstoy in the United States, and hounded sex educator Ida Craddock, author of *The Wedding Night* and *Advice to a Bridegroom*, until she committed suicide. An enthusiastic collaborator of Comstock's was the U.S. Postal Service, which over the years sought to ban works by Ernest Hemingway, John O'Hara, Erskine Caldwell, J.D. Salinger, Alberto Moravia, John Steinbeck, Richard Wright, Norman Mailer, Sigmund Freud, Margaret Mead, and Simone de Beauvoir from the mails. Birth control advocate Margaret

Sanger was indicted for her publications, and Radclyffe Hall's novel about lesbianism, *The Well of Loneliness*, was banned based on the following shocking sentence: "And that night, they were not divided." The works of James Joyce, Henry Miller, and Vladimir Nabokov have all faced court battles in this country.

The list of books that have been prohibited in the United States is too long to give. Though Supreme Court cases in recent years have given the impression that works consisting of text alone cannot be found obscene or otherwise outlawed, there is no shortage of cases at the local level where school boards ban books as diverse as *Huckleberry Finn* and *Heather Has Two Mommies* for the ideas they contain. This treatment of books underlines an unfortunate truth that, though our politicians pay lip service to it, the freedom of speech is not, and has probably never been, very popular in this country. Most people are happy to see the government intervene to end some form of speech they do not like. The drafting of the First Amendment, then, was an example of the Founders giving the American people something they desperately needed but did not know they needed—the kind of leadership that is lacking in all walks of American public life today.

The desire for diversity of the press has not been realized. Newspapers became big business; many merged or vanished, and most of those that remain are owned by conglomerates. Ironically, though broadcast media are more tightly regulated on a "scarcity" rationale, there are many more radio and television stations in this country than newspapers. The *Tornillo* case raised the argument that because newspapers hold monopoly power, they should be made subject to the FCCs Fairness Doctrine. The Fairness Doctrine is the rule that mandates that a candidate who is criticized on radio or TV, or an individual who is personally attacked, must be given air time to reply. Tornillo, who was attacked in the columns of the *Miami Herald* newspaper, submitted a reply which the paper refused to publish. He sued, asking the court to order the *Herald* to print it. The Supreme Court refused to bite into that particular apple, leaving newspapers entirely free to determine their own content.

When we talk about a "free press" in this country, however, we tend to forget that the phrase means only "free of government interference," not necessarily that the press is willing to present every idea or report every incident that may interest us or that its reporters may wish to pursue. As the *Tornillo* court acknowledged, today we have many fewer newspapers than we did 50 years ago, and they tend to be owned by a few families and companies: Newhouse, Gannett, Hearst, and Murdoch. Some of them belong to conglomerates involved in other businesses, which the newspapers may sometimes have occasion to cover; Rupert Murdoch, in addition to the *New York Post*, owns Fox Broadcasting and Harper Collins. NBC, which is owned by GE, has failed to cover stories related to its parent. Like any other large business, the media conglomerates have interlocking ownership and share directors with numerous companies in other fields; in addition, owners and publishers alike may socialize with the powerful people on whom they are supposed to report. In November 1995, the *New York Daily News* ran a headline, accompanied by satirical cover art, calling Speaker Gingrich a "cry baby" for his reaction to being seated in the back of a Presidential plane headed to Israel for Prime Minister Rabin's funeral. The newspaper's publisher, meanwhile, was seated up front, playing cards with President Clinton. In their book, *Manufacturing Consent*, Edward Herman and Noam Chomsky argue that political consent in American democracy is created by a propaganda process carried on by the mass media. "They serve to mobilize support for the special interests that dominate the state and private activity, and...their choices, emphases and omissions can often be understood best, and sometimes with striking clarity and insight, by analyzing them in [propaganda] terms." They studied the frequency with which United States media covered certain international stories and the inconsistent vocabulary used to describe the human rights records of American allies and enemies. "The observable pattern of indignant campaigns and suppressions, of shading and emphasis, and of selection of context, premises, and general agenda, is highly functional for established power and responsive to the needs of the government and major power groups." The media focuses on the victims of our enemies and overlooks the repression, sometimes far worse, practiced by our allies. "It would have been very difficult for the Guatemalan government to murder tens of thousands over the past decade if the United States press had provided the kind of coverage they gave to the difficulties of Andrei Sakharov or the murder of Jerzy Popieluszko in Poland." No conspiracy theory is necessary to explain this; there are a host of political and psychological factors, not least of which is "elemental patriotism, the overwhelming wish to think well of ourselves, our institutions and our leaders. ... If one chooses to denounce Quaddafi...no credible evidence is required. ... But a critical analysis of American institutions...must meet far higher standards; in fact, standards are often imposed that can barely be met in the natural sciences." Barbara Ehrenreich says, "Show me a mainstream journalist today and I will show you a broken creature living in mortal fear of being downsized or dismissed for offending some advertiser, some executive or some company that happens to belong to this poor journalist's ruling media conglomerate." Former FCC Commissioner Nicholas Johnson comments, "A reporter who first comes up with an investigative story idea, writes it up and submits it to the editor and is told the story is not going to run. He wonders why, but the next time, he is cautious enough to check with the editor first. He is told by the editor that it would be better not to write that story. The third time he thinks of an investigative story idea but doesn't bother the editor with it because he knows it's silly. The fourth time he doesn't even think of the idea anymore."

In Fall 1995, the U.S. Postal Service announced new second class mailing rates that would reward huge, wealthy media conglomerates like Time Warner, which can afford to pre-sort its mail and truck it to the local post office, and would penalize small labor-of-love journals like *The Nation* by raising mailing rates 17%. The post office broke with a 200-year tradition of supporting the small press with inexpensive tariffs.

Neil Postman believes that the printing press was the last communications innovation that promoted the organization of thought in a coherent manner. In his essay *Remembering the Golden Age*, Postman amusingly fielded the criticism, leveled by one of his students, that he would have opposed printing as well, if he had lived in the fifteenth century. He said, "Assuming I had the brains to see what was happening in the year 1500, I would certainly have warned the Holy See that the printing press would place the word of God on every Christian's table, and, as a consequence, the authority of the Church's hierarchy would be put in jeopardy. ... I would have warned the Pope that armed with a printing press, Martin Luther was more than a malcontent priest. ... I might also have warned the local princes that their days were numbered, that printing would give form to a new idea of nationhood. ... I would have told [the alchemists] to go into another line of work, that printing would give great impetus to inductive science and that alchemy would not stand against the glare of publicly shared scientific knowledge." He concludes that "the changes brought about by new media benefit some, harm others and to a few don't make much of a difference." Elsewhere, he has said, "Forms of communication are neither good nor bad in themselves. They become good or bad depending on their relationship to other symbols and on the functions they are made to serve within a social order."

The third revolution in communications was the telegraph. Not everyone knows that before the electric telegraph was invented, France led the world in developing an extensive system of optical telegraphy that consisted of lines of towers which could pass a message via semaphores or moving panels. Innovations still in use today, such as the concepts of bits and of error checking protocols, were developed by the early innovators in this field.

France's telegraph system began when the Chappe brothers approached the revolutionary government in 1792 to request funding for their idea. A demonstration version of the telegraph, using moving panels, was destroyed by an angry crowd which was afraid it was "a subversive instrument, meant to send signals to the enemy." Claude Chappe, after fighting an unending battle for government money to complete his line of towers, killed himself at age 42, "to escape life's burdens that crush me." His brothers carried on the work. The invention was used to commit the world's first "wire fraud" when swindlers tricked the Paris financial markets by bribing an operator to transmit false information. Napoleon's first act, after seizing power in Paris, was to send a telegraph message to the rest of the world announcing that Paris was calm and its citizens happy.

Decades later, Ignace Chappe, extremely discontented by the limited range across which optical telegraphs had been built and the trivial information they were typically used to carry, wrote, "The use of novel methods that modify established habits, often hurts the interests of those who profit the most from the older methods. Few people, with the exception of the inventors, are truly interested in helping projects succeed while the ultimate impact is still uncertain. ... Those in power will normally make no effort to support a new invention, unless it can help them to augment their power; and even when they do support it, their efforts are usually insufficient to allow the new ideas to be fully exploited."

Private funding was not an option. Because of a fear of "a proliferation of communications networks, that would be hard to control in the long run, the French government [had] moved to ban the establishment of private telegraphs."

Abraham Edelcrantz was the father of Swedish optical telegraphy. He never met the Chappes, but spent time in Paris and was aware of their work. His political experience was similar to Ignace's and led him to write, "It often happens, with regard to new inventions, that one part of the general public finds them useless and another part considers them to be impossible. When it becomes clear that the possibility and the usefulness can no longer be denied, most agree that the whole thing was fairly easy to discover and that they knew about it all along."

Electrical telegraphy overtook its optical ancestor in the early decades of the nineteenth century, despite one British expert who opined that optical telegraphy was superior because it did not rely on wires that could be cut. Samuel Morse first asked the United States Congress for funding in 1837, and was rejected. It was not until May of 1844 that Morse demonstrated a telegraph connection between Washington and Baltimore, asking his famous question, "What hath God wrought?" One day later, a Baltimore paper, the *Patriot*, used the telegraph to print a story about a Congressional action which had occurred the same day. "This is indeed the annihilation of space," commented the paper. Morse predicted that telegraphy would make "one community of the whole country."

While optical telegraphy took time because a message had to be decoded and re-transmitted by the operator in each tower, electrical telegraphy was instantaneous. Clay Shirky, who calls the telegraph system the first precursor of the Internet, tells the story of its first use for "real-time" communications, when someone thought to wire ahead to see if a train had already reached the next station.

The courts never really saw the telegraph as raising First Amendment issues; it was too costly per word transmitted, too technical, and difficult to decode to be used to transmit literature or political material. Its main impact on the law was in raising common carriage issues such as what communications, if any, could telegraph operators refuse to transmit. Like the phone companies after deregulation, Western Union and other telegraph companies experimented with providing content such as wire services that transmitted news to papers which could not afford their own distant correspondents. To protect this business, telegraph companies sometimes refused to allow newspaper reporters to cable their stories to the papers that employed them. A *Times of London* managing editor commented that wire services provided no substitute for the individual reportage of "a gentleman specially retained to serve a particular journal...we would much rather remain in ignorance of information conveyed in such a manner."

In Britain, the government solved the wire service newspaper shootout by nationalizing the telegraph system, then forbidding it from reporting the news. In the United States, Congress chose a different solution, telegraphy remained in the hands of private enterprise, but was designated a "common carrier" like the railroad. Common carriers, in return for a monopoly on a type of commerce or on a particular geographical area or route, do not have the right to refuse carriage. Therefore, telegraph companies could no longer refuse to transmit anyone's messages. Pool would have us apply this lesson of telegraphy to today's electronic communications. "The government and common carriers should be blind to circuit use...control of the conduit may not become a means for controlling content. What customers transmit on the carrier is no affair of the carrier."

Someone has digitized and posted the first three issues of *Scientific American* on the World Wide Web. Founded in 1845, the magazine represents the enduring American love affair with technology. Each of the issues carries excited news of the "magnetic telegraph." Issue number one, May 1845, also contains the following item about the railroad, itself a means of communication: *"THE POPE ON RAILWAYS. The Frankfort Journal* makes the following... announcement, under date 17th July, from Rome- 'The Pope has declared once for all that he will not allow railways to be established in the Pontical States, for it would be dangerous to allow them in a country where there exists such political agitation'."

Scholars of communications technology agree that the telegraph brought about a transformation of the social landscape almost as important as that caused by the printing press. Media philosopher Marshall McLuhan called the telegraph "the social hormone," meaning that it transformed society into a single nervous system via the instantaneous transmission of information. "The simultaneity of electric communication, also characteristic of our nervous system, makes each of us present and accessible to every other person in the world." But he also pointed out the impact of telegraphy on the way information was presented, drawing a distinction between "literary" and "telegraphic" newspapers: "It is the difference between columns representing points of view, and a mosaic of unrelated scraps in a field unified by a dateline."

Neil Postman believes telegraphy killed something which had only been born with the printing press. "The telegraph made a three-pronged attack on typography's definition of discourse, introducing on a large scale irrelevance, impotence and incoherence. These demons of discourse were aroused by the fact that telegraphy gave a form of legitimacy to the idea of context-free information; that is, to the idea that the value of information need not be tied to any function it might serve in social and political decision-making and action, but may attach merely to its novelty, interest and curiosity." He quotes Henry David Thoreau's famous comment in *Walden*: "We are in great haste to construct a magnetic telegraph from Maine to Texas; but Maine and Texas, it may be, have nothing important to communicate."

Pool, much more of an optimist, draws the parallel between telegraphy and its most modern outgrowth, electronic mail. "Electronic messages cease to be simply curt aids to transactions; they come to be used for news, education, ideas, and discussion. Among scientists and hobbyists"—remember, he was writing in 1983— "electronic mail networks already exist on which the active discussion of ideas takes place.

"If ten or twenty years hence, homes and offices generally have terminals with messages shown on them at costs less than that of a postage stamp, will the courts still treat telegraphy not as a means of expression but as a transport business subject to regulation as commerce? Or will the courts then recognize electronic expression as an activity about which Congress may make no law?"

Pool was prescient; those terminals he foresaw are the personal computers of today. A few years after he wrote, Congress passed the Electronic Communications Privacy Act, protecting electronic mail from Fourth Amendment searches and seizures; but today's battles over legislation such as the CDA illustrate that Congress has not yet taken the next step and confirmed the First Amendment protection of electronic communications.

In 1876, telegraphy giant Western Union declined to purchase Bell's telephone patent for $100,000, regarding the new invention as insignificant. In 1910, the telephone company bought Western Union for $30 million.

The invention of the telephone signaled the fourth communications revolution. "One system with a common policy, common purpose and common action; comprehensive, universal, interdependent, intercommunicating like the highway system of the country, extending from every door to every other door, affording electrical communication of every kind, from every one at every place to every one at every other place." These words, with a simple substitution of "electronic" for "electrical", could be used to describe the Internet today. They were spoken by AT&T president Theodore Vail in 1910 to describe the telephone system.

In the early years of the French phone system, there was uncertainty about the use of women as operators because of the uncertain effect it would have on morals to allow strangers of opposite gender to deal with one another on the phone. Not many people today know that, before radio, attempts were made to use the telephone to broadcast entertainment—Alexander Graham Bell initially thought this would be the main use of his invention. Telephones in Budapest carried music and news bulletins into the home from 1893 until 1918.

When the telephone was first invented, courts, proceeding by analogy, asked the question "whether, at law, the telephone was a new kind of telegraph or something different." This was answered in Britain in the affirmative: the telephone was a telegraph. Accordingly, like the telegraph industry before it, the fledgling telephone industry was nationalized.

The United States Supreme Court, however, at first misapprehended the nature of the new technology, denying it the telegraph's right of way on public lands. It said that the government had an interest in use of the telegraph for its own purposes, but none in the telephone, because "governmental communications to all distant points are almost all, if not all, in writing." After this initial setback, however, American courts generally began applying telegraph and common carrier law to the telephone.

Another novel issue raised by the new technology was whether statements made on the telephone could be introduced in court as evidence of the making of a contract. Courts were at first reluctant to admit testimony as to phone conversations in evidence, on the grounds that it was difficult or impossible to know the identity of the party on the other end. "Eventually, however, the courts adapted to the reality of the vast increase of telephone use in business, and perhaps also to the improved fidelity in telephone reception, by upholding telephoned agreements." In more recent years, courts have struggled with the question of whether a contract could be made via E-mail, and, in fact, whether E-mail could be introduced in evidence as a business record. The result has been, as it was with the telephone, that E-mail is considered a routine form of written communication and receives the same evidentiary treatment as other forms.

McLuhan argues that the telephone brought about the collapse of hierarchical, delegated authority in corporations and government alike, allowing members of different levels of the organization to communicate with each other directly. He quotes Armaments Minister Albert Speer, testifying at Nuremberg: "The telephone, the teleprinter and the wireless made it possible for orders from the highest levels to be given directly to the lowest levels, where, on account of the absolute authority behind them, they were carried out uncritically." McLuhan comments, "One of the most startling consequences of the telephone was its introduction of a 'seamless web' of interlaced patterns in management and decision-making. It is not feasible to exercise delegated authority by telephone. The pyramidal structure of job-division and description and delegated powers cannot withstand the speed of the phone to bypass all hierarchical arrangements, and to involve people in depth." Similarly, E-mail has been described as a great leveler; employees of IBM or Apple who cannot get the big boss on the telephone may still get an E-mail response from him.

The status of the telephone as a common carrier meant that the phone company, like the telegraph company, could not involve itself in the content of the communications carried. However, one exception, dating back to the 1880s, was indecent language. A subscriber's telephone service was canceled because of his foul language and a court held that "If indecent or rude or improper language was permitted, evil and ill-disposed persons would have it in their power to use it as a medium of insult to others, and perchance by some accident, such as the crossing of wires...the same communication might be launched into the midst of some family circle under very mortifying circumstances." Here are the roots of the very dangerous concept that a communication which comes into the house electronically—is "pervasive"—can be dealt with differently than one in a newspaper or book.

The language used by Senator Exon in the CDA is taken from the Communications Act of 1934, which forbids telephoning "any comment, request, suggestion or proposal which is obscene, lewd, lascivious, filthy or indecent."

After the telephone, the next significant development was the advent of broadcasting. At the dawn of the 20th century, radio broadcasting was an amateur art. Early broadcasters talked and played music, waiting for listeners to contact them and verify the distance at which their signals could be heard. In 1920, an amateur broadcast interfered with communications with an airplane lost in fog over the

English Channel, and the British post office, already responsible for telephones, was given jurisdiction over radio as well.

In a one year period, from 1923-24, the number of radio stations in the U.S. increased from 500 to 1105, reaching two million people. The Americans, as they had with telephony, avoided the European bent for nationalization, despite the avid campaigning of the Navy to take over all radio transmitters. In 1924, Admiral W.L. Rodgers asked, "How can radio be better utilized so as to give news of public interest without such exclusive reliance on the press?" Even some voices on the left thought America would be better served if the government took over broadcasting.

In 1925, the entire available radio spectrum was crowded with stations, and Secretary of Commerce Herbert Hoover warned that "[c]onditions absolutely preclude increasing the number of stations in congested areas." It was apparent to everybody that the government would have to involve itself in determining who could have a broadcasting license. Since 1912, the Secretary of Commerce had assigned frequencies to broadcasters to make sure they did not impinge upon each others' signal, but had no authority to refuse a broadcasting license for any reason. Nevertheless, the Secretary was suspected of giving the best frequencies to applicants he favored, while others were relegated to inferior channels.

In 1926, a court held that the Commerce Department did not have legal authority to punish the Zenith Radio Corporation for using an unauthorized frequency. Anarchy resulted as stations began staking their claim to desirable frequencies and interfering with one another. Even in this undesirable situation, there were voices opposing greater government involvement, including Hoover himself, who said that government control of radio would be "in principle the same as though the entire press of the country was so controlled." Industry figures at their annual convention similarly requested that "the doctrine of free speech be held inviolate."

The following year, Congress passed the Radio Act, creating a Federal Radio Commission, predecessor of the FCC. This law established the "Fairness Doctrine," requiring equal treatment by radio stations of rival political candidates. It also stated that nothing in the law gave the Radio Commission "the power of censorship" over radio communications. Immediately contradicting itself, the law stated that "No person...shall utter any obscene, indecent or profane language by means of radio communication."

Today, radio regularly uses the "seven second delay," with a switch allowing an engineer to cut off a speaker who utters inappropriate language. The first such switch was put into use in a Newark station in 1921, which used it to cut off discussion of birth control, prostitution and cigarettes. Radio was already perceived as a pervasive medium, one that posed a potential threat to the purity of children. Hoover, contradicting his own words about freedom of speech, said, "We can protect the home by preventing the entry of printed matter destructive to its ideals but we must doubleguard the radio." President Coolidge added that "there is an opportunity for greater license even than in the use of print, for...radio reaches directly to our children." The industry's third national conference, while opposing censorship, agreed that radio must be "clean and fit for home consumption at all times."

An industry under the threat of government regulation learns to regulate itself. When Secretary of State Charles Evans Hughes heard columnist H.V. Kaltenborn criticize him on the air, he called a contact at AT&T, which owned the station. Kaltenborn's contract was canceled. Kaltenborn later wrote, "Unknown to the general public, there is a thoroughgoing radio censorship already in effect." The ACLU's Morris Ernst summed up the problem succinctly when he said, "So long as the Department can determine which individuals shall be endowed with larynxes it does not need additional power to determine what shall be said." The ability to license was itself, inevitably, a form of censorship. The commission refused to license applicants who had broadcast personal attacks or disputes, a form of discourse well-protected under the First Amendment where the press is concerned. "Listeners," the commission said grandiosely, "have no protection unless it is given to them by this commission, for they are powerless to prevent the ether waves carrying the unwelcome messages from entering the walls of their homes."

In the early 1930s, the Radio Commission denied license renewals to a broadcaster who used the station to sell medical services; another who failed to maintain "a standard of refinement befitting our day and generation"; and a third who criticized government economic policy, the Catholic religion, and the integrity of local officials on the air. The courts consistently supported the commission; in the third case mentioned, an appeals court said that if a broadcast license holder could use the airwaves to "offend the religious sensibilities of thousands, inspire political distrust and civic discord... then this great science, instead of a boon, will become a scourge." Of course, as de Tocqueville observed, this kind of vigorous discourse had long been the specialty of newspapers and was the very speech the First Amendment had been drafted to protect. Scarcity and pervasiveness were being used as excuses not to extend the First Amendment to the airwaves.

Self-censorship continued to prevail as one station informed the American Legion that certain speeches were unacceptable because they tended to "disturb public confidence" in the President, while CBS Radio announced it would not broadcast anything "critical of any policy of the Administration."

In 1934, Congress passed a Communications Act transforming the Radio Commission into the FCC and expanding its powers to cover the telephone and telegraph as well. As mentioned above, the act contained a ban on the transmission of "obscene" or "indecent" language which would become one of the primary means for content regulation of telephone, radio and television. Seven years later, in *NBC v. United States,* ruling on the first free speech challenge to programming regulations imposed under the 1934 Act, the Supreme Court said, "Freedom of utterance is abridged to many who wish to use the limited facilities of radio. Unlike other modes of expression, radio inherently is not available to all. That is its unique characteristic, and that is why, unlike other modes of expression, it is subject to governmental regulation."

This approach has not changed, as the Supreme Court confirmed in a significant 1969 case, *Red Lion Broadcasting Co. v. FCC.* Journalist Fred Cook asked for time to reply to an attack on him by fundamentalist preacher Billy Hargis during the 1964 Goldwater campaign. The FCC sustained Cook's rights under the Fairness Doctrine. The Court said that "broadcast frequencies constituted a scarce resource whose use could be regulated and rationalized only by the government...where there are substantially more individuals who want to broadcast than there are frequencies to allocate, it is idle to posit an unbridgeable First Amendment right to broadcast comparable to the right of every individual to speak, write or publish."

Over the years, the FCC has involved itself—or been dragged into—Fairness Doctrine issues as diverse as cigarette and gasoline ads, opposition to the Vietnam War, violence, and sex. Thus, because of the excuses of scarcity and pervasiveness, the FCC is constantly being asked to intervene in the contents of broadcasts, and sometimes accedes to those requests. In the next section, we will study the most notorious area of intervention—the FCC's role in ensuring that our communications remain "decent."

Many experts agree that the scarcity excuse isn't true any more. Cable has ended any scarcity of the broadcast spectrum by offering an alternative to broadcasting. The number of channels available is limited only by the technology employed by the cable company. Due to improved technology, even scarcity of the radio spectrum is far less of an issue than it was in the 1920s, when much more of the spectrum was devoted to broadcasting than today. Such factors as introduction of the FM band, transmitting equipment which uses a smaller separation between signals, and technology which utilizes previously unusable frequencies, have seriously relieved scarcity. The FCC acknowledged this in 1987 when it ruled that, in light of the decline of scarcity, it now considered the Fairness Doctrine unconstitutional.

Marshall McLuhan called radio "the tribal drum." "Even more than telephone or telegraph, radio is that extension of the central nervous system that is matched only by human speech itself." Radio is a hot medium, stirring more immediate emotion than cool television, promoting the growth of emotional dictators like Hitler. It simultaneously shrinks the world and promotes division among individuals. "Radio provides a speed-up of information that also causes acceleration in other media. It certainly contracts the world to village size, and creates insatiable village tastes for gossip, rumor and personal malice."

Neil Postman agreed that radio has failed to become a medium for rational discourse. "Radio, of course, is the least likely medium to join into the descent into a Huxleyan world of technological narcotics. It is, after all, particularly well-suited to the transmission of rational, complex language. Nonetheless, and even if we disregard radio's captivation by the music industry, we appear to be left with the chilling fact that such language as radio allows us to hear is increasingly primitive, fragmented, and largely aimed at provoking visceral response."

Pool regards radio as a waste of a major opportunity to promote free speech, and blames the assumption that "the government has a positive role to play as licensor and regulator. The optimistic notion that government is to play that role on behalf of citizen freedom rather than against it is not persuasive to those who are skeptical about the power of good will in political processes to guarantee good results."

Indecent speech is treated more leniently by the law than obscene speech. It may be reasonably regulated when attempted over television, radio, or, under certain circumstances, the telephone. It may not be entirely forbidden on any of these media.

The most famous indecency case, *FCC v. Pacifica Foundation*, resulted from a mid-afternoon broadcast by Pacifica Radio of George Carlin's monologue about the seven dirty words "you definitely couldn't say on the air, ever." Carlin had been taped in a performance before a live audience—a venue which, despite the persecution of comedian Lenny Bruce 15 years before, now entitled him to absolute First Amendment protection. The question was not whether Carlin could perform his monologue, but whether Pacifica had the right to put it on the air in mid-afternoon, as part of a serious presentation about broadcast censorship.

The FCC fined Pacifica, citing four justifications in its order: (1.) Children are at home alone and have access to the radio; (2.) Privacy of the home is entitled to extra deference; (3.) Adults not consenting to hear indecent speech may tune in unsuspectingly (in fact, a man who had unwittingly tuned in the broadcast while driving home with his son filed the initial complaint with the FCC); and (4.) Broadcast scarcity. The FCC, in other words, based its decision on three pervasiveness arguments and one scarcity argument.

The Supreme Court upheld the FCC's decision, stating that "a requirement that indecent language be avoided will have its primary effect on the form, rather than the content, of serious communication. There are few, if any, thoughts that cannot be expressed by the use of less offensive language." This solution was possible, of course, only because the FCC's definition of indecency was limited to use of the seven dirty words which Carlin used in his routine. Thus, the Supreme Court felt that the regulations were reasonable, because broadcasters could choose to express the same thoughts, using different words. As we will see, the FCC, precisely because of the choice of other words by broadcasters, would soon broaden its definition of indecency to reach ideas rather than words.

"Our society," said the Court sententiously, "has a tradition of performing certain bodily functions in private, and of severely limiting the public exposure or disclosure of such matters. Verbal or physical acts exposing those intimacies are offensive irrespective of any message that may accompany the exposure." The last nine words of this sentence—"offensive irrespective of any message that may accompany the exposure"—establish that, unlike obscenity, indecent speech is not saved from regulation by having scientific, literary, artistic, or political value. Thus, we have an inherent contradiction: indecent speech at once has *greater First Amendment protection and can be regulated in fewer circumstances, but, when it is regulated, cannot be saved by any inherent value.*

On the other side of the ledger, the Court reaffirmed that indecent language could not be banned from the air, only regulated. It specifically noted that the broadcast was improper in the middle of the day, when children were likely to be listening, but might be permissible at night. In upholding the FCC's action, the Court referred to the "uniquely pervasive presence" of broadcasting. Ithiel de Sola Pool called the Supreme Court's endorsement of the pervasiveness argument "a ticking time bomb. ... This aberrant approach could be used to justify quite radical censorship."

For the next nine years, the FCC continued to ban the seven words during the day, permitting their broadcast after ten at night. Then, in 1987, the agency became aware that certain broadcasters, including Howard Stern, were using innuendo and double entendre to communicate explicit sexual concepts, while avoiding the seven words. The FCC announced a new definition of indecency: "language or material that depicts or describes, in terms patently offensive as measured by contemporary community standards for the broadcast medium, sexual or excretory activities or organs."

Sound familiar? It is, of course, the language that was later used in the Hyde amendment to the Telecommunications Reform Act, just as the CDA's language is borrowed from the Communications Act of 1934. It has two significant effects before you even consider its potential impact on the Internet. First, like the *Pacifica* standard, it creates no exception for speech which has significant scientific, literary, artistic, or political value. However, the safeguard recognized by the Supreme Court in *Pacifica* no longer applies. There, the Court had observed that ideas could still be expressed using other words, because the FCC policy the Court was reviewing banned only certain words, not ideas. Now the F.C.C. had revised its regulations to ban ideas, not words. If an idea could only be communicated by describing sexual or excretory acts or functions, it no longer had any place on the air.

If this doesn't seem like a problem, walk into your local bookstore and look at the shelves packed with books. Now, imagine that every book which depicts or describes sexual or excretory acts or functions, disappears from the shelves. How many books are left? Not only have all the bestsellers and trash fiction vanished, but serious works about AIDS, rape, family violence, sexual fulfillment, and other topics, have also disappeared. Books on how to toilet train your child are gone. Rabelais and many other classic and modern works of fiction are gone. Even the Bible is gone!

Second, although these FCC regulations apply to the national broadcast community, they are in fact always locally tested by jurors in a particular geography—a subjective determination, based on a vague standard. Applying community standards to much more common indecent language means that real nightmares are possible, like the truck driver who was prosecuted in a Southern state for an "Eat Shit" bumper sticker. The only solution, of course, is for radio and television to become safe and bland.

In the *Pacifica* case, the Supreme Court had held that indecent speech, though it could not be banned, could be "channeled." This expression has a different meaning for each communications medium to which it has been applied. Its meaning for the Internet has not yet been established. For broadcast media, channeling indecent speech meant forcing it to the late hours of the night—after 10:00 p.m., as the FCC mandated. Then, in 1988, Congress ordered the agency to institute a 24-hour ban on indecent speech. The FCC obediently found arguments to justify the ban. It said that large numbers of minors listen to or watch broadcast media well into the night and it also suggested that since indecent speech was easily available on cable and videotapes, there was no significant Constitutional harm in banning it from broadcast media. The Circuit Court of Appeals for the District of Columbia, which hears appeals from FCC orders, invalidated the ban as unconstitutional, reaffirming that indecent speech could be channeled, but not prohibited. The FCC then ordered privately owned broadcast stations to show indecent material only after midnight, but allowed public stations—which often cease broadcasting at midnight—to start earlier, at 10 p.m.

In *Action for Children's Television v. FCC*, the court threw out the after midnight ban as unconstitutional and applied the after 10 p.m. rule to all stations. Chief Judge Harry Edwards, dissenting from the judgment, pointed out the inconsistency between Congress's treatment of broadcast and cable and suggested that scarcity no longer justified treating broadcast differently from print media. In addition to alluding to technological developments that have opened up new regions of the broadcast spectrum, he pointed out that there are many more broadcast stations surviving today than newspapers. He quoted a 1987 FCC ruling acknowledging as much: "The scarcity rationale developed in the *Red Lion* decision and successor cases no longer justifies a different standard of First Amendment review for the electronic press...the constitutional principles applicable to the printed press should be equally applicable to the electronic press." Edwards regarded congressional and FCC regulation of broadcast media as an unwarranted interference in a parent's right to decided what a child may read, hear, or see. Edwards wrote, "Simply put, among the myriad of American parents, not every parent will decide, as the Commission has, that the best way to raise its child is to have the Government shield children under 18 from indecent broadcasts. Furthermore, not every parent will agree with the Commission's definition of indecency."

Some other dissenting judges agreed. "In enforcing the indecency regulations, the Commission takes upon itself a delicate and inevitably subjective role of drawing fine lines between 'serious' and 'pandering' presentations. And even a 'serious' presentation of newsworthy material is emphatically not shielded from liability."

In the summer of 1995, even as it was considering the CDA and Senator Feinstein's bomb bill, Congress decided to require that manufacturers of television sets include a "V-chip." This user-programmable device would allow parents to exclude shows based on their sexual or violent content. As the dissenters in *Action for Children's Television* recognized, the V-chip will change the rules of "channeling." If it succeeds, the FCC may no longer need to impose restrictions on the broadcaster, but may instead be persuaded that individual parents should be held responsible for deciding what their children may see or hear. The dissenting judges wrote, "The imminence of 'V-chip' technology to enable parental control of all violence—and indecency—viewing suggests that a draconian ban...is decidedly premature."

By contrast, telephone indecency didn't really become much of an issue until "information providers" started using the telephones to deliver suggestive speech. Carlin Communications (one wonders if the company was named in honor of George Carlin) was one of the most important of the 900 service providers of pre-recorded indecent phone messages. These were billed to the subscriber by the local phone company. The FCC promulgated regulations under the section of the Communications Act of 1934 barring any telephoned "comment, request, suggestion, or proposition which is obscene, lewd, lascivious, filthy or indecent." The intent of these regulations was to "channel" 900 line activities so as to make it unlikely that minors could get access. In a series of lawsuits between the FCC and Carlin Communications, courts threw out various agency attempts to regulate 900 number activities, until Congress attempted in 1988 to ban, not channel, all indecent speech on the telephone.

The Supreme Court, in what has unfortunately been a rather rare blow for freedom for the regulated media, held in *Sable Communications v. FCC*, the successor to the *Carlin* cases, that indecent speech could not be completely banned from the phone lines. First, however, it disposed of *Sable's* argument against the constitutionality of community standards, in language that indicates just how far the Court has to go in understanding national and international media. The Court stated, "There is no constitutional barrier under *Miller* to prohibiting communications that are obscene in some communities under local standards even though they are not obscene in others. If Sable's audience is comprised of different communities with different local standards, Sable ultimately bears the burden of complying with the prohibition on obscene messages." The Court gives no hint how a national information provider should go about predicting the reaction of all fifty states (let alone thousands of localities) to its information; the implicit message is that, as Robert and Carleen Thomas found out, if you communicate sexually explicit material, do so at your own risk.

Next, the Court reviewed the reasoning behind the regulation of indecency, by confirming that minors are the putative victims of indecent speech. "[T]here is a compelling interest in protecting the physical and psychological well-being of minors. This interest extends to shielding minors from the influence of literature that is not obscene by adult standards." Although this interest would justify "narrowly drawn regulations, tailored to achieve" the required ends, the protection of minors did not justify a total ban on indecent phone speech. Citing *Butler v. Michigan*, the Court said that the regulations had "the invalid effect of limiting the content of adult telephone conversations to that which is suitable for children to hear. It is another case of 'burn[ing] the house to roast the pig'".

The Court offered an interesting analysis of the pervasiveness issue which has resonance for the contemporary debate about indecency in cyberspace. *Pacifica*, it said, was different from the case before it because of a "unique" attribute of broadcasting, namely, that it is "uniquely pervasive," intrusive without prior warning, and "uniquely accessible to children." Telephone communications, it said, are "substantially different" because "The dial-it medium requires the listener to take affirmative steps to receive the communication. There is no 'captive audience' problem here...placing a telephone call is not the same as turning on a radio and being taken by surprise by an indecent message." One hundred years of technological development had finally cured the Court of fears that "the crossing of wires" might launch an indecent communication "into the midst of some family circle under very mortifying circumstances." *Sable* offers at least some hope that the Supreme Court will (in ruling some day on the CDA or some equivalent legislation) not find the Internet pervasive in the same sense as broadcast radio.

After *Sable*, Congress and the FCC reverted to attempts to channel indecent phone communications by requiring providers to charge the calls to user's credit cards and by mandating "reverse blocking." The credit cards were merely inconvenient for 900 service providers, who would rather have the local phone company charge the calls to the user's regular phone bill, but "reverse blocking" was a more serious concern. This classic example of bureaucratese meant that all 900 numbers are automatically blocked by the local phone company unless a user requests access. In order to access indecent speech, you have to tell the phone company, in writing, that you want to do so.

In 1991, two federal appeals courts held that these FCC "channeling" regulations were constitutional. In *Information Providers' Coalition v. FCC*, the court noted that "central office blocking," where a subscriber asks the local phone company to block all further calls to 900 numbers, would be inadequate to protect minors because it lets them get through at least once before their parents observe a 900 charge on the phone bill. The court also noted that contacting the phone company to request access to 900 services was analogous to subscribing to a magazine. Thus, reverse blocking was not unduly restrictive. Also, requiring providers of indecent messages to ask users for credit cards was not unconstitutional because phone companies were not legally required to provide billing services for 900 number providers. In *Dial Information Services v. Thornburgh*, a second federal appeals court upheld the new regulations, finding that "a child may have suffered serious psychological damage from contact with dial-a-porn before the child's parents become aware from a monthly telephone bill that there has been access to an indecent message...."

Possibly emboldened by its success in regulating 900 services, Congress next went after indecency on cable television, passing a 1992 law requiring that cable providers either ban indecency on public access and leased channels or implement reverse blocking—a subscriber would have to write the cable company to inform them that he wanted indecent programming. Cable providers typically also create the content that travels over the cable; Congress required them to lease channels to competitors, and to provide at least one public access channel at inexpensive rates to encourage diverse local programming. Because no scarcity consideration exists, Congress, the FCC and the courts have pursued complex and unconvincing rationales to justify the regulation of cable television. Numerous unsuccessful lawsuits have challenged the FCC's jurisdiction over cable; courts have denied these based on findings that broadcast shows are carried over cable, that cable competes with broadcast television, and that "television is television," no matter how it is received in the home. However, while upholding FCC jurisdiction, courts have allowed the agency much less involvement in content than is allowed for broadcast television—and have regularly struck down state cable indecency laws on First Amendment grounds.

In *Alliance for Community Media v. FCC*, a three judge panel of the federal appeals court in Washington, D.C. threw out the new indecency regulations pertaining to cable providers. The court noted that the government could not legally authorize cable providers to ban all indecent speech. It distinguished the telephone indecency cases which had held that the phone companies were not required to provide billing services to 900 service providers. In the event a phone company decided not to provide billing services, a provider could still connect to the telephone network and handle its own billing, but a content provider denied access to a public access channel was prevented from reaching the public. To the objection that a cable provider's decision not to permit the broadcast of indecent material was not government action and therefore could not violate the First Amendment, the court replied, "The government first strips a cable operator of editorial power over access channels, then singles out the matter it wishes to eliminate, and finally permits the cable operator to pull the trigger on that material only." The First Amendment applied because, in such an environment, the cable operator's action was tantamount to government action. On the issue of reverse blocking, the court handed the case back to the FCC for further consideration.

In a poignant footnote, the court warned of the danger posed by indiscriminate indecency regulations, which include in their "sweep material that does not appeal to the prurient interest or that taken as a whole, may be of the highest literary, artistic, political or scientific value. For example, a truly scientific program, not merely a pretext for showing material that appeals to the prurient interest—that discusses the prevention of life-threatening diseases through the use of condoms, could perhaps be considered 'indecent' but would hardly seem to lack...scientific or social value so as to lose protection under the First Amendment."

Unfortunately, the panel's decision was canceled for reconsideration by the entire Court of Appeals—an unusual measure that happens sometimes in highly significant, controversial cases. The decision of the full court, handed down more than a year later, upheld the FCC regulations in every respect. The majority characterized censorship by cable operators as an exercise of free speech. "When an operator decides what programming will appear on its system, the operator engages in free speech." It found that, despite Congress's encouragement, an operator's decision to ban indecent programming was not state action and therefore raised no First Amendment issues. And it held that the reverse blocking of cable broadcasts was similarly constitutional.

"Under the broad definition of 'indecency' used in this regulation," said some dissenting judges, "affected speech could include programs on the AIDS epidemic, abortion, childbirth, or practically any aspect of human sexuality." Referring to the case in which the curator of a Cincinnati museum was indicted for displaying the sexually explicit work of photographer Robert Mapplethorpe, the dissenters said that "a bowdlerized documentary on the Mapplethorpe exhibit which did not include some description or depiction of Mapplethorpe's sexually photographs themselves, for example, would hardly be an informed statement on the artistic and political debate the exhibit engendered." Countering the pervasiveness issue, the judges pointed out that "The FCC itself takes the position that, although cable television too enters the home, it comes as an invited guest." Chief Judge Edwards, also dissenting, questioned Congress's intent in creating indecency regulations that applied to leased and public access channels, but not to the operator's own content. Criticizing the majority's explanation that operators exercise "editorial control" over their own channels, Chief Judge Edwards complained that the amount of indecent programming on main-stream cable was not really much different—or any less of a prob-lem—than that available on leased and public access channels.

Two years earlier, the Supreme Court had discussed the First Amendment's applicability to cable, in a different context. In the case of *Turner Broadcasting System v. FCC*, Time-Warner, a co-plain-tiff and cable operator, sought to overturn an FCC rule requiring it to carry broadcast television over channels in its system. Congress and the FCC had long regarded it as their role to protect broadcast tele-vision against the competition offered by cable. The cable operator, using an argument that the *Alliance* majority might have found sym-pathetic, claimed that its right of free speech allowed it to refuse to carry broadcast television over its cable system. The Supreme Court handed the case back to a lower court for more fact-finding, but dis-cussed the First Amendment before doing so, including an apparent pot-shot at the scarcity argument. "The broadcast cases are inappo-site in the present context because cable television does not suffer from the inherent limitation that characterizes the broadcast medi-um. ... At the heart of the First Amendment lies the principle that each person should decide for him or herself the ideas or beliefs deserving of expression, consideration and adherence. Our political system and cultural life rest upon this ideal."

It remains to be seen what interpretation lower courts will make of these types of Delphic utterances in the years to come. For now, cable remains a strange hybrid, not as shackled as broadcast televi-sion but not as free as the press. The courts, said Ithiel de Sola Pool, "have evaded the logical conclusion that the FCC has no authority whatever to regulate what may be carried on cable systems and can-not have such authority under the Constitution." But, as long as courts intimate that cable operators have a First Amendment right to deny access to others, freedom of speech will not be a reality on cable. "The problem of access may become the Achilles heel of what could otherwise be a medium of communication every bit as free as print." Pool believed that the solution was to make cable operators common carriers and get them out of the content business. Publishers of content could not be denied a right to lease channels any more than Western Union can deny a reporter the right to send a telegram.

Even more so than in the world of newspapers, free speech in broadcast media is subordinated to business interests of various kinds. First, as Postman never tires of pointing out, the television medium itself is better suited, for example, to coverage of an earthquake than a budget debate. Second, broadcast media live by selling ads, and the ads are more tied to the content than with newspapers. Typically, in a newspaper, the juxtaposition of a story and any given ad is a coincidence. On television, "sponsors" know exactly what show they are buying air time for, and have been known to vote with their feet if the content is too controversial.

Television news traditionally came from another side of the house, that was more independent than the entertainment side. In recent years, networks have realized that news is entertainment, and have changed their guidelines accordingly. The personal attractiveness of the correspondents has become more important, and stories have increasingly been chosen for their entertainment rather than news value. The decline and fall of the news division's objectivity was most clearly revealed by the 1992 scandal in which NBC News illustrated a story on the design of GM pickup trucks by rigging one to explode when sideswiped on a test track. NBC said defensively that it was simply "enhancing reality." Lawrence Grossman, who left the presidency of NBC News some years before this incident, commented that "It was a transparently deceptive journalistic practice that would have been utterly unthinkable just a few years earlier, before network news and entertainment had become so thoroughly integrated and intermixed that viewers had a hard time knowing where truth ended and fiction began."

When Grossman first joined NBC, he expected to find an organization with an army of reporters and stringers, constantly searching out news on every continent. He was amazed to discover that NBC, like the other television news organizations, did almost no investigative reporting, but simply attended press conferences, speeches, celebrations, and the like. Grossman said "I could find hardly any news that we ever 'dug up' ourselves except for an occasional soft feature story or oddball color piece, and even most of them originated from press releases, public information directors, or publicity agents."

In recent years, the networks have been trapped in unacknowledged conflicts of interest, pressured not to cover stories concerning their own corporate parents or sister companies owned by the parent. Grossman described the aftermath of General Electric's purchase of RCA, the parent of NBC. "Early on the morning of Tuesday, October 20, 1987, I received an angry, sputtering phone call from my new boss, GE chairman Welch, a chief executive noted for his intensity and quick temper. ... He called me that morning in high dudgeon to complain about how NBC News had reported the sudden stock market collapse of the day before. Welch insisted that our newsmen stop using phrases like 'Black Monday', 'alarming plunge', and 'precipitous drop' to describe Wall Street's October 19 debacle. Their reports were only making the situation worse, Welch said, scaring stockholders and further depressing the price of even the healthiest companies, like GE, NBC's new parent. NBC News should stop fouling its own nest, he told me." A month later, new NBC president Robert Wright, appointed by Welch and formerly of GE, sent out a memo effectively ordering NBC management, executives of the news division included, to contribute to an NBC PAC, which would attempt to influence telecommunications policy in Washington. "Employees who elect not to participate in a giving program of this type should question their own dedication to the company and their expectations." According to Grossman, the news division refused to participate and he himself left NBC the next year.

In recent years, the networks have backed off of First Amendment confrontations, particularly with the tobacco companies, who are taking a very aggressive tack in bringing lawsuits. In November 1995, *60 Minutes*, regarded by many as the last bastion of devil-may-care speech, was ordered by CBS attorneys not to run an interview with a former tobacco executive, for fear his ex-employer would accuse the network of procuring the breach of a nondisclosure agreement. There was speculation in other media that CBS feared that a major lawsuit would prevent a prospective sale of the network to Westinghouse. Many commentators failed to mention that CBS's parent also owned Lorrilard Tobacco, the maker of Vantage cigarettes. P. Cameron DeVore, CBS's outside counsel, defending his advice to CBS not to run the *60 Minutes* piece, commented that "the world is a less ebullient place for free speech than it was 20 years ago." Not long before, ABC had retracted a story it broadcast about Philip Morris and paid a settlement of $2.5 million.

Grossman said, "The mainstream media, by definition, cater to specific audiences and therefore tend to share their readers' and viewers' existing attitudes and views. Rarely do they veer from the path of mainstream thinking to advocate unorthodox views or radical ideas either of the left or the right. They tend to respond to and reinforce public opinion, rather than shape it and lead it. Their effort, understandably, is to interest and please their large audiences rather than risk alienating or offending them." He concluded that the mainstream media are " a difficult environment in which to launch new ideas."

Movies are a medium of communication, and even the most hackneyed film communicates ideas. However, the Supreme Court at first failed to recognize that movies were entitled to First Amendment protection. In a 1915 case, *Mutual Film Corp. v. Industrial Commission*, the Court said that movies are "a business, pure and simple, originated and conducted for profit, like other spectacles, not to be regarded...as part of the press of this country, or as organs of public opinion." It took the Court until 1952 to reverse itself. In *Joseph Burstyn Co. v. Williams*, the Court said that the fact that "books, newspapers, and magazines are published and sold for profit does not prevent them from being a form of expression whose liberty is safeguarded by the First Amendment. We fail to see why operation of profit should have any different effect in the case of motion pictures." The Court also considered, and brushed aside, an early form of the pervasiveness argument. "It is further urged that motion pictures possess a greater capacity for evil, particularly among the youth of a community, than other modes of expression. Even if one were to accept this hypothesis, it does not follow that motion pictures should be disqualified from First Amendment protection." The Court recognized the confusion that ensues whenever a new means of communication comes along. "Each method tends to present its own peculiar problems. But the basic principles of freedom of speech and of the press, like the First Amendment's commandments, do not vary."

Every new technology, even when essentially similar to what has gone before, is misapprehended by courts and by legislators. The copyright laws also illustrate this point. Every new means of expression is originally considered not subject to copyright, no matter how strong the analogy to existing forms which are protected. Piano rolls and computer software embedded in ROM were held, seventy years apart, not to be copyrightable. Yet each was not very different from forms of expression which everyone recognized to be covered by the copyright laws. A piano roll was comparable to a printed sheet of music, while there was little difference between software in ROM and on disk. Each of these results was later reversed as society became more comfortable with new technology. Policy makers must learn that means of communication and forms of expression are protean, "tak-

226

ing all shapes from Mah to Mahi", but remaining essentially alike. An essay is equally protected by copyright whether it is printed on paper, broadcast over the air, recorded on a phonograph, or stored on a computer disk. If a work is protected by copyright regardless of the media in which it is stored or communicated, why would we think differently about the First Amendment? Yet an explicit, polemical essay against pornography, like the work of Catharine MacKinnon, clearly a First Amendment-protected work in newsprint, would fall afoul of the CDA if stored on an Internet server.

McLuhan failed to devote a chapter of *Understanding Media* to the lowly bullhorn, and Neil Postman has never complained that it has damaged the quality of our lives or interfered with the ability of our children to think. But the Supreme Court pondered the social implications of the bullhorn in 1949, when it upheld the constitutionality of a local regulation banning them in *Kovacs v. Cooper.* Justice Hugo Black, dissenting, accused the Court of being prejudiced in favor of mass media such as the press and radio. "There are many people who have ideas that they wish to disseminate but who do not have enough money to own or control publishing plants, newspapers, radios, moving picture studios or chains of show places. Yet everyone knows the vast reaches of these powerful channels of communication which from the very nature of our economic system must be under the control and guidance of comparatively few people. On the other hand, public speaking is done by many men of divergent minds with no centralized control over the ideas they entertain so as to limit the causes they espouse. It is no reflection on the value of preserving freedom for dissemination of the ideas of... newspapers, magazines and other literature to believe that transmission of ideas through public speaking is also essential to the sound thinking of a fully informed citizenry."

Politicians are fond of metaphors, and the pages of the *Congressional Record* swarm with them in every debate on any topic. Judges, writers, everyone staking a position or arguing a point of view loves metaphors—they are one of the basic tools of human expression. The debate over the nature and proper treatment of the Net has thrown off hundreds of metaphors, from Howard Rheingold's utopian "virtual community" to Senator Coats's satanic "porn shop in your child's bedroom."

Whether it happens this year or 20 years from now, the following is the metaphor we are morally certain will—and should—triumph. We are so certain of this we will print it in capitals (which, on the Net, is construed as shouting):

CYBERSPACE IS A CONSTELLATION OF PRINTING PRESSES AND BOOKSTORES.

Every computer connected to the Net is a printing press, which its owner can use to write the next *Common Sense*, the next *Walden* or *Areopagitica*, and send it off to the world. But every computer connected to the Net is equally a bookstore, which can store all these works and make them available to anyone who wants to download them. There is no way of thinking about the Net that makes sense but this. It is not a radio or TV station or a telephone network or the United States post office.

"The First Amendment," said Pool, "came out of a pluralistic world of small communicators." Now, thanks to the power and the economics of the Net, where anyone can be a publisher for less than $100 a month, we have that world back again.

Neil Postman should be thrilled by the Internet. Instead of contributing to the death of public discourse—the final blow in the beating that started with the telegraph— the Net, particularly the World Wide Web, represents the rebirth of typography. "Writing freezes speech," he wrote, "and in so doing gives birth to the grammarian, the logician, the rhetorician, the historian, the scientist—all those who must hold language before them so that they can see what it means, where it errs, and where it is leading." The quality of writing on the World Wide Web—in pages dealing with ethics, politics, law, science, and everything else under the sun—is arguably higher than the quality of writing in the world in general. The Web browser, like the printing press, is a machine for formatting text and presenting it to us in a pleasant, easy to read format, interlaced with graphics, far more accessible than the pre-Web text file of unadorned print requiring special knowledge to download.

Of course, as Clifford Stoll and many others have complained, a computer, even a "notebook," does not replicate the tactile feel, the satisfactions, of a book. At a friend's suggestion, Stoll downloaded a hypertext version of Wells's *The Time Machine*. "Ugh. Can't lie the laptop on my chest...it's cumbersome, clunky, ghastly slow and mechanical. The text isn't hard to read, it just feels unfriendly. ... Book publishers have nothing to worry about." Stoll is probably right. In a recent episode of *Star Trek–Deep Space Nine*, set in the

24th century, a character was portrayed as the author of a best-selling novel. When he proudly showed it to another character, the audience saw not a computer chip, not an electronic clipboard with scrolling text, but a traditional bound book.

Nonetheless, printed books will have to coexist with electronic ones. Electronic books cost next to nothing to produce and distribute, striking a blow for the freedom of information. They are harder to track down and eliminate, striking a blow against censorship. They can never go out of print and their permanent storage in cyberspace incurs no warehouse costs, risks no mildew or yellowing pages. If you want a copy of two out-of-print works of philosophy we looked for recently, Peter Singer's *The Expanding Circle* or Karl Jaspers's *The Question of German Guilt*, you might be out of luck; even the immense main branch of the New York Public Library does not have them. But when we needed to consult Milton's *Aeropagitica*, the elapsed time between the formulation of the desire and its fulfillment was ten minutes—the time necessary to walk upstairs to the computer, connect to the Internet, access and use the Webcrawler search engine, and click on the resulting link to the work.

Postman, of course, is right when he says that a new technology is typically neither good or evil in itself. He raises his voice to oppose technology not because he believes it is unalloyed evil, but because its supporters are everywhere—and unrealistic—and its critics are lacking. "A dissenting voice is sometimes needed to moderate the din made by the enthusiastic multitudes. If one is to err, it is better to err on the side of Thamusian skepticism." But what he may be missing is the fact that the Net is not a step in the direction of amusement, fragmentation, irrelevance (though parts of it, such as Usenet, may seem "telegraphic" in this sense), but back towards the printing press, with its coherent and sober organization of information.

A proof of this statement is that the sins of the Internet are largely the sins of the printing press. Both allow the easier, more widespread distribution of wrong information, irrelevant information, even evil information. Yet few would argue today that the printing press did not provide an overall social benefit and few will argue in the future that the Net was not similarly a boon.

Postman would probably respond that the availability of the *Aeropagitica* on the Web doesn't prove anything, since it is just as easy to find baseball statistics, the Magic 8-Ball, and the Fish Cam. He says that the principal legacy of the telegraph—which he would certainly find multiplied in the Internet by a factor of millions—is the "information glut," which creates a "diminished social and political potency." "You may get a sense of what this means by asking yourself another series of questions such as What steps do you plan to take to reduce the conflict in the Middle East? Or the rates of inflation, crime and unemployment? What are your plans for preserving the environment or reducing the risk of nuclear war? ... I shall take the liberty of answering for you: You plan to do nothing about them. ... Prior to the age of telegraphy...most people had a sense of being able to control some of the contingencies in their lives. ... In the information world created by telegraphy, this sense of potency was lost, precisely because the whole world became the context for news. Everything became everyone's business."

Postman takes a serious misstep here. All of these problems may have been exacerbated by the telegraph, but they were created by the printing press. You can just as easily feel overwhelmed by the information in a bookstore—do you want to read a novel? A work of history or psychology? A cookbook? Some people play into Postman's hands by complaining that every Web-surfing session ends in futility and confusion as they follow links to information of decreasing relevance; but they lack the self-discipline to survive in a library. If you attempted to research any issue by constantly jumping from the book before you to the first book referenced in a footnote, you would soon lose sight of your topic. If you wouldn't do research this way in a library, why use a different approach on the Web? On the Internet, you can find what you need faster, or lose your way faster—it's all up to you.

Anyway, Postman is wrong to suggest, as he did in a recent interview in *Net Guide* magazine, that an information glut makes us helpless. Richard Lanham says, "Speak for yourself, Neil! I do a number of things, from recycling my trash to designing new writing curricula, from talking to my Congressman to giving money. ... Most people act on the information glut."

"Wait," Postman might say, "You are trying to persuade me that the Internet is a constellation of printing presses and bookstores—a revelation that would make me very happy, if true. But it also represents the ultimate convergence of all forms of communication—so it is simultaneously the telegraph, which I detest, and the television, which I really detest. Justify your position that the proper metaphor for regulation of the Internet is the printing press and not any of these other media."

This is easy to do. Ithiel de Sola Pool spotted this issue in 1983 when he wondered if the convergence of press, telephone, and broadcast media—the three major categories receiving different treatment under the law—would lead to more regulation or more freedom. He knew how the question should be answered, "[C]oncern for the traditional notion of a free press [should] lead to finding ways to free the electronic media from regulation. ... A policy of freedom aims at pluralism of expression rather than at dissemination of preferred ideas." And again, "The specific question to be answered is whether the electronic resources for communication can be as free of public regulation in the future as the platform and printing press have been in the past."

Another way to phrase the same thought is that when all media converge, for an idea to gain currency it must exist in cyberspace—we are not very far from this now. The First Amendment then loses all validity if it does not apply to electronic communication as fully as it does to the products of the printing press. It may be that one day, the majority of our public discourse will take place on-line. "The printed book," said Jay David Bolter, "seems destined to move to the margin of our literate culture. The issue is not whether print technology will completely disappear; books may long continue to be printed for certain kinds of texts and for luxury consumption. But the idea and the ideal of the book will change...electronic technology offers us a new kind of book and new ways to write and read." When this is true, when the printing press accounts for a minority of our speech, the First Amendment will become a cast-off shell if we do not bring it with us into cyberspace.

Our review of history reveals some other common themes.

First, each new wave in communications has transformed society, pulling people closer together, promoting the flow of information—but also providing a medium for the transmission of bad or useless ideas along with the good. Writing encouraged the dissemination of "false wisdom." The printing press allowed the proliferation of the "natural history of nonsense" and also gave birth to pornographic literature. The telegraph gave rise to the first wire fraud and also encouraged the transmission of rivers of irrelevant and trivial data. The telephone and radio created the threat of indecency pervading the house.

Second, each communications revolution has been met with bewilderment, confusion, and doubt by people who saw the evil but not the good. Thamus failed to see any benefit from writing. Francois

I, in a rage, banned the publication of books in France. A French mob feared that the telegraph would be used to signal the enemy. The United States Supreme Court didn't see that the telephone would be useful to government. Familiar stories from more recent years recount laughably off-base predictions about the number of mainframe computers, photocopiers, and personal computers that would ever be needed in the world.

Third, the first attempt to make rules governing a new technology is usually hasty and wrong. Legislators and judges who act with care and circumspection have an opportunity to make fair rules by which future generations will remember them with gratitude, the way we recall Cardozo, Brandeis, and Holmes today. Those who rush to institute half-baked policies based on ignorance will be remembered, if at all, for how wrong they were. Senators Exon and Feinstein and their co-sponsors are taking this risk by allowing yesterday to paralyze today, and today to paralyze tomorrow. They would be better advised to follow the advice of Senator Leahy and of Judge Cardozo, to wait a while and examine history before making any rash judgments.

Fourth, as the history of the printing press illustrated, censorship does not work—it merely creates a thriving underground market in the material it seeks to eliminate. The global, distributed nature of the Internet makes it extremely unlikely that any prohibitive scheme of government regulation can succeed. The history of the printing press is repeating itself—already, attempts at repression of certain types of information, such as pornography, have contributed to driving them offshore, where they may remain accessible to Americans who wish to obtain them. The Scientologists' attempt to seize the computers of their enemies did not succeed, as the files the church sought to suppress proliferated to other servers. The oft-quoted statement that "the Net interprets censorship as damage, and routes around it," is absolutely correct.

Fifth, technological change is a wave which must be ridden but cannot be stopped. No attempt to prohibit books or license presses was remotely effective. Another frequently quoted statement is that "information wants to be free." In 1976, evolutionary biologist Richard Dawkins posited that, in some respects, ideas (which he calls "memes") behave like genes, replicating themselves across brains the way genes do across bodies. Writing represented the first effective way to store ideas outside the human brain, so that they could be passed on to human beings who did not have direct contact with the author, and who did not even necessarily live in the same time as she did. Each wave of communications technology since then—printing press, telegraph, telephone, radio, television and Internet—has promoted "memetic reproduction," allowing more information, good and evil, to flow to more people faster. The most optimistic thing one can say about laws like the CDA is that they are as likely to be swept away in short order as the Indiana legislature's attempt at the end of the last century to define pi as 3.00.

Sixth, as De Tocqueville recognized, a large number of competing voices is the best guarantee that no speaker will grow too powerful. Recognizing that the Net warrants full-fledged First Amendment protection will guarantee continuation of the status quo: numerous, diverse voices on the Net. Regulation will make cyberspace too risky for the little guy, and transfer control to a limited number of large businesses, like the broadcast networks.

Our study of the history of communications technology raises a number of threshold issues that must be resolved in determining the right approach to regulation of the Internet. What is the significance of the Net for free speech? What is the significance, and what are the effects, of technological convergence? Is the Internet pervasive in the same sense as radio or television? What is the role of parental supervision in determining what children can see on the Net? Can speech on the Internet effectively be channeled? What technological solutions aid parents in filtering the contents of the Internet for their children? Does fighting speech with speech work on the Net? Why is there so much hysteria about the Internet? Is it primarily to be a vehicle for business or speech (and are these uses inconsistent)? Who should control the Internet? When do we need new laws for the Internet, and when will the old ones suffice?

We do not have completely free speech in America. Print journalists work for owners who frequently restrict the range of topics that they cover and what they can say about those topics. The press follows rather than leads public opinion—an event or person has to gain public notice outside the media before the press will cover it. And with failures and consolidations, there are fewer newspapers in America than ever before, while many of those that survive are owned by a few families or media conglomerates.

The broadcast media are even worse. They share all the weakness of print media, and add some of their own. They are not fully protected by the First Amendment. Licensed by the government, they can be sanctioned or denied a renewal if they fall afoul of content restrictions. They do little investigative reporting and mainly seek out the visual and punchy story, giving the spectator little that is substantive on the complex policy issues of the day.

These days, to track new developments and to observe the groundswell of public opinion that will tell them something is worth reporting, journalists are turning to the Internet. This means that the Net is also the place to which any member of the public can turn to learn the truth, without having to rely on the media as intermediary. Therefore, it is a forum for unvarnished truth and for information that is not pre-digested by the Fourth Estate.

Of course, truth and falsehood, bad and good ideas all co-exist on the Net. But nowhere in the Constitution or elsewhere is it written that the media are exempt from falsehood or bad ideas. No one ever appointed print or broadcast journalists the sole bearers of the beacon of truth. Instead, most people have always relied on the media to tell them what is going on because they had no alternative. The ordinary citizen had neither the time, the money, or the knowledge to do the research. A major technological achievement of the Internet is that it alleviates these problems. It costs little and does not require much time to check many of the primary sources used by the media—the Congressional Record, Supreme Court decisions, and government press releases. But, more valuable still, people can make their own choices, rather than relying on the media's, about what is valuable and worthy of consideration. Many stories which the media has disregarded, or of which it has not yet perceived the importance, are to be found among the rivers of information on the Net.

Here is just one example. As of November 1995, more than three months after the passage of the House version of the Telecommunications Reform Act, the print media were still confused about the impact of what the House had done. Most reporters indicated that Mr. Gingrich had kept his promise and that the CDA had gone down to defeat. Many did not know of the existence of the Hyde amendment, and those that did still failed to understand its impact. No one had reported that the language of the CDA was derived from the Communications Act of 1934 or that the Hyde amendment copied the FCC regulations on broadcast indecency. In other words, the media had missed the heart of the story, that an attempt was being made to apply broadcast style regulation to the Internet.

In August, within days after the House vote, we found word of the Hyde amendment on the Center for Democracy and Technology home pages, **http://www.cdt.org.** More information was forthcoming from Voter's Telecommunications Watch, **http://www.vtw.org**. We sent E-mail to Brock Meeks and Mike Godwin to check details. We wrote a summary of our findings that was distributed in Computer Underground Digest and appeared in the home pages of The Ethical Spectacle, **http://www.spectacle.org**.

We were able to do much of the research for this book on the Net. Among the materials we obtained there were:

- The Congressional Record transcripts of the House and Senate CDA debates, and the Senate bomb bill debate.

- The full text of the CDA, Cox-Wyden, the Hyde amendment, and the bomb bill.

- All Supreme Court cases decided since 1990 which we have quoted here.

- Legal analysis and Usenet posts giving background information on the *Amateur Action* case. In Usenet, we found Keith Henson, who had firsthand knowledge of the arrest and trial of the Thomases.

- Judge Cohen's decision in the *Baker* case, copies of Baker's stories, a roundtable transcript with Professor Catharine MacKinnon and the prosecutor, copies of articles from local newspapers on the case, and information on the University of Michigan proceedings against Baker.

- The writings of Phil Zimmerman, background information on PGP and his case, the transcripts of hearings and federal actions on cryptology and privacy, and contact information for Phil's attorneys.

- Candyman's pages, Usenet posts about bombmaking, the NRA disclaimer and Tanya Metaksas's letter, and the Congressional testimony of Rabbi Hier and Jerry Berman.

- The Marty Rimm study, the *Time* article about it, Usenet posts critiquing Rimm, Hoffman and Novak's analysis, the MacKinnon, Branscomb and Meyer law review articles, the CMU press release, Brock Meeks's reporting, the Press coverage, and virtually everything else we quoted in that chapter.

- The Parental Control FAQ, the American Psychological Association pages on children and television, and sources on the history of the media and of technology.

Although we happened to be reporting a story about the Internet, research we have done on topics as diverse as game theory, evolution, religion, morality, memetics, and gun control have all revealed substantial reference material on the Internet. A medium in its infancy already has enough information on-line to get you started on almost every topic. Although any particular fact may be wrong or idea wrong-headed, the Internet gives you the freedom to judge for yourself, rather than relying on information pre-evaluated by others.

The Internet gives everyone the ability to act as an investigative reporter and to amass all the data necessary—not just officially approved data—to draw a conclusion. It contains the full range of available ideas, not just the more limited range adopted for official consumption by the mass media. As such, the Net is a tremendous force in favor of free speech.

## Technological Convergence

The convergence of television, radio, the phone, and the Internet undercuts the rationale for differing First Amendment treatment and supports strong First Amendment protection of all forms of communication. This convergence has accelerated to light-speed as the battle for predominance on the Information Superhighway is fought by players as disparate as content providers (Time Warner), phone companies (Bell Atlantic), cable companies (TCI) and software giants (Microsoft). Legislators are beginning to notice that any type of content, in fact, any type of service, can be delivered using the Internet as a medium. Though we are still in the early days of this transformation, and prototypes have often been buggy and slow, the Internet has already been used to broadcast radio and movies. A shareware program, *CU-SeeMe*, with the aid of a home video camera and an Internet-connected PC, allows video conferencing; another product, Internet Phone, can be used to make international calls via the Net (you speak into a microphone attached to your computer, which digitizes your voice and sends it out via the modem as a data transmission, carrying your voice to foreign countries without incurring the long distance phone rates you would pay for making a traditional call.)

Each of these other technologies have been affected by the Internet. People use E-mail the way the telegraph was used in prior generations, for the rapid transmission of urgent messages. E-mail is also frequently used in place of a phone call. Electronic communications have even affected the printing press's domain: typography that would have been done mechanically a few years ago is now routinely performed on the computer, using products like Atex, and then electronically transmitted to remote printing plants for local distribution. In recent years, Project Gutenberg and similar efforts have made thousands of public domain works available on-line (Milton's *Aeropagitica*, Paine's *Common Sense* and Thoreau's *Walden* are all on the Internet). Some periodicals are now exclusively published on-line, without corresponding print versions. One of the authors of this book creates a newsletter which is read on the World Wide Web every month by as many as 10,000 people. The total cost, other than the time he puts in, is less than $100 per issue, most of which goes to rent space on an Internet server. The cost of distributing a print publication to that many people would be many thousands of dollars a month.

Reed Hundt, chairman of the FCC, recognizes that the television, telephone, and personal computer are converging. In a recent speech to the Information Technology Association of America, he quoted the *Economist* magazine. "'As the transmission of information is increasingly digitized, the boundaries between the telephone, the television, and the computer are blurring. Put the three together and all sorts of unpredictable new products and services start to evolve from the fun of television, the brain and memory of the computer, and the two-or-more-way human contact of the telephone.' But neither *The Economist* nor I know what to call the combined TV, PC, and telephone." Such coy comments from the FCC chairman are disconcerting. What role does he foresee for the FCC if all the media converge? In a live chat session on America Online, he gave vague, unsettling answers to questions about regulating the Internet:

> "Question: Any ideas on how to censor the Net, while keeping all Constitutional guarantees in place?
>
> REHundt: The Constitution doesn't guarantee any rights at all to obscene communications. On the other hand, censorship is specifically not a power of the FCC."
>
> "Question: You currently cannot define your rules on radio. Can we expect the same vague rules on the Net ?
>
> REHundt: If you're asking about indecency, we have very sound rules on indecency that have been repeatedly upheld by the highest courts in the land."

And, most chillingly:

"Question: What are your ideas [about] censorship?

"REHundt: I start with the idea that the FCC should not stand for the Federal Censorship Commission. On the other hand, shouldn't parents have the power to choose and something to choose for their kids?"

Hundt won't come out and say so, but clearly he thinks that if an older regulated medium converges with a newer, unregulated one, the FCC gets jurisdiction over the new one. If so, this will be fatal to free speech on the Internet, which will take on the intellectually barren semblance of radio and television. The only way to avoid this is by doing the opposite—if regulated media converge with unregulated ones, the FCC should lose jurisdiction, not gain new powers of influence over American speech and thought. The FCC was not created to be an Orwellian Ministry of Information.

## The Chimera of Pervasiveness

As we have already pointed out, there is no scarcity of bandwidth in cyberspace. Anyone who wants to can attach a server to the Net, and no one has seriously suggested that a broadcasting-style licensing approach be applied. Therefore, the sole rationale for applying content regulation born of broadcasting laws is that the Net is pervasive, that, like television and radio, it comes into the living room.

There is a direct line of inheritance from the concern of the court in the first telephone indecency case that foul language "might be launched into the midst of some family circle" to the FCC's pious mission to protect helpless families from the "ether waves carrying the unwelcome messages...entering the walls of their homes," to Senator Coats's description of the Internet as a "porn shop in a child's bedroom."

In recent decades, educators and social critics have spent a lot of time agonizing over the death of reading, wondering why our children don't want to and why our schools can't teach them how to read. "Children come to school," says Postman, "having been deeply conditioned by the biases of television. There, they encounter the world of the printed word. A sort of psychic battle takes place, and there are many casualties—children who can't learn to read or won't, children who cannot organize their thought into logical structure even in a simple paragraph, children who cannot attend to lectures or oral explanations for more than a few minutes at a time." There is an inherent tension between this concern and our legislators' utterances about the pervasiveness of media. To combat the decline of reading, we should want books to be pervasive, to come into the house and be as easily accessible to our children as cartoons or video games. Since the Internet represents the rebirth of typography, of reading, we should welcome its pervasiveness. Its most important benefit is the ability to bring unfettered ideas and communications into the house.

Any scheme of censorship justified by the Net's pervasiveness flouts the First Amendment and tries to hold the ocean back with a broom. It also places us squarely in the domain of the state law invalidated in the Supreme Court case *Butler v. Michigan*—setting the level of all public discourse (for public discourse already takes place on the Net) no higher than what is considered fit for children. Wouldn't it really make more sense to leave the Net alone, and place the burden on parents to determine what is fit for their children?

## Parental Supervision

Experts on childhood all agree that allowing the television set to baby-sit your child is an abdication of responsibility. "It has been calculated," says Dr. Spock, "that three quarters of children's viewing of television is in prime time so that is the time to be vigilant about what your children are watching. Parents can check up every day to make sure the rules are being followed." According to Dr. Haim Ginott, "television, like medication, must be taken at prescribed times and in the right doses." Dr. Lawrence Balter recommends that you "preselect and screen the programs that your child watches." Ellen Galinsky observes, "you must actively guide your children's viewing...think of your role not as a censor but as a socializer conveying values and knowledge to your children." Earl Grollman and Gerri Sweder, advising working parents, comment that "Some youngsters told us that during weekends the family sits down together and plans those programs that are acceptable for viewing after school. Other children mentioned to us that from time to time parents call from work and simply ask what programs they are watching."

Contrast Senator Exon's view that, since children know the computer better, parents cannot monitor their activities. Children are not mindless automatons drawn obsessively to indecency. Parental supervision does not always mean strict moment-to-moment control of activities. It can mean, as these authors all agree, communicating values and then checking from time to time to see if the rules are being followed. A parent does not have to understand the computer to glance into a child's room to see what is on the screen, or to sit with the child and participate in a surfing session. A phone call from work to ask what the child is doing with the computer is a marvelous and practical idea.

Parents certainly have the right to determine what ideas—and what expressions—may enter the home and which must stay outside. A parent can legally decide not to allow books to enter the home. But parents who are glad to have this right must, of course, exercise the concomitant responsibility of supervision. It is ludicrous to suggest, as Senator Exon does, that parents can abdicate all responsibility for what their children do with the computer, while the law steps in to make the computer a safe piece of bedroom furniture.

A computer does not magically connect itself to the Internet. A parent authorizes the purchase of Internet software and the opening of an account. Nowhere is it written that a parent must allow a child to surf the Net at all, or permit the child to connect without any supervision. In the balancing of interests that Congress and the courts must do every day, which makes more sense: to remove Rabelais, Holocaust resources, and AIDS data banks from the Internet or to require a little parental supervision? Removing serious information from the Net makes idiots of us all. Censorship, said Milton, is "to the common people [not] less than a reproach; for if we be so jealous over them, as that we dare not trust them with an English pamphlet, what do we but censure them for a giddy, vicious, and ungrounded people; in such a sick and weak state of faith and discretion, as to be able to take nothing down but through the pipe of a licenser?"

An organization called Voter's Telecommunication Watch distributes a "Parental Control FAQ"; "As will always be true, the most effective method of getting comfortable with your child's Internet access is to guide them as a parent. No other human being except you knows best what is and isn't appropriate for them. By learning to use the Internet with your child (either one of you can teach the other) you can instill in them the values that you want them to use when selecting material in the Internet, or on television, radio, or in print media. The respect built between you and your child will function when no one is around, and will survive software upgrades, eternally-changing international law, and other unpredictable events."

We do not believe that the Internet is a medium which Congress is permitted to regulate under the First Amendment. But, even if it is, permissible regulation must be narrowly drawn and tailored to achieve compelling ends. Hence the law of "channeling," of causing indecent communications to flow into a corner where, or a time when, it is not likely children will be exposed to them. At no point in the Congressional debate did the supporters of the CDA ever suggest how it is possible to channel speech on the Internet. The clear and savage effect of the CDA, or other indecency legislation, would be to turn off, not channel, speech on the Internet. And adults and children alike would be much poorer as a result.

## Channeling

Traditional concepts of channeling, from the telephone and broadcast cases, have only limited application to the Internet. Although it is technically possible to make a server, or certain information on it, available only at night, a child living ten time zones away may access it in the middle of her day. Today the purveyors of hard-core pornography, such as the Thomases of *Amateur Action*, do not attach their BBSs to the Internet precisely so they can use traditional means of channeling, such as application forms (effectively "reverse blocking") and credit cards, to screen out minors. However, the philosophy of the Internet itself is that "information wants to be free" and will route itself around censorship. This latter concept might be called "reverse channeling." Therefore, solutions such as application forms or credit cards are not applicable to most aspects of the Net, including Usenet and the World Wide Web. Imposing a "reverse blocking" obligation on access providers would require them to sift through hundreds of thousands of Web, FTP and Telnet sites and Usenet groups to determine what is indecent.

An examination of the client/server paradigm in computing, however, gives some insights into how channeling may be applied to the Internet.

## Immense Server, Fat Client

In the not-so-remote old days, all data resided and all processing took place on the mainframe. A "dumb terminal" on your desk displayed information from the server but was not capable of handling any computation of its own.

The client server paradigm refers to the development of smarter desktop machines such as x-terminals, PCs, and workstations, capable of handling part of the work. While some of these desktop or "client" machines handle only the computation inherent in presenting a graphical user interface, others, known as "fat clients," can handle much of the application's processing, relieving the load on the mainframe. A major design issue in any system is how much of the responsibility to place on the server and how much on the client. Pieces of the application intended to be uniform for all users might be placed on the server. Features that may vary according to user preferences can more profitably be placed on the client machine.

Herein lies the parallel. Modern broadcast media are the equivalent of the mainframe economy from pre-client server days. Your TV or radio is the dumb terminal—in fact, it has often been said that these two appliances are the stupidest in your house, lacking the microchips now built in to your microwave and your coffee maker. The computer, and the television with V-chip installed, represent fat clients, capable of being customized to assist you in making choices about the information you wish to see. Software like Surfwatch is already on the market to assist parents in protecting their children from indecent speech on the Internet. In the world of the fat client, which makes more sense—to expunge the information some people do not wish to see from the server, so that no one can get it? Or to put the onus on each adult to utilize the intelligence now built into the computer or television to decide what information comes into the house? To promote freedom of speech, the clear choice is to place the responsibility on the individual, abetted by the fat client, to filter information.

The client server paradigm also includes the concept of a three tiered architecture. Sometimes the server contains only a massive collection of information, and for performance reasons, we delegate certain watchdog or organizational responsibilities to a third machine in between the server and client. Such third tier machines are already springing up to provide our children with safe access to the Internet. Prodigy and Bessnet, described below, are two such services, filtering the Net's contents to ensure that children can surf safely, while adults who wish to can access the Net directly through an unfiltered service.

## Filtering

Parents who would like the assistance of the child's PC in screening out objectionable content may install a software program like SurfWatch which will block access to a list of sites determined to contain indecent material. Software is also available to block any materials containing certain words or phrases. Some of the on-line services which have entered the Internet access business also provide filtering as a free service to parents. For example, Prodigy, which presents itself as a family-oriented service, restricts users "from posting messages either in public forums or in chat rooms that are deemed inappropriate for children. This includes George Carlin's famous 'Seven Dirty Words'. Internet access from Prodigy is not allowed except with authorization from the parent account holder (using a credit card). In addition, Prodigy keeps a log of which sites the child has visited for parental review. Prodigy's parental control service is free." Another such service is Bessnet, "an Internet service provider designed specifically for kids, families, and schools. Bess blocks access to areas of the net that are inappropriate for children. Bess monitors new sites and adds them to the list of blocked sites on a daily basis; no maintenance is required on the part of the subscriber."

However, filtering software can go overboard and, in the immortal words of *Butler v. Michigan*, may burn the house down to roast the pig. The systems administrator for a nonprofit group home for boys recently installed a Web browser and one of the filtering programs. He deleted the latter when it wouldn't permit another staff member to access a Web page for battered women. "Guess we'll just have to fall back on good old adult supervision," he commented.

## Fighting Speech with Speech

When we really dislike something, think it is evil, inimical to everything we stand for, and dangerous to our children, it is a natural reaction to want the government to regulate or ban it. Each of us has his or her own devil: pornography, Communism, sexual harassment, violence, abortion, welfare, poverty, religion in the classroom, or the lack of religion in the classroom. If we hate a thing and wish to ban it—or if it is already banned by the law, as violence, obscenity, religion in the classroom, and sexism in the workplace are— then it is also human nature to wish to ban speech about it. After all, talking about a thing may cause people to want it; it may be attractive precisely because forbidden. If no one can talk about it, no one may ever learn it exists.

The First Amendment is a stop sign. It says, "You cannot," in almost all cases in which we think about banning speech. It stands for the proposition that no one is God-like enough, no one can be trusted, to decide which speech to ban. Its message is, if you don't like someone's speech, speak up and tell them, and tell everyone else who is listening, and get them to tell everyone they know too.

Each chapter in this book has focused on a situation in which speech was thought to have crossed the line, leaving the First Amendment's zone of protection entirely because it is categorized as: obscenity (*Amateur Action*), a threat of action (Jake Baker), a munition (Phil Zimmerman), a copyright infringement (Scientology), likely to cause imminent lawless action (Candyman), or libel (Prodigy). We did not write a chapter on hate speech and denial of the Holocaust, because as yet no Senator Exon or Feinstein has come forward to claim that such speech is not protected by the First Amendment. However, Nazi and skinhead propaganda on the Net made the newspapers frequently this year and is much on the mind of people like Rabbi Hier of the Wiesenthal Center. "Cyberspace offers direct instantaneous, cheap, mainstream communications in the marketplace of ideas," he told Senator Feinstein and the Senate Judiciary subcommittee during the bomb bill hearing. "Young people—a target group for racists—are especially drawn to this cutting edge of technology." The rabbi, who is obviously in conflict because he is committed to the First Amendment as much as he hates hatred, wants government to find ways to combat these groups even though he knows their speech cannot be banned. He wants on-line services to refuse to carry their material. He wants private citizens everywhere to feel outrage against them. Rabbi Hier, saying these things to Congress and in editorials, is fighting speech with speech.

You can find some very disturbing speech on the Internet. Since the Oklahoma City bombing, Usenet has been awash in speculation that the government itself, or the Anti-Defamation League (a Jewish organization), committed the bombing. A typical message lists a series of allegedly unexplained aspects of the bombing, like the "fact" that a black helicopter was seen hovering over the building just before the explosion. The Patriot gopher server contains a miasma of files about conspiracies, the New World Order, and the militias. The Institute for Historical Review web site contains a series of unctuous documents which explain, in calm, technical language, that no Jews were deliberately killed during the Holocaust, that Auschwitz was a prison camp, not a death camp, and that most of the small number of deaths there were from disease, especially after the inconsiderate Allies bombed the Germans so badly that they could no longer care for the Jews properly. No one could possibly have been gassed in the showers or burned in the ovens. And so on.

Ken McVay is famous on the Internet for his ceaseless campaign against hate and Holocaust denial. First, he wrote the Auschwitz FAQ, which he posts to Usenet every time someone claims there is no proof the Holocaust occurred. Later, he created the Nizkor Project web site, which is a gateway to gigabytes of Holocaust-related materials on the Internet. Trusting in McVay's belief that speech will overcome speech, and wanting the reader to know just what it is he is opposing, Nizkor contains links to the Institute for Historical Review and other hateful sites.

In an E-mail interview, McVay spoke of his electronic crusade and what he has learned from it.

> "Q: What makes the 'revisionists' tick? I've used the link from your pages to visit the IHR pages, and noticed that, instead of the ravings you'd expect, the whole thing is pitched so low key that it would persuade a certain number of people who know nothing about the Holocaust. What is their agenda?"
>
> "A: Surely you understand that I can't begin to speak for them—all I can do is speculate. For many of them, in my view, the agenda is simply to indulge in Hitler-cleansing, in order to make fascism respectable. However, so long as the Holocaust remains as unquestioned historical reality, nothing these people either do or say will convince anyone that Adolf Hitler was really a rather nice chap, albeit misunderstood.
>
> I think this is about power - nothing more, nothing less."
>
> "Q: What got you interested in going after the revisionists?"
>
> "A: They offended my humanity. It's that simple..."
>
> "Q: Do you think human beings are far more capable of perpetrating evil than of remembering, understanding, or avoiding it?"
>
> "A: Man has a horrid capacity to do evil, almost as if he cannot avoid it - a genetic marker gone bad, perhaps..."
>
> "Perhaps one thing that I should note, because authors often sensationalize the hate mongering on the Net, is that, for all their vitriol,

these people are only a tiny handful of the 30-40 million users on the Internet. I am weary of seeing their activities blown out of proportion, as I am weary of seeing the issue of 'child porn' blown out of proportion...."

"We are dealing with a few dozen cynical activists, trolling the net for money and cannon fodder. Even if *all* of the estimated 20,000 or so Fascists on the continent became active on the Net, they *still* would represent no more than a small ripple in the Internet pond. In spite of that, the press continues to sensationalize their presence, using it as an excuse for black headlines, and the Canadian and American governments dutifully blather about 'controlling the Internet,' presumably for 'our own good.'

Speaking for myself, I wish to make it crystal clear that I don't *want* to be 'protected' by government thought police. Everywhere we turn, governments are pushing and prodding our lives, and I'm far more concerned about *them* attacking the Net, and thus our freedom, than I am about watching the Nazis do it."

# Hysteria

Gold is discovered and the rush begins. The people who flock to the new territory include the adventurous, the greedy, the loners, the hungry, the violent, and those with something to hide. Some will get rich; some will see their dreams evade them; some will go to prison; and some will die. Inconvenient indigenous people will be eliminated if they stand between the newcomers and the gold. A force—greed, curiosity, the shock of the new—transforms everybody's lives. Later, the territory will become a community like any other. But now, all the usual rules are suspended, and as a result, all human characteristics seem to be warped or magnified. Beauty and ugliness are extreme. People you have never met before and will never see again cannot be trusted. Merchants sell you shoddy products because they are in too much of a hurry to make them well, or because they think they only have a day to make a dollar before everyone else arrives.

Sound familiar? It is the Internet today. The pages of the press, and the electrons of the Net itself, are full of optimistic expectations, hype, exaggerated claims, and grotesque condemnations. "There's always another mind there. It's like...the corner bar, complete with old buddies and delightful newcomers and new tools waiting to take home and fresh graffiti and letters. ... I just invoke my telecom program and there they are. It's a place." But it's also "a porn shop in a child's bedroom." It turns the entire world into a single nervous system; but it also isolates us and makes us antisocial. It gives us the ability to find whatever we need quickly and cheaply, track public affairs, communicate with our leaders; but it also overwhelms us with information glut and makes us passive and irresponsible.

A company, which for some years has been a well-respected Internet access provider for businesses, tries to stake a claim in the low end of the market by releasing a browser so full of bugs that it crashes every session, cannot save files, and garbles HTML forms. A pair of immigration lawyers "spam" Usenet, blasting out tens of thousands of self-promoting messages to all newsgroups. Advertising banners begin to appear on World Wide Web pages. Marty Rimm rides into town with bottles of a distasteful patent medicine, which he markets simultaneously as an aphrodisiac and as a sexual appetite suppressant. FCC chairman Reed Hundt prowls around in the background, hoping that Congress will ask him to be the sheriff of the Internet. Federal prosecutors grapple with the problem of applying export laws to an instantaneous, worldwide network. Senators inveigh against "pornographers, pedophiles, and predators" on the Internet, though for most people, it is very difficult to find any.

We have examined the incidents in this book from a legal, ethical, and political standpoint. But it is possible to place them in a larger context: the Internet is the modern Yukon and everyone wants a piece of the action. Are the issues real, or are they only pretexts for a battle of interests? "The odds are always good," says Howard Rheingold, "that big power and big money will find a way to control access to virtual communities; big power and big money have always found ways to control new communications media when they emerged in the past. What we know and do now is important because it is still possible for people around the world to make sure this new sphere of vital human discourse remains open to the citizens of this planet before the political and economic big boys seize it, censor it, meter it, and sell it back to us."

The cases and incidents we discuss in this book represent the first shots fired by an advance party intent on a land grab.

## Business or Speech... What is the Internet for?

For those of us who post to Usenet, exchange E-mail, update Gopher servers, or maintain Web pages, it is the "pluralistic world of small communicators" that was 18th century America, born again. A biographer of Thomas Jefferson commented that, if Jefferson lived today, he would be an obscure university professor, and would never dare enter politics. By contrast, if Thomas Paine lived today, he would almost certainly publish only on the Internet. Paine, having failed as a sailor, staymaker, shopkeeper, and customs official in Britain, came to America where he was an obscure schoolteacher and journalist. His anonymously printed pamphlet, *Common Sense*, electrified Americans with its argument, pitched in the right tone at the right moment, that their destiny was to separate from Britain. "No pages was ever more eagerly read, nor more generally approved. People speak of it with rapturous praise," said one contemporary.

In today's world of media conglomerates and executives desperate for the sure thing, how many modern Thomas Paines fail to get heard—unless they make their reputation on the Internet first? Paine self-published the second edition of *Common Sense* because he was unhappy with the publisher's efforts with the first. You can potentially reach millions of people at little expense by self-publishing on the Internet. Paine would have a Web page and a FAQ posted to Usenet—where he would also have the opportunity to be read, debated and believed by millions of people.

The proof is the proliferation of essays, newsletters, and other original texts of scholarship and advocacy on the Net. *The Network Observer, Computer Mediated Communications Journal,* and *The Ethical Spectacle* are just three of the monthly publications that exist only on the Net, with no newsprint equivalent. They cover the social import of technology, the dangers of censorship, the collisions between ethics, law and politics in America. With the raise in postage prices, struggling noncommercial journals with something of importance to say may soon have to join their electronic brethren on the Web, where stamps are not necessary and where they can reach a potential audience of millions at a fraction of the cost of mailing to thousands.

The National Organization for Women, the Christian Coalition, Greenpeace, and the NRA are on the Web. While some who surf may be looking for the Nude of the Month or **playboy.com**, many others are simply starved for the kind of discourse they can't find in *Time, 60 Minutes,* or *The Bridges of Madison County.*

But there is another, competing view of the Net. It is the view of Chairman Hundt, who sees a shiny new appliance, a "converged" TV, telephone and computer, clean, regulated by the FCC, allowing you to order pizzas in the privacy of your home. In *To Renew*

*America,* Newt Gingrich reveals that he may not have been overly concerned by the Hyde amendment because his view of the Net is all about markets, markets, markets. The Internet, says Speaker Gingrich, gives you the opportunity to dominate a corner of the information market. "You may know more than anyone else about the incorporation laws of Zaire and offer advice to anyone attempting to set up a business in that country." He concludes that "the United States can profit enormously by being the leader in the development of the new goods, services, systems, and standards associated with a technological revolution of this scale."

Listen to the words chosen by investment banker Daniel Burstein and *Wired* contributing writer David Kline in *Road Warriors:*

> "Can the Internet's wild frontier be tamed and made 'safe' for Big Business?..."
>
> "[C]yberspace may eventually turn out to be the greatest new market opportunity in history ...."
>
> "But what is far less certain is whether it can be effectively molded to serve corporate America's key financial and business-to-business requirements."

Most ominously, and apparently unaware of the obnoxious significance of their metaphor, they write that "in between those eastern farms and the hills of California there lies a long, long stretch of 'Indian country.'" The Indians who must be eliminated for the safety of the newly arriving settlers are the hacker denizens of the Internet.

Journalist Steve Levy, chronicler of the early history of the personal computer revolution, offers a ray of hope. He notes that big media mergers intended to create mega-companies with important stakes in the Information Superhighway are failing, while small software companies specializing in the Internet are thriving. The Bell Atlantic and TCI merger fell apart and companies are pulling the plug on set-top box projects, and discontinuing the wiring of local communities with optical fiber ready for video on demand; but companies such as Netscape are thriving. The financial markets, driven by people who understand stocks but not the Net, will continue to thrash for a while, but the set-top box vision of the Information Superhighway, where interactivity is limited to ordering a pizza or a movie, may be dead. Levy says a different vision of the media future has the potential to "pull the plug on the 500-channel dream." He quotes EFF co-founder John Perry Barlow: the current mass media merger epidemic is "the re-arrangement of deck chairs on the Titanic." "The iceberg, of course," adds Levy, "is the Internet."

The set-top box vision is not synonymous with business on the Net. While the broadcast and cable companies are trying to apply the metaphor they understand, bookstores, record stores, florists, overnight package companies, banks, and numerous others are already doing business on the World Wide Web, even taking credit card orders without a great deal of fuss. If the settlers and Indians couldn't co-exist in America, it was mainly because of the rapaciousness and fanaticism of the former; if business and speech can't coexist in cyberspace, it will be for the same reasons. Saying that the Internet must be cleaned up for business is like saying that we must eliminate *The Nation* magazine to clear the way for *Money* or *People*. It is like saying that in order for businesspeople to use the phone, we must eliminate chatting, flirtation, or political discussion. Only if you regard business on the Net exclusively in light of the broadcast metaphor, does the conflict make sense. Broadcast regulation and free speech cannot co-exist, but business and free speech can.

## Control of the Internet

Each of the incidents we relate in this book must be seen in the context of an epic battle for control of the Internet. David Dirmeyer, whether he understood it or not, was battling to ensure that nothing could be posted anywhere in cyberspace that would violate Tennessee standards. Michigan prosecutors, the university, and Professor Catharine MacKinnon wanted Jake Baker out of the way for writing vile short stories on Usenet. Senator Exon is trying to apply broadcast-style regulation to the Net, while Reed Hundt coyly waits to see if someone will offer him the job. The Church of Scientology doesn't simply want to fight speech with speech; it wants to use all the technical and legal tools at its disposition to stamp out opposition on the Net. The Scientologists, Stratton Oakmont, and the Christian Coalition all advanced the proposition that the electronic bookstore should be held liable for the misdeeds of the author, so we can more effectively stamp out bad speech on-line. Rabbi Hier ambivalently says that he doesn't want the government raiding the bookstore; he wants the bookstore to be a good citizen and censor itself. Senator Feinstein and law professor Cass Sunstein don't want bad speech to compete in the electronic marketplace of ideas. The

Justice Department and the FBI don't want Phil Zimmerman, or anyone else, to publish anything cryptology-related which might get on the Net and might get downloaded abroad. And Marty Rimm shows up to sell refreshments to the contestants and spectators on both sides of the issue.

The question, "Who should control the Internet?" may be seen in an entirely different light if we remember the operative metaphor. If the Internet is a constellation of printing presses and bookstores, then what we are really asking is, "Who should control the press? Who should control free speech?" That question is easily answered by the First Amendment: "Congress shall make no law respecting an establishment of religion, or prohibiting the free exercise thereof; or abridging the freedom of speech, or of the press; or the right of the people peaceably to assemble, and to petition the government for a redress of grievances."

In fact, because of its distributed nature, control of the Internet is probably impossible, and, if attempted, can result only in its destruction. Nicholas Negroponte compares the Net to ducks flying in V formation. "[T]hat order is not imposed by a head duck. If a hunter shoots the head duck, the V shape reforms, and the ducks continue on. ... Tensions between the government and the Internet are often caused by this decentralization. The government can't attack the Internet leader. In fact, to fight the net—as Sen. Exon...seem[s] determined to do—there is really no alternative except to shoot all the ducks."

In an age where all public discourse will take place on the Internet, where our print publications and broadcast journalism have failed us and where there are significant truths which can be found only on the Net, nobody must control it. Don't let history repeat itself; instead preserve the "pluralistic world of small communicators" for more than another 200 years. The Internet must remain free.

## New Laws

Again, the operative metaphor sets the stage for any discussion. What new laws were necessary to govern the printing press or the bookstore? The First Amendment establishes that laws affecting speech are heavily disfavored. In the circumstances where they are permitted, they must be content-neutral and narrowly tailored to serve a compelling government interest.

Because of the hysteria surrounding a new technology which is causing a social transformation, our lawmakers have lost sight of the fact that most of the old laws work just fine. Yet history illustrates the principle that old laws are mostly shaped, not thrown away, when a new technology emerges. The telegraph was like a railroad. The telephone was a form of telegraph. Television was radio with pictures. When the automobile was introduced, existing laws governing the theft of personal property were easily applied or adapted to protect automobile owners. There was no significant difference between the theft of a horse drawn carriage and that of an automobile. It is not necessary to remake our laws from scratch every time we create something new, yet there are people apparently blind to metaphor who always want to rush in and do exactly that.

Some people have been on-line, exchanging mail and files since the 1970s. Seventeen years of the personal computer and the growth of cyber-institutions like CompuServe and Fidonet provided fertile ground for precedent-seeking and dispute resolution even before the recent Internet boom. Every time the issue has risen, lawyers and policy makers have eventually discovered how easily existing laws can be applied. There is no meaningful legal distinction to be made between making an illegal copy of a book using a photocopier and making an illegal copy of software using your disk drive—or by E-mailing it via the Net. Prodigy's liability for a libelous statement should be no more, and no less, than that of the owner of your community bookstore. Child pornography can be prosecuted the same way whether it is in a magazine or a GIF stored on a server.

Sometimes a feature or effect of a new technology will render a law obsolete, or will require a new one. This happens extremely rarely, far less often than people such as Senator Exon or Senator Feinstein think. Perhaps speed limits were not necessary until cars came along. Scarcity of the original radio spectrum required a scheme for allocating frequencies. The threshold question is what features or effects of the Internet evade or invalidate old laws? Possible answers are the Net's pervasiveness, its ability to reach millions of users, its universal and instantaneous nature. As we have demonstrated, the Net's pervasiveness should not be an excuse for regulation if we value the First Amendment. As for the idea that the Internet is "dangerous" because it reaches so many, Cass Sunstein's argument, that controversial or disfavored speech is acceptable as long as it reaches only a few people, is contradicted by all prior First Amendment jurisprudence and must fail.

Only the Internet's universal, instantaneous presence requires changes to existing law. The Internet as a global "nervous system" renders futile and inapplicable the Supreme Court's *Miller* standard and the Justice Department's attempt to apply export laws to software. When something placed on a server in Milpitas, California is instantaneously available to users in Memphis and France, the laws must be changed to adapt.

## Advice for the Perplexed

Most of the following points are directed to judges and legislators who are making decisions affecting cyberspace. The last recommendation is our request, directed to our fellow citizens of the on-line world, for good citizenship.

**The First Amendment applies in cyberspace**. Avoid double standards and knee jerk reactions. Ask yourself whether you would react differently to the same speech in a different medium. If the material you are ruling or basing legislation upon would be First Amendment-protected if disseminated in a book or magazine, there is no rationale for treating it differently on the Internet. Robert Thomas's distribution of obscene GIFs is no different than if he had distributed obscene magazines. Jake Baker's case would be identical if he had handed out leaflets containing his stories rather than posting them to Usenet. Candyman's Web pages and Barricade Books' *Anarchist Cookbook* are the same in the eyes of the law. Using a computer does not, and should not, make anything illegal that is legal if done without a computer.

**Free speech is a good thing**. Our existing mass media are ever fewer in number, run for profit, and very constrained. They do not offer us the full spectrum of available ideas for our evaluation. Moreover, they stand between us and the facts, acting as self-appointed interpreters of information we now have the capacity to obtain and evaluate for ourselves. As the newest mass medium, the Net presents unprecedented opportunities for diversity of speech and for the free flow of information. Please do not stifle this new medium.

**Don't rush in!** History shows that the first attempt to regulate a new technology is almost always disastrously wrong. Instead of constantly repeating the mistakes of the past, why not take a deep breath, review the situation, and give the technology's creators and users time to work out the wrinkles? Senator Leahy's suggestion that the government study the situation a little while, giving the denizens of the Net time to design their own native forms of channeling, was a good one. Senator Exon's proposal, to rush right in and end all serious intellectual discussion on the Net, was a bad one.

Duke University professor Stanley Fish points out that First Amendment protections serve "a function that is not at all negligible; they slow down outcomes in an area in which the fear of overhasty outcomes is justified by a long record of abuses of power. ... there is some comfort and protection to be found in a procedure that requires you to jump through hoops—do a lot of argumentative work—before a speech regulation will be allowed to stand."

**Indecency regulation has no place on the Net.** If you derive only one message from this book, let it be the following: due to human nature, serious discourse at some point or another will depict or describe sexual or excretory acts or organs, as metaphor, as history, or as information. Cleansing the entire Net of material that falls afoul of this extremely broad standard would leave only intellectual pabulum and would deprive the public of the most serious uses of the newest mass medium. It's the wrong thing to do. Please take a stand in support of free speech and recognize the First Amendment's full, unconditional applicability to the Internet.

**The time has come to overrule Miller.** *Miller* is the hand of the past strangling the present. It was an antiquated and inappropriate standard when the Supreme Court adopted it in 1973. It makes even less sense today. It serves only to let the most conservative community in the United States determine the content of the entire Net. A global, instantaneous network cannot be governed by local standards of obscenity. A national standard and, ultimately, an international convention (similar to the evolution of copyright law) is the only approach that makes sense. Applying the standards of electronic communities who themselves are the users of the pornographic material effectively repeals obscenity laws (in which case we might just as well overtly do so) or, conversely, invites the same abuses inherent in the application of geographical community standards. The channeling of pornographic speech should be recognized as a defense to liability for obscenity just as it is for indecency; if the Robert Thomases of the world can show that they took measures to exclude minors and that their material was viewed and used only be consenting adults, they should be left alone. Moreover, the introduction of obscenity laws into the on-line world is an excellent opportunity to revisit the intentions and effects of obscenity regulation in general. The important questions to consider are: is there any logic in classifying obscenity as something other than speech? Is it really possible to define obscenity? Can obscenity rules be made sufficiently explicit that a content provider can seek the limits of free speech without needing to fear that he or she will inadvertently sail over the constantly shifting boundaries, or be dragged into court in a foreign jurisdiction? Who is the victim? Exactly what social interests are we seeking to advance?

We do not know if it will happen next year or 20 years from now, but we are completely confident that the Supreme Court will overrule *Miller* and replace it with a national standard.

**Keep the FCC far away from the Net.** Reed Hundt probably wouldn't say no if you asked him to regulate the Net. Don't do it. In the near future, the Internet may be a more important source of reading material than the bookstore for most of us. (For many, it already is.) Electronic print on a screen is still print. If you wouldn't want the FCC telling you what you can and can't stock in a bookstore, then you shouldn't want it involved in the Internet. "Truth and understanding," said Milton, "are not such wares as to be monopolized and traded in by tickets and statutes and standards."

**Don't allow government to chill information distributors.** The *Eckstein, Mountain Bell,* and *Alliance for Community Media* cases tell a frightening story. The government is increasingly pressuring information providers to act as censors. They are inexperienced at this job, have relatively little ability to carry out a First Amendment analysis, and, as profit-making businesses, have no reason to invest time and money defending free speech. Thus, they will inevitably institute overbroad censorship schemes, throwing out legal speech along with the illegal or indecent. "Yet his very office and his commission enjoins him to let pass nothing but what is vulgarly received already," said Milton.

**When you seize a computer, you seize a printing press.** In cases such as *Amateur Action* and *Steve Jackson Games,* authorities have seized computers and held them for evidence, or sought their forfeiture. Insufficient consideration was given to the fact that by taking the computer, you restrain all the other speech it is being used to produce. Each of these seizures shut down communities of individuals who used these machines to exchange mail with each other. They may, as in the *Amateur Action* case, be communities we disapprove of, but our dislike doesn't tarnish their First Amendment rights. Their speech to one another, consisting of written words, was not obscene even if the GIFs stored on the computer were. The police can search a computer without taking it away just as they can search a house without uprooting it. As for forfeitures, developments in this area have encouraged immoderate behavior by some law enforcement authorities in recent years as cars and homes have been taken away with little justification. Just as you should not require forfeiture of an entire bookstore because the owner sold one obscene book, you should not take away a computer system which is used for constitutionally protected speech just because some illegal speech took place there.

**Be cautious about prior restraints.** There have been a number of cases, such as *Baker* and *Elansky*, where judges rather casually ordered defendants not to post to the Internet or to BBS's, or to avoid certain kinds of speech when they did post. It is an easy mistake to make if you do not remind yourself that the computer is a printing press. Imagine an order granting bond or probation which instructed a defendant to stop writing columns for *The Nation* or the *National Review*. There is no difference.

**New laws are almost never necessary.** Most laws are drafted generically. Laws applying to personal property don't have to be modified every time a new type of personal property is invented. Existing laws pertaining to obscenity, libel, and fighting words can be used appropriately in connection with speech on the Net. Laws discriminating against on-line speech—criminalizing speech which is legal in a newspaper or magazine—are always based on misconceptions or on impermissible distinctions. The most dangerous of these is Cass Sunstein's suggestion that speech can be outlawed based on its success in reaching a mass audience. Can an idea that is legal in a newsletter with a circulation of 500 people be banned from appearing in *Time* ? Obviously not. The First Amendment, and the fabric of free speech in our society, is founded on the assumption that the good speech will win.

The only circumstances in which new speech-related laws are required is when a new technology changes the landscape by rendering prior rules inapplicable. In general, new laws to restrict speech should not be necessary but new laws to protect speech may be. Two examples are the *Miller* standard and the export laws, neither of which accord well with the realities of speech on a global, instantaneous network.

**The owner of the wire is a common carrier.** Rabbi Hier, the Christian Coalition, and the Justice Department have all expressed interest in "encouraging" information distributors to think twice about the distribution of disfavored speech. If Internet access providers are free to pick and choose the speech that may reach the Internet, by implication they may join together to determine that certain categories of speech, though legal, will never see the light of day. This is the moral equivalent of the telegraph companies refusing to transmit telegrams from reporters to their newspapers; it is wrong and must not be permitted. While companies that sell not only access but content of their own, such as CompuServe, America Online, and Prodigy, must be treated as distributors and have the right to delete disfavored speech, others, such as Performance Systems International and Netcom, who sell only a connection to the Internet, must be treated as common carriers. They must be denied the right to bar anyone from the Internet and, conversely, must be held blameless for the content of the speech that passes over the wires they own.

**Anonymity is socially useful.** The publishers of Protestant literature and of Rabelais left their names off the books to avoid persecution. *Common Sense* was published anonymously. A seminal essay on policy toward the Soviets was published in the late 1940s under the name X; the author made his identity known 40 years later, and his work was still being quoted as the Soviet Empire fell. Many great, if controversial, works of literature and political advocacy have been published anonymously or under pseudonyms, which amounts to the same thing. Frequently, the best way to advance an unpopular idea without receiving social sanction is to disseminate it anonymously. If pseudonyms cannot legally be outlawed in print literature, there are no grounds for forbidding them on the Net. Requiring people to "take responsibility" for their ideas on the Net is really a way of ensuring that they will utter, or endorse, only popular ideas. An idea will stand or fall on its own merits in the marketplace, regardless of the identity of its "owner." Most crimes, as Phil Zimmerman said, leave footprints in the real world: Criminal acts on the Internet can always be investigated, and, in many cases, identities of the criminals discovered, without the necessity of forcing all users of the Net to declare themselves.

**Cryptography is also socially useful.** There can be no better justification of the importance of cryptography to free speech than the government's desire to get rid of it. The right of free speech under the First Amendment is not restricted to speech that is uttered loudly and slowly in a public place within earshot of the government. We also have a right to speak to each other in whispers, in slang, innuendo, or code, and to keep our speech private. There is no difference between the government's Clipper and Digital Telephony proposals and a law requiring all new houses to be built with a bug in every room. In the entire history of this country, from the framing of the Constitution to the present day, the government has never dared suggest that a mass medium collaborate widely in allowing it to listen to the speech of every American. If the FBI can flip a switch and listen to any call, it will do so, regardless of any promise always to obtain a warrant.

We are not prepared to say that all software should not be considered subject to export laws. However, we strongly believe that it serves no useful purpose, and cripples the ability of American software companies to compete, to ban the export of software using keys of more than 40 bits. Cryptology software should be exempted from the definition of a "munition" and should be freely exportable like other commercial software.

Phillip Zimmerman has never been indicted and it is possible the government is using the grand jury activity to chill his rights of free speech, travel, and free association. Obviously, it should not be considered a crime to publish a program that someone else places on the Net. Even if Zimmerman had placed PGP on the Net himself, the anomalous application of United States export laws to a global network would dictate that nothing could be placed on the Internet which could not legitimately be sent abroad. Since PGP may be freely distributed domestically, and the Internet is a prime means of distribution, the effect is to chill Zimmerman from distributing it— even from publishing it—for fear it may go out of the country. This is not the behavior we expect in an open society and highlights the necessity of easing export restrictions. The category of software that cannot be posted to the Net—if it is necessary to have such a category at all—should be very narrowly defined.

**Channeling, if required, should take place at the client level.** Technology now offers us a marvelous series of options for customizing the information that enters our house. This allows parents to make individual choices about the speech their children are allowed to hear, without requiring the rest of us to delete all adult information from every computer on the Internet in order to make the world safe for children. Please note that set-top box and V-chip technology make this solution practical for cable and broadcast television as well. Under the circumstances, laws aimed at the "server"—the entire Internet, or the provider of broadcast or cable content—flunk the First Amendment test requiring that regulation be narrowly tailored. The most narrowly tailored laws will be those which aim at increasing flexibility at the client level—building "regulatory intelligence" into the TV set or computer—rather than banning speech on the server.

**Good citizenship involves creating a non-restrictive way to channel the Net.** As we have already said, we do not believe that the government can legally apply indecency regulations to the Internet, any more than it could to print publications. Therefore, it is tempting to say that we must be vigilant against any attempt, a la *Eckstein, Mountain Bell,* or *Alliance for Community Media,* to bully us into self-censorship.

Nevertheless, we believe that voluntary self-rating would not harm anyone's rights, and in fact represents the only form of channeling universally valid for cyberspace. A <rating=""> tag could be added to the next generation of HTML. Ratings, which would be self-imposed by the creator of each Web site, might approximate those assigned to movies: G, PG, R and NC-17. A parent installing a Web browser could follow simple instructions to set the level of material that the browser would accept from the server. The browser could also be set to refuse any pages lacking the <rating> tag. Says Alex Stewart, one of the first to propose an HTML self-rating system: "We, as a community of informed, responsible people have a duty not only to the rest of the world but to ourselves to show that our community can be responsible and responsive to the concerns of parents, teachers, and others of the larger world in which we also live." The same ratings could be used for Usenet news groups or individual messages and for telnet and FTP sites.

The *Amateur Action* case illustrates the probable success of such an approach. Purveyors of explicit sexual material typically do not want minors or the unwary to stumble on their merchandise. Robert Thomas did everything he reasonably could to "channel" the pornographic material he carried, including requiring a written application, a credit card and a phone conversation before he granted access to the BBS. Most providers of intentionally explicit material will gladly apply the most restrictive voluntary rating if it means that their target audience of adults will still find them, while the "cyber-cops," public and private, search elsewhere for the socially irresponsible.

What about the hardcore incurable, the pedophile who insists on applying a G rating because he wants children to visit his pages of innuendo and double entendre? Since human nature encompasses a wide range of evil characters, we believe he is out there somewhere, though we have never seen anyone like him on the Web. Parents can guard against him by the use of filtering software or by obtaining Internet access for their children through services like Bessnet. We also believe that the Internet community would team up to fight speech with speech, exposing such an individual and urging him out of the public eye. Finally, if he crossed the line, he could be indicted for child pornography.

We believe that a combination of these approaches will make cyberspace a very comfortable place for families and children, while preserving its outspoken, human, varied and sometimes explicit character. The Net, as the press was at our country's founding, is a "pluralistic world of small communicators," and should remain so.

# EPILOGUE

The stories we tell are not over. The CDA was struck down as unconstitutional in 1996 by a panel of three federal judges in Philadelphia; however, the case is being appealed and will be heard by the Supreme Court in early 1997. The Jake Baker case is also being appealed by the government. The Church of Scientology is still litigating furiously against its critics. The Clinton Administration still considers powerful cryptography as munitions and is pushing for key escrow schemes. In addition, new cases are being filed every day that could affect the future of the Net.

We have set up a web site at http://www.spectacle.org/freespch/ to bring you continuing coverage of these events. The site follows the organization of the table of contents of this book. In each section, you will find a summary of the chapter, links to the online materials we consulted, and updates and afterthoughts on the cases we discussed in the book.

We also invite readers to contact us via E-mail at markm@bway.net for Mark Mangan and jw@bway.net for Jonathan Wallace.

# BIBLIOGRAPHY

It was a pleasure to write a book that allowed us to quote Plato, Milton, De Tocqueville, and McLuhan and that united subjects as diverse as the First Amendment, the history of technology, media criticism, and the history of communications. The following are the books on which we relied a great deal and which we recommend for further reading.

Above all, we recommend Ithiel de Sola Pool's *Technologies of Freedom* (Cambridge: Harvard University Press, 1983). This remarkable book qualifies for no fewer than three of the following categories; published 12 years ago, it is about cyberspace, freedom of speech, and media.

## CYBERSPACE

Nicholas Negroponte, *Being Digital* (New York: Alfred Knopf, 1995). Negroponte explains, in simple language, the transformations resulting from increased bandwidth, technological convergence, and the triumph of bits over atoms.

Howard Rheingold, *The Virtual Community* (New York: Harper Perennial, 1994). Rheingold is the original Internet cheerleader. His book is simultaneously a history of cyberspace and a paean to its possibilities.

Lance Rose, *Netlaw* (New York: McGraw-Hill, 1995). Rose is an expert in on-line law, and this book, aimed at system operators and information providers, includes coverage of copyright, First Amendment issues, obscenity, and searches and seizures.

Peter H. Salus, *Casting the Net* (Reading, Mass.: Addison Wesley, 1995). This little-noticed book is a documentary history of the Internet from its earliest days.

Clay Shirky, *Voices from the Net* (Emeryville, Calif.: Ziff-Davis, 1995). Shirky, like Rheingold, provides an intelligent tour of the social topography and promise of the Internet.

Bruce Sterling, *The Hacker Crackdown* (New York: Bantam, 1992). This is a disorganized but highly readable history of the first federal prosecutions involving on-line crimes; it includes the founding of the Electronic Frontier Foundation.

# FREEDOM OF SPEECH

Stanley Fish, *There's No Such Thing as Free Speech* (New York: Oxford University Press, 1994). Fish is a law professor and Miltonist, a strange combination. In several essays, including the one from which the book takes its title, he advances an idiosyncratic and somewhat irritating—but highly thought-provoking—analysis of First Amendment law.

Kent Greenawalt, *Fighting Words* (Princeton: Princeton University Press, 1995). Columbia Law professor Greenawalt summarizes First Amendment jurisprudence, concentrating on *Brandenburg* and the theory of "fighting words."

Jethro K. Lieberman, *The Evolving Constitution* (New York: Random House, 1992). A one-volume encyclopedia of the Supreme Court's rulings, alphabetical by topic.

Robert J. Wagman, *The First Amendment Book* (New York: Pharos Books, 1991). A layman's history of First Amendment case law, with chapters on obscenity, libel, and broadcast regulation.

# MEDIA

Lawrence K. Grossman, *The Electronic Republic* (New York: Viking, 1995). Grossman is a former president of PBS and NBC News. He combines insights into the limitations of regulated media with some fascinating stories of his own experiences.

Edward S. Herman and Noam Chomsky, *Manufacturing Consent* (New York: Pantheon, 1988). Herman and Chomsky maintain that the mass media usually tell the official government story where foreign affairs are concerned.

Marshall McLuhan, *Understanding Media* (Cambridge: The MIT Press, 1994). Half the time, McLuhan is babbling incoherently; the rest of the time he is advancing remarkable insights into the nature of human communications.

Neil Postman, *Amusing Ourselves to Death* (New York: Penguin 1985), *Conscientious Objections* (New York: Vintage, 1988), *Technopoly* (New York: Vintage, 1993). Postman is an eloquent, sarcastic critic of media and always a pleasure to read. However, his dislike of computers has caused him to misunderstand the Internet grievously; he thinks it is a form of telegraph, overloading us with a glut of irrelevant information.

# PORNOGRAPHY

Edward deGrazia, *Girls Lean Back Everywhere* (New York: Vintage Books, 1992). An anecdotal history of the use of obscenity laws to censor literary works, by an attorney who defended Henry Miller and William Burroughs, among others.

Susan M. Easton, *The Problem of Pornography* (London: Routledge, 1994). A British law professor struggles with the question of how to regulate pornography without chilling speech.

Catharine A. MacKinnon, *Only Words* (Cambridge: Harvard University Press, 1993). This is a brilliant, savage polemic against pornography, by a law professor who believes that free speech is at war with the equality of women.

Wendy McElroy, *XXX: A Woman's Right to Pornography* (New York: St. Martin's Press, 1995). McElroy is the counter-MacKinnon; she argues that pornography is healthy and must not be regulated.

Susan Sontag, *Styles of Radical Will* (Anchor Books, 1991), contains the essay "The Pornographic Imagination," which argues that pornography, though repellent, has literary value.

Adele Stan, editor, *Debating Sexual Correctness* (New York: Delta, 1995) is a collection of essays presenting all feminist positions for and against pornography.

Nadine Strossen, *Defending Pornography* (New York: Scribner, 1995). Strossen is the president of the American Civil Liberties Union and presents the civil libertarian perspective that pornography is First Amendment–protected speech.

# CRYPTOGRAPHY

Philip R Zimmerman, *The Official PGP User's Guide* (Cambridge: MIT Press, 1995) is Zimmerman's own guide and history to PGP.

Simson Garfinkel, *PGP (Pretty Good Privacy)* (Sebastopol, CA: O'Reilly & Associates, 1995) is another fine resource on the capabilities of and story behind PGP.

# CITATIONS

## CHAPTER 1  MEMPHIS RULES

Except where otherwise specified, our account of the events before trial is  based on Dirmeyer's affidavit in support of the search warrant, dated January 14, 1992, filed before Magistrate Brazil in the U.S. District Court for the Northern District of California,  and  our account of the trial is based on the court file, including the trial transcript,  in *United States v. Robert and Carleen Thomas*,  94-20019-G, United States District Court for the Western District of Tennessee, Western Division.

*Page 2*

"I'm requesting your assistance...." Distributed  in July 5 1995 message of J. Keith Henson, in comp.org.eff.talk, misc.legal and alt.sex.

"This file had been prepared by J. Keith Henson...." We interviewed Henson by phone on August 7, 1995.

*Page 10*

"In fact, he thought that Dirmeyer might really be...." Henson Usenet post.

*Page 11*

"On Friday, just as Henson...." Henson Usenet post.

*Page 12*

"On crutches from an injury...."and "He advised me...." Henson Usenet post.

*Page 13*

"On April 18, Williams filed a motion to dismiss..." *Miller v. California*, 413 U.S. 15 (1973).

*Page 14*

"He based his argument on *Xcitement Video*...." *U.S. v. Xcitement Video*, 982 F. 2d 1285 (1992 ).

*Page 17*

"Originally the states were left free...." Jethro K. Lieberman, *The Evolving Constitution* (New York: Random House 1992) p. 354.

*Page 18*

"Of the first two prongs, the 'prurient appeal' part of the test...." Prof. Kathleen Sullivan, quoted in Nadine Strossen, *Defending Pornography,* (New York: Scribner 1995), pp. 53-54.

*Page 28*

"In his brief, Nolan  cited a  Tenth Circuit case...." *U.S. v. Carlin Communications*, 815 F.2d 1367 (10th Cir. 1987).

*Page 29*

"Jumping into the fray...." The appeal was  *Robert and Carleen Thomas v. U.S.,* nos. 94-6648 and 6649, in the United States Court of Appeals for the Sixth Circuit.

"He cited *Cubby v. Compuserve*...." 776 F. Supp. 135 (SDNY 1991).

*Page 30*

"In its famous *Butler v. Michigan* decision...." 352 U.S. 380 (1957).

# FOOTNOTES

*Page 33*

"This argument is well supported...." For background on the prosecution of works of literature under obscenity laws, see generally Edward De Grazia, *Girls Lean Back Everywhere* (New York: Vintage Books 1992).

*Page 34*

"In the 1950's, the Post Office undertook a crusade...." *Roth v. U.S.*, 354 U.S. 476 (1957), see also De Grazia, 273-94.

"In 1986, the Justice Department...." Strossen, pp. 94-95.

*Page 36*

"The Court said that, with regard to unsolicited mailings...." *Consolidated Edison v. Public Service Commission*, 447 U.S. 530 (1980).

"The Supreme Court also invalidated...." *Erznoznik v. City of Jacksonville*, 422 U.S. 205 (1975).

*Page 37*

"Although the recent 'cyberporn' debate...." *Paris Adult Theaters v. Slaton*, 413 U.S. 49 (1973).

"In 1993, she published a book...." Catharine A. MacKinnon, *Only Words* (Cambridge: Harvard University Press 1993).

"What pornography does...." MacKinnon, p. 15.

"The law of equality...." MacKinnon, p. 71.

*Page 38*

"The law was adopted in a few municipalities...." Strossen, pp. 73-81.

"Over the years, the Supreme Court has overturned...." *R.A.V. v. City of St. Paul*, 112 S. Ct. 2538 ( 1992); the Skokie case, Lieberman, *The Evolving Constitution*, p. 241.

*Page 39*

"In *Stanley v. Georgia*...." 394 U.S. 557 (1969).

"John Stuart Mill said...." *On Liberty* (New York: Bantam Books, 1993), p. 12.

# CHAPTER 2  THE GOVERNMENT'S KEYS

Most of the research for this chapter was taken from online sources of information, principally the following: http://www.hotwired.com/ clipper/; http://epic.org/crypto; http://www.quadralay.com/www/Crypt/.

*Page 43*

"In his book *The Puzzle Palace*,..." James Bamford, *The Puzzle Palace* (New York: Penguin, 1983).

*Page 45*

"They introduced their discovery..." Whitfield Diffie and M.E. Hellman. "New Directions in Cryptography." *IEEE Transactions on Information Theory* IT-22 (1976).

*Page 46*

"The magic words are squeamish ossifrage." Simon Garfinkel, *PGP* (Sebastopol: O'Reilly & Associates, 1995) p. 115.

*Page 47*

"As Zimmerman puts it, ..." Philip R. Zimmerman, *The Official PGP User's Guide* (Cambridge: MIT Press, 1995).

*Page 49*

"As he says,..." Ibid.

"As Zimmerman says, 'I think...,'" "Hero or Villain?" by Jeff Ubois, *Internet World.* August 1995.

*Page 51*

"Nicolas Negroponte, the founder..." *Wired.* November 1995.

"The government right to wiretap...." *Olmstead v. U.S.*, 277 US 438 (1928).

*Page 52*

"In *Goldman v. U.S....*" 316 US 129 (1942).

"This was again upheld in 1954...." *Irvine v. California*, 347 US 128 (1954).

"However, in 1961...." *Silverman v. U.S.*, 365 US 505 (1961).

"It was not until 1967...." *Katz v. U.S.* 389 US 347 (1967).

*Page 55*

"John Perry Barlow, co-founder of the EFF..." http://www.seas.gwu.edu:80/seas/instcts/docs/book/ book.html.

"The document explicitly says that..." http://icg.stwing.upenn.edu/cis590/topic.regulation.kumbhani.html.

*Page 56*

"Barlow, who also wrote the introduction..." http://vip.hotwired.com/Lib/Privacy/wired.letter.html.

"Given the small number of currently available wiretaps..." A reply to Dorothy Denning in *Newsday* editorial, February 25, 1995, http://www.hotwired.com/clipper/denning-rivest.html.

"Brock Meeks points out that..." "Same Old Shit, The Government's Not-So-New Clipper II: a train wreck waiting to happen," Brock Meeks, *Wired*, November 1995.

*Page 57*

"Mike Godwin of the EFF points out..." http://cec.wustl.edu/~cs142/articles/ENCRYPTION/clipper-notes—godwin.

"Historically, law enforcement..." Ibid.

"Wouldn't it make sense..." Ibid.

"In support of one's right..." "Hero or Villain?" by Jeff Ubois, *Internet World*, August 1995.

*Page 58*

"In July 1994, Brock Meeks announced..." http://vip.hotwired.com/Lib/Privacy/meeks/dispatch.8.html.

"In a letter to Representative Maria Cantwell..." http://cec.wustl.edu/~cs142/articles/ENCRYPTION/son-of-clipper.

"The *New York Times* ran a front page article..." "F.B.I Wants Advanced System To Vastly Increase Wiretapping," by John Markoff, *The New York Times*, November 2, 1995.

*Page 59*

"They are still apparently married to the idea..." "Same Old Shit, The Government's Not-So-New Clipper II: a train wreck waiting to happen," Brock Meeks, *Wired*, November 1995.

"In a paper hailing the Clipper..." "Resolving the Encryption Dilemma: The Case for Clipper," by Dorothy E. Denning, *Technology Review*, July 1995.

"Mark Rotenberg, the director..." http://cpsr.org/cpsr/privacy/epic/wiretap/wiretap_alert.txt.

"It seems clear to me that Digital Telephony..." http://cec.wustl.edu/~cs142/articles/ENCRYPTION/clipper-notes—godwin.

*Page 61*

"FBI director Freeh asserts..." "F.B.I Isn't Trying to Increase Wiretaps," (letter to the editor) by Louis J. Freeh, *The New York Times*, November 3, 1995.

"A recent *Newsweek* article..." *Newsweek*, April 24, 1995.

# CHAPTER 3   A STALKER IN CYBERSPACE

For the legal proceedings against Jake Baker, we relied on the file in *United States of America v. Jake Baker and Arthur Gonda*, No. 92-80106, E.D. Mich, S. Div. A Web page maintained by P.J. Swan at http://krusty.eecs.umich.edu/people/pjswan/Baker/Jake-Baker.html contained some legal materials, many articles about the case, and copies of Baker's stories.

*Page 63*

"When I saw the story I thought..." "Terror by E-Mail" by David Grogan, *People Magazine*, March 6, 1995 pp. 59-60.

*Page 65*

"The alt.sex newsgroup had been created...." Peter H. Salus, *Casting the Net* (Reading, Mass: Addison Wesley 1995) pp. 140-147.

*Page 66*

"Baker's roomate Jesse Jannetta later remarked,..." "Crossing the Line on the Info Highway," by Megan Garvey, *The Washington Post*, March 11, 1995.

*Page 67*

"David Cahill, the attorney..." "U-M Expelling Student for Internet Fantasy" by Judson Branam, *The Ann Arbor News*, February 4, 1995.

"As Captain James Smiley of the DPS..." Ibid.

*Page 68*

"MacKinnon specifically commented on the Baker case..." http://www.umich.edu/~umlaw/mttlr.html.

"Although the stories were all prefaced..." "FBI Has Contacted U-M," by Stephen Cain, *Ann Arbor News*, February 3, 1995.

*Page 69*

"We're still assuming it..." "Student With Online Fantasy Can't Go To Class," by Judson Branam, *Ann Arbor News*, February 7, 1995.

"Meanwhile, Baker commented to reporters..." *Ann Arbor News*, February 4, 1995.

*Page 70*

"In response to one angry..." "Fantasy Writer Pleads Not Guilty to Threat Charge," by Arthur Bridgeforth, Jr., *Ann Arbor News*, February 18, 1995.

"He protested the detention order..." "Internet Writer Arrested," by Judson Branam and Arthur Bridgeforth, Jr., *Ann Arbor News*, February 10, 1995.

*Page 71*

"Cahill told the press..." "U-M Expelling Student for Internet Fantasy," by Judson Branam, *Ann Arbor News*, February 4, 1995.

*Page 72*

"She later remarked that..." "Internet Writer Arrested," by Judson Branam and Arthur Bridgeforth, Jr., *Ann Arbor News*, February 10, 1995.

*Page 72-73*

"He asserted that Baker's..." "Rape-Torture Fantasy Author Indicted in Federal Court" by William B. Treml, *Ann Arbor News*, February 15, 1995.

*Page 73*

"We will present the court with the same release conditions..." "Prosecutors Push Baker Indictment," by Josh White, *The Michigan Daily*, February 14, 1995.

*Page 74*

"Janetta, Baker's former roomate..." "Student Called 'A Very Quiet Guy,'" by Josh White, *The Michigan Daily*, February 15, 1995.

# FOOTNOTES

"He wrote that Baker's Internet..." "Fantasy Writer Pleads Not Guilty to Threat Charge," by Arthur Bridgeforth, *Ann Arbor News,* February 18, 1995.

"When asked about her son's explicit..." "U-M fantasy Writer to Remain in Jail," by Arthur Bridgeforth, Jr, *Ann Arbor News,* February 11, 1995.

"The FBI was convinced..." "Mystery Man Sought in U-M Rape Story," by John Bebow and Dave Farrell. February 17, 1995.

"Cahill had remarked that..." "Grand Jury Sets New Indictments Against Writer," by Stephen Cain, *Ann Arbor News,* March 16, 1995.

*Page 75*

"I am sorry to have used a real person's name..." "Jake Baker released on 10K Bond" by Josh White, *The Michigan Daily,* February 13, 1995.

"Jake's Stepfather, David Hutchinson..." "Baker Tells Story of Life Behind Bars," by Josh White, *Michigan Daily,* February 13, 1995.

*Page 76*

"Chadwell, who made no objections..." "Judge Frees Sex Fantasist on Bond," by Arthur Bridgeforth, Jr, *Ann Arbor News,* February 11, 1995.

*Page 78*

"In his decision, Cohn..." *United States v. Kelner,* 534 F. 2d 1020 (2d Cir.), cert. denied, 429 U.S. 1022 (1976).

*Page 80*

"Paul Denenfeld, Legal Director of the ACLU..." "Internet Author's Charges Dismissed" by Jim Schaefer and Maryanne George, *Detroit Free Press,* June 22, 1995.

*Page 81*

"An ACLU brief prepared...." *Whitney v. California,* 274 U.S. 357 (1927).

"As Justice Oliver Wendell Holmes said...." *Abrams v. US,* 250 US 616 (1919).

# Chapter 4  The Unruly Bookstore

For our account of the *Prodigy* proceedings, we consulted the file in *Stratton Oakmont v. Prodigy Services Company,* No. 031063/94 in New York State Supreme Court, Nassau County. Justice Stuart Ain's summary judgment decision was dated May 23, 1995. We relied heavily on attorney Martin Garbus' motion for renewal and reargument and attached documents, dated July 7, 1995.

*Page 85*

"On the question of the liability...." *Cubby v. Compuserve ,* 776 F. Supp. 135 (SDNY 1991).

*Page 86*

"Judge Leisure based his decision...." *Smith v. California,* 361 U.S. 147 (1959).

*Page 90*

"Texts on the law of the on-line world...." Lance Rose, *Netlaw* (New York: McGraw Hill 1995).

*Page 91*

"Garbus is one of the elite group...." DeGrazia, *Girls Lean Back Everywhere,* p. 446.

*Page 94*

"For example, a feminist newsgroup...." Clay Shirky, *Voices From the Net* (Emeryville, Ca: Ziff-Davis, 1995), pp. 52-53.

*Page 95*

"Howard Rheingold echoed this...." Howard Rheingold, *The Virtual Community* (New York: Harper Perennial, 1993), p. 43.

*Page 96*

"In September 1995...." "After Apology From Prodigy, Firm Drops Suit," by Peter Lewis, *New York Times,* October 25, 1995.

*Page 97*

"While the *Prodigy* case was being decided...." *Stern v. Delphi Internet Services Corp.*, decision of Justice Emily Jane Goodman, New York State Supreme Court for New York County, April 20, 1995.

*Page 98*

"Seven FBI agents entered...." *Eckstein v. Melson*, 18 F3d 1181 (4th Cir. 1994).

*Page 99*

"In 1987, an Arizona district attorney...." *Carlin Communications v. Mountain States Telephone and Telegraph*, 827 F.2d 1291 (9th Cir. 1981).

"The chilling effect of cases...." "Prodigy Libel Ruling Changes Online Scene", *Newsday*, May 28, 1995, p. 4.

# CHAPTER 5 INQUISITION ON THE NET

For our accounts of the court proceedings in the Erlich, Lerma, and FACTNet cases, we relied on the court files respectively in *Religious Technology Center v. Netcom On-Line Communications, et al*, C-95-20091, U.S. District Court, Northern District of California; *Religious Technology Center v. Arnaldo Pagliarini Lerma et al.*, U.S. District Court for the Eastern District of Virginia, 95-1107-A; and *Religious Technology Corporation v. FACTNet et al*, U.S. District Court, District of Colorado 95-B-2143.

All of the relevant court documents and many national news articles have been placed on the World Wide Web and are linked off a page maintained by R. Newman at http://www.cybercom.net/~rnewman/scientology/home.html.

*Page 101*

"The purpose of the suit is to harass..." *Magazine Articles on Level O Checksheet*, by L. Ron Hubbard, pg.55 (http://www.skeptic.com/03.3.jl-jj-scientology.html#ruin).

"In 1991, Scott Goehring...." "Dissidents Use Computer Network to Rile Scientologists," by Mike Allen, *The New York Times*, August 14, 1995.

*Pages 103-104*

"The Internet reacted to the attack...." and "In China FTP servers...." "Internet Gospel: Scientology's Expensive Wisdom Now Comes Free," by Mike Allen, *The New York Times*, August 20, 1995.

*Page 104*

"On February 2, 1995, CoS approached Julf Helsingius...." "Postcard from Cyberspace: The Helsinki Incident and the Right to Anonymity," by Daniel Akst, *The Los Angeles Times*, February 22, 1995.

*Page 105*

"I objected...." and following quotes, February 13, 1995 Usenet post by Ehrlich.

"In a 1986 case...." *Religious Technology Center v. Wollersheim*, 796 F.2d 1076, 1077 (9th Cir. 1986), cert. denied 479 U.S. 1103 (1987).

*Page 110*

"He quoted *Smith v. California*...." 361 U.S. 147 (1959).

*Page 117*

"I engaged in taking illegal drugs..." "Enforcing 'Truth': How the Scientologists Try to Impose Their Version of the Truth on Members, Defectors—and on Journalists," By Richard Leiby, *The Washington Post*, December 25, 1994.

*Page 118*

"This case is somewhat out of control...." "Scientology Reined In," By Charles W. Hall, *The Washington Post*, September 16, 1995.

*Page 119*

"In March 1995, Lawrence Wollersheim..." March 26, 1995 Usenet post by Wollersheim.

*Page 121*

"We are not...." "Scientologists Deleted Data Before Returning Computers", by Tillie Fong, *Rocky Mountain Press*, September 26, 1995.

"In many respects...." "Scientologists lose battle over seized computers", by James Brooke, *New York Times*, September 14, 1995.

"In a press release issued later that day..." "Police and members of Scientology church enter offices of XS4ALL Amsterdam" issued September 5, 1995.

*Page 122*

"On November 8, COS brought suit...." *Church of Spiritual Technology and Religious Technology Center v. Dataweb et al.*, November 8 1995 filing in county court in The Hague.

"In a column for a newspaper, Het Parool..." Karin Spaink, "Squeezed", *Het Parool*, October 8, 1995.

# CHAPTER 6 THE BARNUM OF CYBERPORN

Links to most of the sources used for this article are gathered at Donna Hoffman and Thomas Novak's *Project 2000* Web pages, http://www2000.ogsm.vanderbilt.edu/.

*Page 125*

"Senior Time writer...", *Hotwired* interview with Gary Brickman, July 4th weekend, http://www.hotwired.com.

*Page 127*

"The Time editors were convinced..." Brock Meeks, "Jacking in from the 'Point-Five Percent Solution' Port", *Cyberwire Dispatch*, http://www.cyberwerks.com , July 7, 1995.

*Page 128*

"The Press reported...." "Is Rimm's Porn Study 'Cyberfraud?'", *Press of Atlantic City*, July 11, 1995; "Cyberporn Researcher Linked to Atlantic City Pranks," ibid., August 29, 1995. Both articles are by Ray Robinson and are available on the *Press* web site at http://www.acy.digex.net.

*Page 129*

"Commenting on the approach...." *Press of Atlantic City*, supra, July 11, 1995.

*Page 132*

"Discrete [sic], ain't we?" Meeks, *Cyberwire Dispatch*, July 7, 1995.

"When Meeks asked how he was able to obtain...." "Time Fails," by Brock Meeks, in *Hotwired*, http://www.hotwired.com.

*Page 133*

"Unknown to Meeks...." Mike Godwin Usenet post reprinted in Computer Underground Digest, 7-59, available at http://www.soci.niu.edu:80/~cudigest/.

*Page 139*

"As Mike Godwin would point out...". "The Rimmjob Method," by Mike Godwin, in *Hotwired*, October 1, 1995, http://www.hotwired.com.

*Page 141*

"That was probably a screw up...." Meeks, "Time Fails", supra.

*Page 145*

"Brian Reid was also extremely distressed...." Rimm, "Response to Letter from Brian Reid," available on the *Project 2000* Web site.

*Page 147*

"Rimm would later attack Donna Hoffman personally...." Meeks, "Time Fails", supra.

"Mike Godwin of EFF..." "The Shoddy Article," by Mike Godwin, in *Hotwired*, http://www.hotwired.com.

*Page 150*

"In July, Carnegie Mellon Provost..." July 14 Usenet post from Bruce Gerson.

"On July 11, in a typically acerb piece..." "Jacking in from the 'Mr. Toad's Wild Ride' Port," by Brock Meeks, *Cyberwire Dispatch*, July 13, 1995.

*Page 151*

"Illinois University professor Jim Thomas wrote...." and "On August 8...." " Some Thoughts On Carnegie Mellon's Committee Of Investigation", by Jim Thomas, in *Computer Underground Digest* 7-59 (September 15, 1995).

"Rimm would later claim ingenuously...." Rimm, "Response to Letter from Brian Reid", on *Project 2000* Web site.

*Page 152*

"Mike Godwin had the last word on Rimm..." Meeks, "Jacking in from the 'Mr. Toad's Wild Ride' Port" , supra.

# CHAPTER 7 BOMB SPEECH

The text of Senator Feinstein's bomb speech bill, and the transcript of the Senate debate, were obtained from the Library of Congress' Thomas service at http://www.thomas.loc.gov. Jerry Berman's testimony before the subcommittee was available on the Center for Democracy and Technology Web page at http://www.cdt.org, and Rabbi Marvin Hier's testimony was posted on the Wiesenthal Center Web page at http://www.wiesenthal.org. Additional subcommittee testimony was obtained from the Westlaw service.

*Page 153*

"The Candyland pages...." Candyman's pages are at http://www.mcs.net/~candyman/http/boom.html.

*Page 156*

"To the immense embarassment of the National Rifle Association...."
Quoted by Senator Feinstein in the Congressional Record for June 5, 1995.
Cass Sunstein, "Is Violent Speech a Right?", *The American Prospect*, Summer
1995 gives the name "Warmaster."

*Page 157*

"On May 5, Tanya Metaksas...." Metaksas' letter is posted on the NRA
Web Site, http://www.nra.org.

"Member agrees to use the GUN-TALK service...." Log on screen from
the GunTalk BBS, accessed in October 1995.

*Page 158*

"You can find it in some bookstores or...." *Anarchists Cookbook* ad in
Nov. 6, 1995 *Nation*.

"Another well-known distributor...." Erik Larson, *Lethal Passage* (New
York: Vintage 1994).

pp. 174-175.

"Larson interviewed Billy Blann..." *Lethal Passage*, p. 176.

"According to Larson, investigators...." *Lethal Passage*, p. 175.

*Page 159*

"In a 1969 case,*Brandenburg v. Ohio*...." 395 US 444 (1969).

"You can't say they can't print...." *Lethal Passage*, p. 180.

"University of Chicago law professor Cass Sunstein...." Sunstein, "Is
Violent Speech a Right?", *The American Prospect* , Summer 1995.

# FOOTNOTES

*Page 160*

"This is the opposite of Justice Holmes...." Holmes, dissenting in *Abrams v. US*, 250 US 616 (1919).

*Page 161*

"One federal law is on the books...." 18 United States Code 231.

"In a 1972 case...." *U.S. v. Featherston*, 461 F. 2d 1119 (1972).

"The Court of Appeals rejected...." *Dennis v. United States*, 341 U.S. 494 (1950).

"As NYU law professor Kent Greenawalt notes...." Kent Greenawalt, *Fighting Words* (Princeton, N.J.: Princeton University Press 1995), p. 6.

*Page 162*

"Nevertheless, at least one BBS sysop...." Lance Rose, *Netlaw* (New York: McGraw Hill 1995), p. 238.

"'It appears,' said David Banisar..." and "Mike Godwin of EFF added...." "Free speech and computers central to bomb recipe case", by John M. Moran, *The Hartford Courant*, September 27, 1993.

"Benfry was never chargd with any crime...." "Tapping into Trouble," by Mike Gordon, *Montreal Gazette*, December 20, 1993.

"After spending more than three months...." "West Hartford Man May Get 3-Year Term in Bomb Recipe Case", by Matthew Kaufman, *The Hartford Courant*, October 23, 1993.

"Judge Thomas Miano sentenced him..."""Interest in Explosives Nets 28-month Term", by John M. Moran, *The Hartford Courant*, Nov. 20, 1993

*Page 163*

"Feinstein was the target..." Feinstein comments, *Congressional Record* for June 5.

"Tuerkheimer, as a young Wisconsin prosecutor...." *U.S. v. The Progressive*, 467 F. Supp. 990 (W.D. Wisconsin 1979).

# Chapter 8  The New Comstock

We obtained the Senate debate and the text of the CDA from the *Congressional Record,* available on the Thomas service at http://www.thomas.loc.gov.

*Page 174*

"In 1971, the Supreme Court overturned...." *Cohen v. California,* 403 U.S. 15 (1971).

*Page 175*

"In 1978, the Court upheld the right...." *F.C.C. v. Pacifica Foundation,* 438 U.S. 726 (1978).

"In 1989, the Supreme Court threw out this law...." *Sable Communications v. F.C.C.,* 492 U.S. 115 (1989).

*Page 181*

"Feingold did not cite *Butler v. Michigan...*" 352 U.S. 380 (1957).

*Page 183*

"However, Meeks says....." September 29, 1995 email from Meeks.

*Page 187*

"In his book, *To Renew America....*" (New York: HarperCollins 1995) pp. 55-56.

"In an interview...." "Friend and Foe", *Wired* Magazine, August 1995.

"A few weeks prior to the Senate's debate...." PBS interview with David Frost on May 31, 1995.

"The week after the Senate adopted...." Appearance on National Empowerment Television, June 20, 1995.

"That week, Senator Exon appeared...." Macneill-Lehrer News Hour, June 22, 1995.

# CHAPTER 9 A COMPASS FOR CYBERSPACE

*Page 193*

"Cardozo said...." Benjamin A. Cardozo, *The Nature of the Judicial Process* (New Haven: Yale 1991) p. 53; Maitland quote, p. 54.

*Pages 193-194*

"The book states, 'Each new advance....'" Ithiel de Sola Pool, *Technologies of Freedom* (Cambridge, Mass: Harvard University Press 1983) pp. 7-10.

*Page 195*

"Plato, whose life...." Plato, *Phaedrus*, in Edman, The Works of Plato (tr. Jowett) (New York: Modern Library 1928), pp. 322-323. We found this quote in Neil Postman, *Technopoly* (New York: Vintage Books 1992).

"Postman states, 'Thamus' error...'" Neil Postman, *Technopoly*, New York: Vintage Books 1992), p. 4.

"An apocryphal story...." Elizabeth L. Eisenstein, *The Printing Revolution in Early Modern Europe* (Cambridge: Cambridge University Press, 1983.), p. 19.

*Page 196*

" Elizabeth Eisenstein, foremost scholar...." Eisenstein,  p. 155.

"Within a few years..." Lucien Febvre and Henri Jean Martin, *The Coming of the Book* ( London: NLB 1976), tr. David Gerard, p. 244ff.

'Eisenstein says, 'Given the existence...." Eisenstein, p. 170.

"Lutheranism was from the beginning..." Eisenstein, p. 145.

*Page 197*

"They said, 'Among the real victims...'" Febvre and Martin, pp. 311-312.

"'Nothing,' say Febvre and Martin.... " Febvre and Martin,  p. 307.

"The number of books liable..." Febvre and Martin,  p. 246.

"It is evident..."Febvre and Martin,  p. 247.

"In England in 1643..." Preamble to *Aeropagitica.*

*Page 198*

"Cardinal Richelieu substituted...." Eisenstein  p. 95.

"Thus, when 'technology'..." Eisenstein, p. 139.

*Page 199*

"Historian Daniel J. Boorstin...."  Daniel J. Boorstin, "Printing and the Constitution", in *Cleopatra's Nose* (New York: Vintage  1994) pp. 63-73.

"Ithiel de Sola Pool lamented...." Pool, p. 74.

"First Amendment scholar Zachariah Chafee..." *Free Speech in the United States* (1942)  p. 381, quoted in *Tornillo v. Miami Herald* 418 US 241 (1973).

"Writing 182 years later...." *Tornillo v. Miami Herald* 418 US 241 (1973).

*Page 200*

"Thomas Jefferson commented...." quoted in Boorstin, "Printing and the Constitution," p. 69.

"In 1831, Alexis de Tocqueville...." *De la Democratie en Amerique* (Paris: GF-Flammarion, 1981), pp. 264-269 (tr. by the authors).

"In his recent book...." Newt Gingrich, To Renew America (New York: Harper Collins 1995) p, 57.

"A Senate report of 1832" and "The poisoned sentiments...."  Pool, p. 269, fn. 9.

# FOOTNOTES

*Page 201*

"In 1859, philosopher John Stuart Mill...." Mill, *On Liberty* (New York: Bantam 1993) p. 12, 19-20.

*Page 203*

"In their book, *Manufacturing Consent*...." Edward S. Herman and Noam Chomsky, *Manufacturing Consent* (New York: Pantheon Books 1988) pp. xi, xv, 6, 305.

*Page 204*

"Barbara Ehrenreich says...." Barbara Ehrenreich, "Media Matters" column, *The Nation*, Dec. 4, 1995, p. 698.

"Former FCC commissioner...." "Routine Somersaults of Self-Censorship", by Jeff Cohen and Norman Solomon, "Media Beat" column for September 13, 1995, available on the FAIR home page at http://www.fair.org.

"Neil Postman believes...." "Remembering the Golden Age" in *Conscientous Objections* (Vintage, NY 1988), pp. 116-117. "Forms of communication are neither good nor bad..." "Future Schlock", ibid., p. 173.

*Page 205*

"A demonstration version...." Gerard J. Holzmann and Bjorn Pehrson, *The Early History of Data Networks* (Los Alamitos Ca.: IEEE Computer Society Press 1995), p. 57.

"Decades later, Ignace Chappe....", Holzmann and Pehrson, p. 92.

"Because of a fear...." Holzmann and Pehrson, p. 91.

"His political experience...." Holzmann and Pehrson, p. 179.

*Page 206*

"This is indeed the annihilation..." and "Morse predicted...." Neil Postman, *Amusing Ourselves to Death* (New York: Penguin 1985), p. 65-66.

"Clay Shirky...." *Voices From the Net* (Emeryville, Ca.: Ziff-Davis Press 1995) p. xvi.

"To protect this business...." Pool, p. 93.

*Page 207*

"Pool would have us apply...." Pool, p. 248.

"McLuhan wrote...." and "But he also pointed out...." Marshall McLuhan, *Understanding Media,* (Cambridge: MIT Press 1995), pp. 248-249.

"Postman stated that...." Postman, *Amusing Ourselves to Death,* p. 65.

*Page 208*

"Pool, much more of an optimist...." Pool, 99-100.

"In 1876..." Pool, p. 29.

"One system with a common policy..." Pool, p. 29.

*Page 209*

"When the telephone was first invented...." and "The United States Supreme Court, however...." Pool, p. 100.

"Eventually, however...." Pool, p. 101.

*Page 210*

"He quotes Armaments Minister..." McLuhan, p. 247.

"McLuhan comments...." McLuhan, p. 270.

"A subscriber's telephone service was cancelled...." Pool, pp. 106, 274.

*Page 211*

"In 1924, Admiral W.L. Rodgers...." Pool, p. 111.

"In 1925...." Pool, p. 113.

"Even in this undesirable situation...." Pool, p. 116.

"Industry figures at their annual convention...." Pool, p. 117.

# FOOTNOTES

*Page 212*

"Hoover, contradicting his own words...." and "President Coolidge added...." Pool, p. 120.

"The industry's third national conference...." Pool, p. 121.

"Kaltenborn later wrote...." Pool, p. 121.

"The ACLU's Morris Ernst...." Pool, p. 122.

"'Listeners,' the Commission said...." Pool, p. 123.

"In the early 1930's...." Pool, pp. 125-126.

*Page 213*

"Self-censorship continued to prevail...." Pool, pp. 127-128.

"Seven years later...." *NBC v. United States*, 319 US 190 (1943).

"This approach has not changed...." *Red Lion Broadcasting v. FCC*, 395 US 367 (1969).

*Page 214*

"Such factors as..." Wagman, *The First Amendment Book* (New York: Pharos Books 1991), p. 133-134.

"Marshall McLuhan called radio..." McLuhan, p. 302.

"Radio provides a speed-up..." McLuhan, p. 306.

"Postman stated..." Postman, *Amusing Ourselves to Death*, p. 112.

"Pool regards radio...." Pool, p. 135.

*Page 215*

"The most famous indecency case...." *FCC v. Pacifica Foundation*, 438 US 726 (1978). The seven words, in case you're curious, are shit, piss, fuck, cunt, cocksucker, motherfucker and tits. Printing this list is perfectly legal in this book, but under the indecency legislation pending as this book went to press, could earn us up to five years in prison and a $100,000 fine for echoing these words on our Web site, http://www.spectacle.org/freespch/.

*Page 216*

"Ithiel de Sola Pool called...." Pool, p. 134.

"The FCC announced...." Wagman, p. 136.

*Page 217*

"The Circuit Court of Appeals...." *Action for Children's Television v. FCC*, 852 F.2d 1332 (DC Cir. 1988).

"In *Action for Children's Television v. FCC*...." 58 F.3d 654 (DC Cir. 1995).

*Page 219*

"The Supreme Court, in what has...." *Sable Communications v. FCC*, 492 U.S. 115 (1989).

*Page 220*

"In *Information Providers Coalition v. FCC*...." 928 F2d 866 (9th Cir. 1991).

"In *Dial Information Services v. Thornburgh*...." 938 F.2d 1535 (2d Cir. 1991).

*Page 221*

"Numerous unsuccessful lawsuits...." Wagman, p. 138.

"In *Alliance for Community Media v. FCC*...." 10 F3d 812 (DC Cir 1993).

*Page 222*

"The decision of the full court...." *Alliance for Community Media v. FCC*, 58 F3d 654 (DC Cir. 1995).

*Page 223*

"In the case of *Turner Broadcasting System v. FCC*...." 114 S. Ct. 2445 (1993).

"The courts, said Ithiel de Sola Pool...." Pool, p. 165.

# FOOTNOTES

"The problem of access..." Pool, p. 166.

*Page 224*

"The decline and fall...." Lawrence K. Grossman, *The Electronic Republic* (New York: Viking 1995), p. 109.

"Grossman said, 'I could find hardly...'" Grossman, p. 86.

*Page 225*

"Early on the morning of Tuesday...." Grossman , pp. 84-85.

"Many commentators failed to mention...." Counterspin radio program for 11/17/95, hosted by Laura Flanders and Janine Jackson, partial transcript on FAIR Web pages, http://www.fair.org.

"P. Cameron DeVore...."    "60 Minutes Case Part of a Trend of Corporate Pressure, Some Analysts Say," by William Glaberson, *New York Times*, Nov. 17, 1995, p. B14.

"Grossman said, 'The mainstream media by definition....'" Grossman, p. 85.

*Page 226*

"In a 1915 case...." *Mutual Film Corporation v. Industrial Commission*, 236 US 230 (1915).

"It took the Court until 1952...." *Joseph Burstyn Inc. v. Wilson*, 343 US 495 (1951).

*Page 227*

"But the Supreme Court pondered...." *Kovacs v. Cooper,* 336 U.S. 77 (1949).

*Page 228*

"'The First Amendment,' said Pool...."   Pool, p. 5.

"Writing freezes speech...." Postman, *Amusing Ourselves to Death*, p. 12.

"Stoll downloaded...." Clifford Stoll, *Silicon Snake Oil* (New York: Doubleday 1995), p. 41.

*Page 229*

"A dissenting voice is sometimes needed..." Postman, *Technopoly*, p. 5.

"He says that the principal legacy...." and "You may get..."Postman, *Amusing Ourselves to Death*, pp. 68-69.

*Page 230*

"Anyway, Postman would not only...." Postman interview, *Net Guide*, August 1995.

"Speak for yourself...." Richard Lanham, *The Electronic Word* (Chicago: University of Chicago Press 1993).

*Page 231*

"[C]oncern for the traditional notion..." Pool, p. 8.

"And again...." Pool, p. 10.

"'The printed book,' said Jay David Bolter...." Jay David Bolter, *Writing Space: The Computer, Hypertext and the History of Writing* (Hillsdale, N.J.: Erlbaum 1991), p. 2. We found this quote in Lanham, *The Electronic Word*, supra, p. x.

*Page 232*

"In 1976, evolutionary biologist...." Richard Dawkins, *The Selfish Gene* (New York: Oxford University Press, 1976), chapter 11.

*Page 237*

"Reed Hundt...." We obtained all the Hundt quotes from the FCC Web page, http://www.fcc.gov.

*Page 238*

"Children come to school..." Postman, *Technopoly*, pp. 16-17.

*Page 239*

"It has been calculated...." Dr. Benjamin M. Spock, *A Better World for our Children* (Bethesda, Md: National Press Books 1994) p. 78.

# FOOTNOTES

"According to Dr. Haim Ginott...." Dr. Haim Ginott, *Between Parent and Child* (New York: Avon 1969) p. 140.

"Dr. Lawrence Balter recommends...." Dr. Lawrence Balter with Anita Shreve, *Dr. Balter's Child Sense* (New York: Poseidon Press 1985) p. 129.

"Ellen Galinsky observes...." Ellen Galinsky amd Judy David, *The Preschool Years* (Ballantine Books, New York 1988), p. 86.

"Earl Grollman and Gerri Sweder...." Earl Grollman and Gerri Sweder, *The Working Parent Dilemma* (Boston:Beacon Press 1986), p. 157.

*Page 240*

"Censorship, said Milton...." Milton, *Aeropagitica*.

"An organization called Voter's Telecommunications Watch...." http://www.vtw.org.

*Page 243*

""For example, Prodigy...." and "Another such service...." Parental Control FAQ, at http://www.vtw.org.

"Guess we'll just have to fall back..." Email communication to the authors, October 1995.

*Page 244*

"Cyberspace offers direct, instantaneous...." Rabbi Hier's testimony is on the Wiesenthal Center Web page at http://www.wiesenthal.org.

*Page 245*

"In an email interview...." The McVay interview is in *The Ethical Spectacle* for June 1995, http://www.spectacle.org/695/mcvay.html.

*Page 246*

"There's always another mind...." Howard Rheingold, *The Virtual Community* (New York: Harper Perennial, New York 1993), p. 24.

*Page 247*

"The odds are always good...." Rheingold, p. 5.

*Page 248*

"No pages was ever more eagerly read...." Isaac Kramnick, introduction to Thomas Paine, *Common Sense* (London: Penguin 1986) p. 29.

*Page 249*

"The Internet, says Speaker Gingrich...." Newt Gingrich, *To Renew America* (New York: Harper Collins 1995) pp. 57-58.

"Listen to the words chosen...." Daniel Burstein and David Kline, *Road Warriors* (New York: Dutton 1995), pp. 104, 118, 126, 129.

"Journalist Steven Levy...." "How the Propellor Heads Stole the Electronic Future", by Steven Levy, *New York Times Sunday Magazine*, September 24, 1995, p. 58.

*Page 251*

"Nicholas Negroponte compares...." "MIT's Lab Rat," Interview by Bob Berger with Nicholas Negroponte, in *Net Guide*, Dec. 1995, p. 183.

*Page 254*

"Duke University professor Stanley Fish...." Stanley Fish, *There's No Such Thing as Free Speech* (New York: Oxford University Press, 1994) p. 113-114.

*Page 255*

"Truth and understanding...." Milton, *Aeropagitica*.

"Yet his very office..." Milton, *Aeropagitica*.

*Page 259*

"We as a community..." Alex Stewart, proposal at http://www.crl.com/~riche/IVSR/proposal.html.

# INDEX

# INDEX